Mastering Self-Employed Taxes

A Comprehensive Guide to Financial Freedom

WealthWise

WealthWisePublications.com

Copyright © 2024 by WealthWise

All rights reserved.

No portion of this book may be reproduced in any form without written permission from the publisher or author, except as permitted by U.S. copyright law.

This publication is designed to provide accurate and authoritative information in regard to the subject matter covered. It is sold with the understanding that neither the author nor the publisher is engaged in rendering legal, investment, accounting, or other professional services. The information provided in this book is for general informational purposes only. WealthWise makes no representations or warranties of any kind, express or implied, about the completeness, accuracy, reliability, suitability, or availability of the information contained in this book for any purpose. Any reliance you place on such information is strictly at your own risk. The content is not intended as, and shall not be construed as, financial advice.

While the publisher and author have used their best efforts in preparing this book, they make no representations or warranties with respect to the accuracy or completeness of the contents of this book and specifically disclaim any implied warranties of merchantability or fitness for a particular purpose. No warranty may be created or extended by sales representatives or written sales materials. Neither the publisher nor the author shall be liable for any loss of profit or any other commercial damages, including but not limited to special, incidental, consequential, personal, or other damages.

About WealthWise

WealthWise Publications is revolutionizing the world of financial education. Founded with the vision of empowering individuals to achieve financial independence and security, WealthWise harnesses the power of expert insights and cutting-edge technology to deliver comprehensive, accessible, and actionable content on a wide range of financial topics.

At the core of WealthWise's mission is a deep commitment to leveraging the collective knowledge of top financial minds and innovative technology to democratize financial education. By collaborating with renowned experts and utilizing advanced data analysis tools, WealthWise has created a platform that delivers high-quality, customized financial guidance, making it accessible to readers worldwide.

What sets WealthWise apart is its unwavering dedication to bridging the gap between financial expertise and everyday life. Our expert-driven content is meticulously crafted to break down complex financial concepts into digestible, easy-to-understand insights, empowering readers to make informed decisions and take confident steps toward their financial goals.

As your trusted companion on the path to financial mastery, WealthWise Publications is dedicated to empowering you with the insights, strategies, and inspiration you need to unlock your financial potential and create the life you've always envisioned. Join us on this exciting journey as we redefine the landscape of financial education and pave the way for a more financially literate, confident, and prosperous future for all.

Visit
WealthWisePublications.com

Contents

Introduction	1
1. The Basics Of Self Employed Taxes	4
Defining Self-Employment Income	
The Self-Employment Tax Explained	
Key Tax Forms for the Self-Employed	
2. Tracking Income And Expenses	20
Setting Up an Efficient Record-Keeping System	
Categorizing Business Expenses	
Using Technology to Simplify Tracking	
3. Claiming Deductions	37
Common Deductions for Freelancers and Contractors	
Home Office Deduction: What You Need to Know	
Maximizing Vehicle and Travel Deductions	
4. Understanding Quarterly Taxes	52
Calculating Estimated Taxes	
Deadlines and Penalties for Late Payments	
Strategies for Managing Quarterly Payments	
5. Retirement Planning For The Self Employed	68
Exploring Retirement Account Options	
Tax Benefits of Retirement Contributions	
Creating a Long-Term Retirement Strategy	
6. Healthcare Options For The Self Employed	84

Navigating Health Insurance Marketplaces

Understanding the Self-Employed Health Insurance Deduction

Evaluating Healthcare Sharing Plans

7. Legal Considerations And Business Structures   101

Choosing the Right Business Entity

Legal Protections and Liability

The Impact of Business Structure on Taxes

8. Avoiding Common Tax Mistakes   118

Misclassifying Income and Expenses

Ignoring Deadlines and Penalties

Overlooking Deductions and Credits

9. Working With Tax Professionals   135

When to Hire an Accountant

Finding the Right Tax Advisor

Collaborating Effectively with Your Accountant

10. Tools And Resources For Tax Management   151

Essential Software for Self-Employed Taxes

Utilizing Online Tax Preparation Services

Staying Updated with Tax Law Changes

11. Building A Tax Strategy   167

Setting Financial Goals

Developing a Year-Round Tax Plan

Adjusting Your Strategy as Your Business Grows

12. The Bigger Picture Of Financial Independence   183

Creating Multiple Streams of Income

Investing in Your Future

Achieving Work-Life Balance

13. Success Strategies   199

Interviews with Financially Independent Freelancers

Inspirational Case Studies

Lessons Learned from Tax Challenges

14. Staying Organized And Motivated   215

   Developing Effective Time Management Skills

   Maintaining Financial Records Throughout the Year

   Staying Motivated on the Path to Financial Freedom

Conclusion   231

  Recap of Key Takeaways

  Encouragement for Continued Growth

  Final Tips for Mastering Self-Employed Taxes

Resources   236

References   240

WealthWise's Mission   244

Introduction

Try to imagine waking up each morning, invigorated by the freedom to chart your own course, unburdened by the constraints of a traditional 9-to-5 job. This is the life of the self-employed, a realm filled with promise and potential, but also with its fair share of challenges and intricacies, particularly when it comes to taxes. One fascinating aspect of this journey is the sheer variety of people who take the plunge into self-employment: from creative freelancers and gig workers to seasoned independent contractors. Yet, despite their diverse backgrounds, they all share a common goal: achieving financial freedom through diligent and proactive financial management.

Financial freedom is more than just a lofty ideal; it's a tangible goal that can transform your life. It allows you to pursue your passions, invest in meaningful projects, and secure a comfortable future. But this journey is not without its hurdles. For many self-employed individuals, the complexity of taxes can be a significant roadblock. Navigating the maze of self-employment taxes requires a solid understanding of various rules and regulations, as well as a proactive approach to managing your finances.

In my years of experience as a financial advisor specializing in self-employment, I've seen countless individuals struggle with the burden of tax obligations, often feeling overwhelmed and ill-equipped to handle them. This book aims to bridge that knowledge gap, providing you with the tools and insights needed to master self-employed taxes and, ultimately, achieve financial independence. Understanding the tax landscape is crucial for anyone embarking on the journey to financial freedom. This book will serve as your roadmap, guiding you through the intricacies of self-employed taxes, from tracking income and expenses to claiming deductions and understanding quarterly payments. By mastering these aspects, you'll be well on your way to financial independence, free from the stress and uncertainty that can accompany self-employment.

The self-employed tax landscape can be daunting, but it's essential to comprehend its key components to navigate it effectively. Unlike traditional employees, self-employed individuals are responsible for calculating and paying their own taxes, which includes both income tax and the self-employment tax. The latter encompasses Social Security and Medicare taxes, which are usually withheld by employers for their employees but must be managed independently by self-employed individuals.

This dual responsibility can be intimidating, but understanding the basic principles can demystify the process. For instance, knowing which tax forms to use, such as the Schedule C for reporting income and expenses or the Form 1040-ES for estimated tax payments, is foundational. Moreover, recognizing the importance of accurate record-keeping and categorization of business expenses can significantly streamline your tax preparation efforts. Throughout this book, you'll find detailed explanations and practical tips to help you grasp these concepts. From setting up efficient record-keeping systems to leveraging technology for tracking expenses, each chapter is designed to equip you with the knowledge and tools necessary for effective tax management.

Proactive financial management is the cornerstone of successful self-employment. It involves not only understanding your tax obligations but also planning ahead to minimize liabilities and maximize deductions. By taking a proactive approach, you can avoid common pitfalls such as missing deadlines, incurring penalties, or overlooking valuable deductions. One of the most critical aspects of proactive financial management is staying informed about tax law changes and updates. The tax landscape is constantly evolving, and keeping abreast of new regulations can help you make informed decisions and optimize your tax strategy. This book will provide you with the latest information and insights, ensuring that you remain compliant and make the most of available opportunities. Another key component of proactive financial management is retirement planning. Unlike traditional employees who may have access to employer-sponsored retirement plans, self-employed individuals must take the initiative to establish and fund their own retirement accounts. This book will explore various retirement options, such as SEP IRAs and Solo 401(k)s, and highlight the tax benefits associated with retirement contributions.

Healthcare is another area where proactive planning can make a significant difference. Navigating health insurance marketplaces, understanding the self-employed health insurance deduction, and evaluating alternative healthcare options are essential steps for securing your well-being and financial stability. By

INTRODUCTION

addressing these topics, this book will empower you to make informed choices and safeguard your health. Ultimately, the goal of this book is to empower you with the knowledge and tools needed to master self-employed taxes and achieve financial freedom. By understanding the self-employed tax landscape and adopting a proactive approach to financial management, you can navigate the complexities of self-employment with confidence and ease.

Throughout the chapters, you'll encounter personal anecdotes, success stories, and expert interviews that add depth and authenticity to the content. These real-life examples will illustrate the principles discussed and provide valuable insights into the experiences of others who have successfully navigated the journey to financial freedom. As you embark on this journey, remember that achieving financial independence is not an overnight process. It requires dedication, discipline, and a willingness to learn and adapt. This book will serve as your guide, offering practical advice, actionable strategies, and the encouragement needed to stay motivated and focused on your goals.

So, whether you're just starting out on your self-employment journey or looking to refine your tax strategy, this book has something for you. The insights and knowledge you'll gain will not only help you master self-employed taxes but also pave the way for a financially secure and fulfilling future. Welcome to "Mastering Self-Employed Taxes: A Comprehensive Guide to Financial Freedom." Let's embark on this journey together and unlock the potential for financial independence and peace of mind.

Chapter One

The Basics Of Self Employed Taxes

U nlocking the secrets of self-employed taxes can feel like discovering a hidden treasure map, guiding you towards financial freedom. Imagine Jane, a freelance graphic designer who once felt overwhelmed by the maze of tax forms and regulations. She felt like she was constantly treading water, trying to keep her head above the chaos of invoices, receipts, and deadlines. But once she began to understand the basics of self-employed taxes, Jane found herself navigating her financial journey with newfound confidence and clarity. Her story is not unique; countless freelancers and independent contractors face similar challenges. This chapter sets out to demystify the world of self-employed taxes, turning confusion into empowerment.

In our quest to understand the essentials, we'll explore what constitutes self-employment income and why it's crucial to differentiate it from other types of earnings. The self-employment tax itself can seem daunting at first, but breaking it down into manageable pieces reveals its purpose and how it fits into your overall tax obligations. Navigating the labyrinth of tax forms is another critical step; knowing which documents to prepare and when to file them can save you time, stress, and potentially significant sums of money. Each component is a piece of the puzzle that, when assembled, provides a comprehensive view of your financial landscape.

These foundational elements are more than just technical details—they are the keys to taking control of your financial destiny. Understanding the basics allows you to make informed decisions, avoid costly mistakes, and seize opportunities that enhance your financial well-being. By mastering these concepts, you set the stage for a proactive approach to managing your taxes, ultimately paving the way to financial independence and peace of mind. The journey may begin with understanding the basics, but the destination is a future where you are the master of your financial fate.

Defining Self-Employment Income

Imagine you're walking through a bustling marketplace, each stall representing a different facet of your self-employment journey. One stall is loaded with freelance design projects, another with income from your Etsy shop, and yet another with payments for consulting gigs. This lively scene mirrors the diverse streams of self-employment income that many freelancers and independent contractors juggle daily. It's not just about selling a product or service; it's about understanding and managing every dollar that flows into your pocket. In this section, we explore the myriad sources of self-employment income, shedding light on how to identify and report each one accurately.

Understanding the source and nature of your self-employment income isn't just a matter of curiosity—it's a fundamental step toward mastering your financial obligations and maximizing your tax benefits. Whether it's distinguishing between what qualifies as business income versus personal earnings or learning how to report income from multiple streams, every bit of knowledge empowers you to make smarter financial decisions. So let's dive in and uncover the essential components of defining self-employment income, ensuring you have a solid foundation for the chapters ahead.

Identifying Sources of Self-Employment Income

Self-employment income encompasses a diverse array of revenue streams, each uniquely contributing to the financial landscape of freelancers, gig workers, and independent contractors. This income is often derived from project-based work, consulting services, or freelance gigs, which differ substantially from traditional salaried employment. For instance, a freelance graphic designer may earn from designing logos, creating marketing materials, and managing social media content for various clients. Understanding these sources of income is crucial for accurate financial reporting and ensuring compliance with tax obligations.

Diversification is a hallmark of self-employment income. Individuals may find themselves juggling multiple roles and projects simultaneously. A writer, for example, might generate income from writing articles, ghostwriting books, and conducting workshops. Recognizing and categorizing these different income streams is essential for maintaining organized financial records. It not only facilitates accurate tax reporting but also helps in identifying the most profitable ventures, thereby enabling more strategic business decisions.

A key aspect in defining self-employment income is distinguishing it from personal earnings. This distinction can sometimes be nebulous, especially when personal and business activities overlap. For example, an individual who rents out a portion of their home on a short-term rental platform needs to clearly delineate the rental income from their personal funds. Establishing separate bank accounts for business transactions can simplify this process, ensuring that personal and business finances remain distinct and easily traceable.

Reporting income from multiple sources requires meticulous record-keeping and a thorough understanding of tax forms and regulations. Each stream of income may necessitate different reporting methods and documentation. For instance, income from freelance writing might be reported using a 1099-NEC form, while rental income might require a Schedule E. Familiarity with these forms and the specific requirements for each type of income is critical for avoiding errors and ensuring that all income is accurately reported to the IRS.

In an era of digital transformation, new opportunities for self-employment income continue to emerge. The rise of the gig economy, driven by platforms like Uber, Etsy, and Upwork, has expanded the avenues through which individuals can earn. Staying abreast of these trends and understanding their tax implications is vital for modern self-employed individuals. By leveraging technology and innovative platforms, self-employed professionals can maximize their income potential while maintaining compliance with evolving tax regulations. This proactive approach not only ensures financial stability but also empowers individuals to take full control of their financial destinies.

Distinguishing Between Business and Personal Earnings

Distinguishing between business and personal earnings is crucial for any self-employed individual aiming to maintain financial clarity and compliance

THE BASICS OF SELF EMPLOYED TAXES

with tax regulations. Understanding this distinction helps in accurately reporting income, maximizing allowable deductions, and avoiding potential audits. One of the fundamental steps is to maintain separate bank accounts for business and personal transactions. This segregation simplifies the tracking of income and expenses, ensuring that personal expenditures don't inadvertently get mixed with business finances.

To illustrate, consider a freelance graphic designer who receives payments from clients for design projects. Any income generated directly from these projects qualifies as business earnings. Conversely, money received as a gift from a friend or an inheritance should be categorized as personal income. This clear delineation is not only vital for accurate tax reporting but also for strategic financial planning, allowing the individual to reinvest business profits effectively and manage personal finances prudently.

Advanced financial tools and software can further streamline this process. Platforms like QuickBooks or Wave allow self-employed individuals to tag transactions as either business or personal. Utilizing such tools enhances accuracy and saves time, ensuring that every dollar is appropriately categorized. Furthermore, these tools offer insights into spending patterns, helping freelancers and contractors make informed decisions about their business finances.

It's also essential to recognize the tax implications of mixing business and personal finances. Misclassification of income can lead to complications during tax season, potentially resulting in penalties or missed opportunities for deductions. For instance, if personal expenses are mistakenly claimed as business deductions, it could trigger an audit or disallowance of those expenses. On the other hand, failing to claim legitimate business expenses can lead to higher taxable income and increased tax liability.

To foster a comprehensive understanding, let's consider a scenario: A freelance writer receives payment for an article and uses part of that payment to purchase a new laptop. The income from the article is business income, and the expenditure on the laptop, if used primarily for business purposes, can be claimed as a business expense. However, if the writer uses the laptop equally for personal and business activities, only the business-use portion can be deducted. This nuanced understanding of business versus personal usage and income is essential for minimizing tax burdens and optimizing financial strategies.

By clearly distinguishing between business and personal earnings and effectively utilizing financial tools, self-employed individuals can navigate the complexities of their finances with greater ease and confidence. This meticulous

8　　　　　MASTERING SELF-EMPLOYED TAXES

approach not only ensures compliance with tax laws but also fosters sustainable financial growth, paving the way for long-term success and stability in their entrepreneurial endeavors.

Reporting Income from Multiple Streams

For self-employed individuals, reporting income from multiple streams can seem daunting, but it's a crucial aspect of maintaining accurate financial records and staying compliant with tax regulations. Self-employment often means juggling diverse sources of income, such as freelance projects, consulting gigs, and sales from online platforms. Each income stream must be meticulously tracked and reported to ensure a comprehensive and accurate financial picture. Properly managing this can prevent underreporting, which may lead to hefty penalties and interest charges. Therefore, understanding the nuances of reporting varied income streams is pivotal for any self-employed professional aiming to achieve financial stability and avoid unwelcome surprises during tax season.

One of the first steps in reporting income from multiple streams involves distinguishing between taxable and non-taxable income. Taxable income includes earnings from freelance work, contractual projects, and any other business activities. Conversely, certain forms of income, like hobby income or casual earnings, might not be taxable if they don't meet specific criteria set by the IRS. For example, if you occasionally sell handmade crafts as a hobby and earn minimal income, it might not be considered self-employment income. However, if you consistently sell these crafts with the intent to profit, it would be classified as business income. This distinction is essential, as it dictates which earnings need to be reported and how they should be documented.

Accurate reporting also involves using the appropriate tax forms for different types of income. The IRS requires self-employed individuals to use Schedule C (Form 1040) to report profit or loss from business activities. This form aggregates income from all business-related activities, providing a clear snapshot of total earnings. Additionally, if you receive payments from clients totaling $600 or more in a year, they should issue a Form 1099-NEC, which you must include in your tax return. It's also vital to keep detailed records of smaller payments that don't meet the 1099 threshold, as all income, regardless of amount, must be reported. Proper documentation, including invoices, receipts, and bank statements, is indispensable for this process.

One practical strategy for managing multiple income streams is to use specialized accounting software designed for self-employed individuals. Tools like QuickBooks Self-Employed or FreshBooks can automate the tracking of income, categorize transactions, and generate reports that simplify tax filing. These platforms also facilitate the separation of personal and business finances, which is crucial for accurate reporting. By integrating these tools into your daily operations, you can streamline the process of recording income from various sources, ensuring that nothing slips through the cracks. Leveraging technology in this way not only saves time but also reduces the risk of errors, making tax season far less stressful.

To further enhance your financial strategy, consider consulting with a tax professional who specializes in self-employment. They can provide tailored advice on managing income from multiple streams and help identify potential deductions that you might overlook. A tax expert can also offer insights into optimizing your tax strategy, such as making estimated tax payments throughout the year to avoid a large bill in April. By investing in professional guidance, you can ensure that your income is reported accurately and efficiently, positioning yourself for long-term financial success.

The Self-Employment Tax Explained

Let's dive into the heart of self-employment tax, a crucial element for anyone navigating their own financial seas. Picture this: Jennifer, a talented graphic designer, left her corporate job to pursue freelancing full-time. She quickly discovered the freedom of setting her own hours and choosing her projects, but she also encountered the uncharted waters of self-employment tax. Like Jennifer, many freelancers and independent contractors are initially blindsided by the complexities of this tax, often feeling overwhelmed and uncertain about how to handle it. It's not just about paying taxes—it's about understanding what you're paying and why.

Self-employment tax is more than just a line item on your tax return; it's a combination of Social Security and Medicare taxes that are typically withheld by employers in traditional job settings. For the self-employed, this means taking on both the employer and employee portions of these taxes. Understanding the components of self-employment tax is vital, as it helps you anticipate your tax liability and plan accordingly. By breaking down the calculation process and

MASTERING SELF-EMPLOYED TAXES

exploring strategies to reduce your tax burden, you can transform a daunting task into a manageable part of your financial routine. So, let's unpack these elements and equip ourselves with the knowledge to tackle self-employment tax head-on.

Understanding the Components of Self-Employment Tax

Self-employment tax consists of two main components: Social Security and Medicare taxes, which are typically withheld from wages for traditional employees. However, self-employed individuals must handle these contributions independently, encompassing both the employee and employer portions. This dual responsibility means self-employed workers pay a higher percentage o verall—15.3%—split into 12.4% for Social Security and 2.9% for Medicare. Understanding these components is crucial, as they impact not only your annual tax liability but also your future benefits under the Social Security system.

For example, consider a freelance graphic designer earning $80,000 annually. Unlike a traditional employee, who shares the tax burden with an employer, the freelancer must shoulder the entire 15.3% self-employment tax. This equates to $12,240 annually, a significant figure that underscores the importance of careful financial planning. It's essential to recognize how these taxes are calculated and to factor them into your overall budgeting strategy. Comprehensive financial software or a dedicated tax professional can assist in accurate estimations, ensuring you remain compliant and avoid unexpected tax bills.

Advanced strategies exist to mitigate the impact of self-employment tax, such as forming an S-Corporation. This structure allows you to pay yourself a reasonable salary, subject to payroll taxes, while distributing remaining profits as dividends, which are not subject to self-employment tax. However, this approach requires meticulous adherence to IRS guidelines and may necessitate additional administrative work and costs. Consulting with a tax advisor can help determine whether this strategy aligns with your financial goals and business operations.

Recent developments in the gig economy and remote work paradigms have also influenced self-employment tax policies. Legislative changes, like the potential for increased Social Security contribution caps, could further affect tax liabilities for high earners. Staying informed about these trends is vital, as they can directly impact your financial planning. Subscribing to industry newsletters or joining professional associations can provide timely updates, ensuring you remain ahead of any shifts in the tax landscape.

Engaging with diverse perspectives can also yield innovative approaches to managing self-employment tax. For instance, some experts advocate for the strategic use of retirement accounts like Solo 401(k)s or SEP IRAs, which offer significant tax deferral benefits. These accounts not only reduce your taxable income but also build a nest egg for your future, demonstrating a dual advantage. By exploring and implementing such advanced tactics, you can more effectively manage your self-employment tax, paving the way for greater financial stability and freedom.

Calculating Your Self-Employment Tax Liability

Calculating your self-employment tax liability is a critical skill for any freelancer or independent contractor. This process begins with understanding that self-employment tax is essentially a combination of Social Security and Medicare taxes. Unlike traditional employees who share these costs with their employers, self-employed individuals are responsible for the entire amount. The current rate stands at 15.3%, with 12.4% allocated for Social Security and 2.9% for Medicare. To calculate this tax accurately, you must first determine your net earnings from self-employment, which involves subtracting your business expenses from your gross income. This net figure forms the basis for your self-employment tax calculation.

Once you have your net earnings, the next step is to apply the self-employment tax rate to this amount. For instance, if your net earnings are $50,000, you would multiply this by 15.3%, resulting in a self-employment tax liability of $7,650. However, there's a crucial detail to note: the IRS allows you to deduct the employer-equivalent portion of your self-employment tax when calculating your adjusted gross income. This deduction is typically 50% of your total self-employment tax, which would reduce your taxable income and, consequently, your overall tax burden. This means that from the $7,650 calculated, you can deduct $3,825 when determining your adjusted gross income.

To further refine your tax calculations, consider the income thresholds and caps that might affect your liability. For example, Social Security tax is only applied to the first $142,800 of net income for the 2021 tax year, which means any income above this threshold is not subject to the 12.4% Social Security tax. However, the 2.9% Medicare tax applies to all net earnings, with an additional

0.9% Medicare surtax on earnings over $200,000 for single filers or $250,000 for married couples filing jointly. This layered approach ensures that your calculations are precise and reflect all applicable tax regulations.

Incorporating advanced strategies can also help mitigate your self-employment tax liability. One such strategy involves setting up an S-Corporation, which allows you to split your income into a reasonable salary and distributions. Only the salary portion is subject to self-employment tax, potentially lowering your overall tax liability. Another approach is maximizing your business deductions to reduce your net earnings effectively. Keeping meticulous records of all deductible expenses, from office supplies to travel costs, can significantly lower your taxable income and, by extension, your self-employment tax.

Staying updated with the latest tax laws and leveraging professional advice can be game-changers. Tax laws evolve, and what was applicable last year might not hold this year. Subscribing to tax updates or consulting with a tax professional who specializes in self-employment can provide you with cutting-edge insights and ensure compliance. For instance, recent changes in tax code or new deductions introduced could offer opportunities to further reduce your tax liability. By maintaining an informed and proactive approach, you can navigate the complexities of self-employment tax with confidence and precision, ensuring that you keep more of your hard-earned money.

Strategies for Reducing Self-Employment Tax

Reducing self-employment tax liability can be a game-changer for freelancers and independent contractors aiming to maximize their earnings. One of the most effective strategies is to fully leverage business deductions. By carefully documenting and claiming all eligible expenses—such as office supplies, travel costs, and software subscriptions—you can significantly lower your taxable income. This not only reduces the amount of self-employment tax you owe but also ensures you are not overpaying on your federal and state income taxes. A meticulous approach to record-keeping, using tools like expense-tracking apps or accounting software, can streamline this process and make it less daunting.

Another powerful strategy involves structuring your business entity in a way that minimizes tax liability. For instance, operating as an S Corporation rather than a sole proprietorship can offer substantial tax benefits. In an S Corp, you can classify part of your income as a salary and part as a distribution. While the salary portion is subject to self-employment tax, the distribution is not, effectively reducing the overall tax burden. However, it's crucial to ensure that the salary portion is reasonable according to IRS standards to avoid potential penalties. Consulting with a tax professional can help you determine the most advantageous business structure for your specific circumstances.

Retirement planning also plays a critical role in reducing self-employment tax. Contributing to retirement accounts such as a Simplified Employee Pension (SEP) IRA or a Solo 401(k) not only helps secure your financial future but also provides immediate tax benefits. Contributions to these plans are tax-deductible, lowering your taxable income and, consequently, your self-employment tax. For example, in 2023, you can contribute up to 25% of your net earnings to a SEP IRA, with a maximum contribution limit of $66,000. This dual benefit of tax savings and retirement security makes it a highly effective strategy for self-employed individuals.

Health insurance premiums can also be a significant deduction for self-employed individuals. If you pay for your own health insurance, you're likely eligible to deduct the premiums, which can substantially reduce your taxable income. This deduction is available whether you itemize your deductions or not, making it accessible to a wide range of self-employed workers. Additionally, Health Savings Accounts (HSAs) offer another tax-advantaged way to manage healthcare expenses. Contributions to an HSA are tax-deductible, and withdrawals used for qualified medical expenses are tax-free, providing a dual benefit that can further reduce your tax liability.

Staying informed about tax credits and incentives can provide additional opportunities for reducing self-employment tax. For instance, the Qualified Business Income (QBI) deduction allows eligible self-employed individuals to deduct up to 20% of their qualified business income from their taxable income. This deduction can be particularly beneficial for those in certain service professions. Additionally, keeping an eye on legislative changes and new tax policies can help you take advantage of emerging opportunities. Regularly consulting with a tax advisor ensures you remain compliant while optimizing your tax strategy, ultimately paving the way for greater financial freedom.

Key Tax Forms for the Self-Employed

Let's dive into the heart of what makes self-employment both liberating and a bit daunting: the tax forms. Picture this: You've just landed a fantastic freelance gig, the kind that lets you work in your pajamas while sipping coffee at your favorite cafe. The freedom is intoxicating. But as the year progresses, the thought of tax season begins to loom over you like a dark cloud. You might wonder, "How do I even start to tackle all these forms?" This chapter aims to demystify that process, transforming the intimidating maze of paperwork into a manageable and even empowering part of your financial journey.

At first glance, the myriad of tax forms might seem like a confusing jumble of numbers and jargon. However, understanding these forms is essential to ensuring you're not only compliant but also making the most of your self-employed status. By mastering Form 1040 and Schedule C, you can accurately report your income and expenses. Navigating Schedule SE will help you get a grip on the self-employment tax, which is crucial for funding your Social Security and Medicare benefits. And finally, grasping the role of Form 1099-NEC will clarify how nonemployee compensation is reported, ensuring you leave no stone unturned. Each of these forms plays a pivotal role in your financial ecosystem, and this chapter will guide you through them, step by step, making the process as straightforward as possible.

Understanding Form 1040 and Schedule C for Reporting Income and Expenses

Form 1040, often considered the cornerstone of individual tax returns, is the primary document self-employed individuals must understand. This form serves as the comprehensive summary of all income, deductions, and credits for the tax year. For freelancers and independent contractors, it's not just about reporting wages; it's about detailing every source of income, including business revenue. Understanding Form 1040 is crucial because it sets the stage for accurately reporting your financial activities and ensuring compliance with tax regulations. A thorough grasp of this form can prevent common errors and potential audits, providing a solid foundation for more advanced tax strategies.

Accompanying Form 1040 is Schedule C, which specifically addresses Profit or Loss from Business. This supplementary form is vital for detailing income and expenses directly related to self-employment. Schedule C allows you to categorize and list all business-related expenses, ranging from office supplies to travel costs, which can significantly reduce your taxable income. For example, if you spent $2,000 on advertising and $1,500 on office supplies, these expenses would be itemized here, directly reducing your business profit and, consequently, your tax liability. Properly completing Schedule C not only aids in minimizing taxes owed but also provides a clear financial snapshot of your business operations.

Navigating the nuances of Schedule C requires a keen understanding of what constitutes a deductible expense. The IRS defines allowable deductions as those that are both ordinary and necessary for your business. Ordinary expenses are common and accepted in your trade, while necessary expenses are helpful and appropriate for your business. For instance, a graphic designer can deduct software subscriptions and design tools, while a freelance writer might deduct research materials and professional memberships. Misclassifying expenses or failing to claim legitimate deductions can result in overpaying taxes. Conversely, attempting to deduct non-qualifying expenses could trigger an audit, underscoring the importance of meticulous record-keeping and a thorough understanding of allowable deductions.

Advanced tax planning strategies often involve leveraging Schedule C to maximize deductions legally. One emerging trend is the use of home office deductions, which have become more prevalent with the rise of remote work. If part of your home is used exclusively for business, you can claim a portion of your mortgage, rent, utilities, and other related expenses. This deduction can be significant, but it requires precise calculations and adherence to IRS guidelines to avoid pitfalls. Additionally, staying current with tax law changes, such as those introduced by the Tax Cuts and Jobs Act, can provide new opportunities for deductions and credits, further reducing taxable income.

To ensure accuracy and optimize tax benefits, many self-employed individuals consider using tax software or consulting with a tax professional. These tools and experts can help you navigate complex forms, identify all possible deductions, and ensure compliance with evolving tax laws. For instance, sophisticated tax software can integrate with accounting tools, automatically populating Schedule C with categorized expenses from your financial records. This not only saves time but also reduces the likelihood of errors. Engaging with a knowledgeable tax advisor can provide personalized strategies tailored to your unique financial situation, fostering proactive tax planning and long-term financial success. By mastering Form 1040 and Schedule C, self-employed individuals can take control of their tax obligations and pave the way to financial independence.

Navigating the Self-Employment Tax with Schedule SE

Navigating the self-employment tax with Schedule SE can seem daunting, but understanding its intricacies is crucial for any freelancer or independent contractor aiming for financial mastery. Schedule SE is an essential form that calculates the self-employment tax, which comprises Social Security and Medicare taxes. Unlike traditional W-2 employees who split these taxes with their employers, self-employed individuals bear the full burden. This tax is pivotal because it directly impacts your future Social Security benefits and Medicare eligibility. By comprehensively understanding how to accurately complete Schedule SE, you can ensure compliance and optimize your contributions toward long-term financial security.

It's important to grasp the structure of Schedule SE. The form is divided into two parts: Part I for short computation for self-employment tax and Part II for long computation. Most self-employed individuals will use Part I unless they fall into specific categories such as church employees who are exempt from Social Security and Medicare taxes. This section calculates your net earnings from self-employment, which are derived from your net profit reported on Schedule C. Notably, only 92.35% of your net earnings are subject to self-employment tax, a nuance that often surprises newcomers. This percentage accounts for the deduction allowed for the employer-equivalent portion of your self-employment tax.

An illustrative example can clarify this further. Suppose you have a net profit of $50,000 from your freelance business. You will multiply this amount by 92.35% to get $46,175, which is the amount subject to self-employment tax. Next, you'll apply the current self-employment tax rate of 15.3%, yielding a tax liability of $7,064.78. This total comprises 12.4% for Social Security and 2.9% for Medicare. However, keep in mind that the Social Security portion only applies to earnings up to a certain annual limit, which adjusts yearly based on inflation and other economic factors. Staying updated on these thresholds is critical for accurate tax planning.

Advanced insights into optimizing your Schedule SE involve strategic income management. For instance, some self-employed individuals might explore the benefits of forming an S-Corporation, which allows for splitting income into salary and distributions, potentially reducing the self-employment tax burden. It's essential to weigh the administrative costs and compliance require-

THE BASICS OF SELF EMPLOYED TAXES 17

ments of such a structure against the tax savings. Additionally, incorporating retirement contributions into your tax strategy can significantly impact your self-employment tax calculations. Contributions to a SEP-IRA or Solo 401(k) reduce your net earnings, thereby lessening the amount subject to self-employment tax while simultaneously bolstering your retirement savings.

Reflecting on diverse perspectives, some experts advocate for a more dynamic approach to managing self-employment tax. For example, leveraging accounting software that integrates tax planning features can provide real-time insights into your tax obligations and potential savings. Emerging tools use artificial intelligence to predict tax liabilities based on income trends, offering a proactive rather than reactive approach to tax management. By adopting these innovative resources, you not only streamline the tax filing process but also gain a strategic edge in financial planning. This proactive stance can transform the often overwhelming task of navigating self-employment tax into an integral component of your journey toward financial freedom.

Exploring Form 1099-NEC and Its Role in Reporting Nonemployee Compensation

Form 1099-NEC, or Nonemployee Compensation, has become a cornerstone document for the self-employed, transforming the way independent contractors report their earnings. This form, revived in 2020, specifically delineates income paid to individuals who are not traditional employees but provide services as freelancers, gig workers, or independent contractors. Its reintroduction underscores the increasing prevalence of the gig economy and the need for clarity in tax reporting. Unlike Form 1099-MISC, which covered a broader spectrum of miscellaneous income, the 1099-NEC provides a focused lens on nonemployee compensation, ensuring that the IRS has a clear record of earnings that bypass traditional payroll systems.

The practical implications of Form 1099-NEC are profound. When a business pays an independent contractor $600 or more in a given tax year, it is required to issue this form, reflecting the total amount paid for services rendered. This requirement extends to various forms of remuneration, whether it's for freelance writing, consulting, or other professional services. It's vital for the self-employed to understand that the information reported on Form 1099-NEC directly influences the income reported on their Schedule C of Form 1040. Any discrepancies between these forms can trigger audits or inquiries from the IRS, making accurate and consistent reporting paramount.

Navigating the nuances of Form 1099-NEC can be a game-changer for those aiming to optimize their tax strategy. One advanced insight is the importance of maintaining meticulous records of all earnings and corresponding 1099-NEC forms received. This becomes particularly crucial when juggling multiple clients or projects. Implementing robust financial tracking tools can streamline this process, ensuring that every dollar earned is accounted for and reported correctly. Moreover, understanding the timing of these forms is equally critical. Businesses are required to furnish Form 1099-NEC to independent contractors by January 31st of each year, providing a narrow window for contractors to reconcile their records before tax filing deadlines.

From a strategic standpoint, Form 1099-NEC also opens avenues for proactive financial planning. For instance, if you anticipate receiving substantial nonemployee compensation, you might consider how this impacts your quarterly estimated tax payments. Rather than being caught off guard by a hefty tax bill in April, aligning your tax payments with your earnings cycle can alleviate financial strain and foster a more balanced cash flow throughout the year. Additionally, understanding the role of Form 1099-NEC can aid in identifying legitimate business expenses that can be deducted, thus reducing taxable income. This is where the interplay between different tax forms, such as Schedule C and Schedule SE, becomes apparent, highlighting the intricate web of self-employed tax obligations.

To deepen your understanding, consider the broader economic landscape and emerging trends in independent work. The rise of remote work and digital platforms has exponentially increased the issuance of Form 1099-NEC. Staying informed about regulatory changes and tax reforms that may impact how nonemployee compensation is reported will keep you ahead of the curve. Engaging with tax professionals who specialize in self-employed taxes can also provide tailored advice and innovative strategies, ensuring that you not only comply with tax requirements but also leverage them to your financial advantage.

In bringing this chapter to a close, the foundational elements of self-employed taxes become clear. Understanding what qualifies as self-employment income, grasping the intricacies of the self-employment tax, and familiarizing oneself with the essential tax forms are all crucial steps in navigating your financial landscape. These basics serve as the cornerstone for a more sophisticated tax strategy that not only ensures compliance but also optimizes your financial potential. By demystifying these initial concepts, the path toward financial freedom begins to take shape, empowering you to make informed decisions about your earnings and obligations.

As you digest these foundational principles, it's important to view them as the building blocks of a larger financial framework. Each piece of information, from income definitions to tax forms, contributes to a clearer, more manageable picture of your financial responsibilities. Reflect on how this newfound knowledge can transform your approach to your business finances, setting a proactive tone for the chapters ahead. Are you ready to take the next step in mastering the complexities of self-employed taxes? Embrace this journey with confidence, knowing that each chapter will further illuminate the path to financial independence and peace of mind.

Chapter Two

Tracking Income And Expenses

Peering into the heart of financial freedom, imagine Sarah, a graphic designer who recently made the leap from a secure corporate job to the exhilarating yet daunting world of freelancing. Sarah's mornings now begin with a cup of coffee and a laptop in her favorite local café, where creativity flows freely. However, amidst the newfound freedom, she quickly discovers that managing her finances is far more complex than she had anticipated. Sarah's journey highlights a common challenge faced by many self-employed individuals: the art of tracking income and expenses effectively.

As we dive into this chapter, you'll find that mastering the skill of meticulous record-keeping is not just a mundane task but a cornerstone of financial success. From setting up an efficient system that works seamlessly with your lifestyle to categorizing business expenses in a way that maximizes deductions, this chapter will guide you through the essentials of financial organization. By embracing technology and leveraging modern tools to simplify the tracking process, you can transform a daunting chore into a streamlined routine. This approach not only saves time but also provides clarity, enabling you to make informed decisions that propel your business forward.

In the world of self-employment, thorough tracking is more than just a means to an end; it is a proactive strategy that lays the foundation for long-term financial health. As you read on, you'll uncover practical tips and insights designed to empower you. Whether you're a seasoned freelancer or just starting, this chapter offers valuable guidance to help you navigate the complexities of income and expense management with confidence and ease. So, let's embark on this journey together, transforming your financial practices into a robust system that supports your path to financial freedom.

Setting Up an Efficient Record-Keeping System

Imagine a painter trying to create a masterpiece with a cluttered, disorganized palette—colors blending where they shouldn't, brushes scattered, and no clear plan in sight. This chaotic scene is not unlike the financial life of a self-employed individual who lacks an efficient record-keeping system. Just as a painter needs a well-organized workspace to bring their vision to life, you too need a structured approach to manage your income and expenses effectively. A closer examination shows that the foundation of financial success lies in meticulous record-keeping, transforming what may seem like a mundane task into a powerful tool for achieving financial freedom.

To begin, let's consider the myriad benefits of setting up a streamlined record-keeping system. Not only does it save time and reduce stress when tax season rolls around, but it also provides a clear picture of your financial health, allowing you to make informed decisions about your business. Think of this system as a well-oiled machine, where each component—from choosing the right accounting software to establishing a consistent filing method—plays a crucial role in maintaining accuracy and efficiency. Implementing regular audits ensures that your records are always up-to-date, preventing small errors from snowballing into significant issues. As we explore these essential subtopics, you'll discover practical strategies to transform your financial management from chaotic to composed, setting the stage for long-term success and peace of mind.

Choose the Right Accounting Software for Your Needs

Selecting the ideal accounting software is a pivotal step in establishing an efficient record-keeping system. Unlike traditional methods, modern accounting software offers a plethora of features tailored to the needs of freelancers, gig workers, and independent contractors. These tools automate many time-consuming tasks, enabling users to focus on their core activities. For instance, platforms like QuickBooks Self-Employed and FreshBooks are specifically designed for self-employed individuals, offering functionalities such as income and expense tracking, invoice generation, and even tax estimation. These platforms streamline financial management, ensuring that users can easily monitor their financial health without the labyrinthine complexity of traditional bookkeeping.

When choosing accounting software, it's essential to consider the unique requirements of your business. Some software options cater to specific industries, offering tailored features that can provide a competitive edge. For example, creatives and designers might benefit from software that integrates seamlessly with their project management tools, while those in consulting might prioritize platforms with robust time-tracking capabilities. Furthermore, scalability should be a key consideration. As your business grows, your accounting software should be able to adapt to increased complexity, offering advanced features like multi-currency support, comprehensive reporting, and integration with other business tools.

Advanced functionalities such as AI-driven insights and machine learning are becoming increasingly prevalent in accounting software, offering predictive analytics and personalized recommendations. These cutting-edge features can help identify spending patterns, forecast cash flow, and even suggest ways to optimize tax deductions. For instance, Zoho Books utilizes AI to automate routine tasks and provide actionable insights, helping users make informed decisions based on real-time data. Embracing these innovative tools not only enhances efficiency but also empowers self-employed individuals to make strategic decisions that drive financial growth.

Security is another critical factor to consider when selecting accounting software. Given the sensitive nature of financial data, it's imperative to choose a platform that offers robust security measures, such as encryption, two-factor authentication, and regular security audits. Cloud-based solutions often provide enhanced security features and the added benefit of accessing financial data from any location, ensuring that your records are both secure and readily available. Xero, for example, offers bank-level encryption and multiple layers of security, providing peace of mind that your financial information is well-protected.

Cost and customer support should not be overlooked. While some software options may come with a steeper price tag, they often offer superior features and support that can save time and prevent costly mistakes in the long run. It's crucial to evaluate the total cost of ownership, including any hidden fees for additional features or customer support. Many platforms offer free trials or

TRACKING INCOME AND EXPENSES

tiered pricing plans, allowing users to test the software and choose a plan that aligns with their budget and needs. Excellent customer support can be invaluable, especially during the initial setup and as you navigate complex financial scenarios. QuickBooks, for instance, offers various support options, including phone support, chat, and a comprehensive knowledge base, ensuring that help is always within reach. By carefully considering these factors—specific business needs, advanced functionalities, security, and cost—you can select the accounting software that best aligns with your goals, ultimately setting the foundation for a robust and efficient record-keeping system.

Establish a Consistent Filing and Categorization System

Establishing a consistent filing and categorization system is fundamental for any self-employed individual aiming to maintain clarity and control over their financial records. By ensuring all financial documents are systematically organized, freelancers and gig workers can streamline their tax preparation process, reduce stress, and minimize the risk of errors. The first step in this process involves creating a dedicated space—whether physical or digital—where all financial documents are stored. Digital storage solutions such as cloud-based services offer the advantage of easy access and enhanced security. For those who prefer physical documentation, clearly labeled folders or binders are essential. This initial organization lays the groundwork for an efficient filing system that can handle the complexities of self-employed finances.

A robust categorization system is the next critical component. By dividing expenses into specific categories such as office supplies, travel, and marketing, individuals can gain a clearer understanding of where their money is going and identify potential areas for tax deductions. This categorization should align with IRS guidelines to ensure compliance and facilitate the tax filing process. Advanced accounting software can automate much of this categorization, reducing the time and effort required. However, it's important to periodically review and adjust these categories to reflect any changes in business activities or tax regulations. Staying proactive in this aspect can prevent misclassification and ensure that all expenses are accurately recorded.

Regular audits and updates are indispensable in maintaining the accuracy of a filing and categorization system. Setting aside time, perhaps monthly or quarterly, to review financial records ensures that any discrepancies are caught early. This practice not only aids in keeping the records up-to-date but also provides an opportunity to reassess the financial health of the business. During these audits, individuals should verify that all income and expenses are correctly categorized and that all receipts and invoices are accounted for. This routine check-up can also serve as a moment to reflect on financial goals and make necessary adjustments to budgeting and spending habits.

Implementing technology can significantly enhance the efficiency of a filing system. Modern accounting software offers features such as receipt scanning, automated categorization, and real-time financial reporting. These tools can save a substantial amount of time and reduce the likelihood of human error. For instance, apps that integrate with banking systems can automatically track transactions and categorize them based on predefined rules. Embracing these technological advancements not only simplifies the record-keeping process but also provides valuable insights through data analytics, helping individuals make informed financial decisions.

To ensure the long-term success of a filing and categorization system, it's essential to cultivate disciplined habits. This includes setting regular times for updating records, consistently backing up digital files, and reviewing financial statements. Encouraging self-discipline in these practices can be challenging, but the benefits are significant. By maintaining an organized and accurate financial record, self-employed individuals can confidently navigate tax season, make strategic business decisions, and ultimately work towards achieving financial independence. Consistency and attention to detail are the cornerstones of an effective record-keeping system, paving the way for a smoother, more manageable financial journey.

Implement Regular Audits and Updates to Maintain Accuracy

Implementing regular audits and updates to maintain accuracy in record-keeping is not merely a best practice but a cornerstone of financial integrity for the self-employed. By systematically reviewing your financial records, you ensure that your income and expenses are accurately documented, which is critical not only for tax purposes but also for making informed business decisions. Regular audits help identify discrepancies, such as unrecorded expenses or misclassified transactions, that could otherwise lead to costly mistakes. For instance, a freelance graphic designer might discover through an audit that several small business lunches were mistakenly categorized as personal expenses, thereby missing out on potential deductions. Adopting a disciplined approach to audits ensures

TRACKING INCOME AND EXPENSES

that your financial records reflect the true state of your business, fostering both compliance and strategic planning.

Incorporating technology into your auditing process can significantly streamline this task. Numerous accounting software solutions offer automated features that can flag inconsistencies and generate real-time reports. For example, advanced software like QuickBooks or Xero allows users to set up rules that automatically categorize transactions, reducing the manual effort required. These platforms often include reconciliation tools that compare your bank statements with your financial records, highlighting any mismatches that need attention. Leveraging these technological tools not only saves time but also enhances the accuracy of your audits, making it easier to keep your records up-to-date and error-free.

Periodic updates to your record-keeping system are equally essential. The financial landscape is continuously evolving, and staying abreast of changes—whether in tax laws, industry standards, or your own business operations—requires an adaptable approach. For instance, if new tax deductions become available, your record-keeping system should be updated to capture the relevant data needed to claim these benefits. Regularly updating your categories and templates ensures that your system remains relevant and efficient. An online entrepreneur might find it beneficial to create new expense categories for digital marketing tools as their business grows, ensuring that all relevant costs are tracked and deductible.

Beyond the technical aspects, fostering a routine audit culture within your business can yield significant benefits. Setting aside dedicated time each month or quarter for a thorough review of your financial records instills a habit of meticulousness. This proactive stance helps you catch and rectify errors before they snowball into larger issues. Consider the case of an independent consultant who schedules quarterly reviews; this practice allows for timely adjustments and ensures alignment with their financial goals. Regular audits also provide an opportunity to reflect on your business performance, offering insights into spending patterns and potential areas for cost-saving.

Engaging with a tax professional periodically to review your audits can add an extra layer of assurance. Professionals bring an external perspective and specialized knowledge that can uncover issues you might overlook. They can also provide guidance on optimizing your financial strategies based on the latest regulatory changes and industry trends. For instance, a tax advisor might suggest more efficient ways to structure your expenses or advise on new tax credits relevant to your field. By integrating professional advice into your regular audit routine, you can enhance both the accuracy and strategic value of your financial records, ultimately driving your business towards sustained growth and compliance.

Categorizing Business Expenses

At the core of mastering self-employed taxes is understanding how to categorize your business expenses effectively. Imagine you're a freelance graphic designer, juggling multiple projects and client meetings. One day, you receive a payment for a large project and think, "I've really got this freelance thing figured out." But when tax season rolls around, you find yourself buried in a mountain of receipts and struggling to remember which expenses were directly tied to that project and which were just the cost of running your business. Sound familiar? You're not alone. Many freelancers and independent contractors face this very predicament, and it often results in missed deductions and higher tax bills.

To prevent this scenario from becoming your reality, it's essential to develop a keen eye for distinguishing between direct and indirect expenses. By doing so, you can unlock the potential for maximum deductions and keep more of your hard-earned money. It's not just about saving a few bucks here and there; it's about creating a systematic approach to expense tracking that simplifies your financial life and ensures you're always prepared for tax time. With the right strategies and tools, categorizing expenses can become a seamless part of your routine, freeing up mental space and energy to focus on what you do best—growing your business. So, let's dive into the nuances of expense categorization and explore how advanced tracking software can become your new best friend in the world of self-employment.

Distinguishing Between Direct and Indirect Expenses

Understanding the distinction between direct and indirect expenses is fundamental to effective financial management for the self-employed. Direct expenses are those costs that can be directly attributed to the production of goods or services. Examples include materials for a craftsperson, software for a graphic designer, or travel expenses for a consultant visiting a client. These expenses are critical to track accurately because they directly impact the cost of goods

TRACKING INCOME AND EXPENSES

sold (COGS) and, consequently, the gross profit margin. A keen awareness of direct expenses enables freelancers to price their services appropriately, ensuring profitability.

Indirect expenses, on the other hand, are costs that support the overall operations but are not directly tied to any specific product or service. These include rent for office space, utilities, and general office supplies. Indirect expenses, while not linked to a specific client project, are essential for maintaining a functional business environment. Understanding these expenses is crucial for a holistic view of the business's financial health. By categorizing these costs correctly, freelancers and independent contractors can gain insights into their operational efficiency and identify areas to optimize spending.

To maximize deductions and ensure compliance with tax regulations, it's imperative to categorize business expenses meticulously. The IRS provides guidelines on what constitutes deductible expenses, and distinguishing between direct and indirect costs plays a significant role. For instance, home office expenses can often be partially deducted if the space is used exclusively for business purposes. Similarly, costs like internet service might be split between personal and business use. Keeping detailed records and clear categorizations helps in substantiating these deductions during tax time, minimizing the risk of audits and ensuring that all eligible expenses are claimed.

Advances in technology have made tracking these expenses more accessible than ever. Modern expense tracking software can seamlessly integrate with bank accounts, automatically categorizing transactions based on predefined rules. This automation reduces the administrative burden, allowing freelancers to focus more on their core work. Additionally, many of these tools offer customizable reports that provide insights into spending patterns, helping to identify potential savings and optimize cash flow. Leveraging such technology not only ensures accuracy but also provides a competitive edge in managing finances efficiently.

Consider this scenario: A freelance photographer uses an online platform to manage their expenses. By setting categories for direct costs like camera equipment and indirect costs like office rent, they can generate detailed reports at the click of a button. This clarity not only aids in tax preparation but also offers a strategic overview of their financial health. Are they spending too much on travel? Is there a spike in indirect costs that needs addressing? By maintaining a nuanced understanding of direct and indirect expenses, freelancers can make

Utilizing Expense Categories for Maximum Deductions

Maximizing deductions is paramount for self-employed individuals, and categorizing business expenses efficiently can lead to substantial tax savings. One of the keys to achieving this is understanding how different expense categories can be leveraged for maximum benefit. By meticulously organizing expenses into well-defined categories, freelancers and independent contractors can ensure that no deductible cost goes unnoticed. This process not only simplifies tax filing but also provides a clearer picture of where money is being spent, allowing for better financial planning and management.

Direct expenses are those that can be attributed directly to a specific project or service. These might include materials, labor costs, and subcontractor fees. By distinguishing these from indirect expenses, which are more general business costs like rent and utilities, self-employed individuals can more accurately track project profitability. For example, a freelance graphic designer might categorize software subscriptions, design supplies, and client-specific printing costs as direct expenses. This clear distinction aids in pinpointing which projects are most lucrative and where adjustments might be needed to maintain profitability.

To maximize deductions, it's essential to utilize a comprehensive list of IRS-approved expense categories. These include but are not limited to office supplies, travel, meals, home office expenses, and professional development. Each category has its own set of rules and limitations, so a deep understanding is crucial. For instance, meals and entertainment can only be deducted at 50%, while home office expenses must be proportionate to the space used exclusively for business. Proper categorization ensures that each expense is deducted to the fullest extent allowed by law, reducing taxable income significantly.

Advanced expense tracking software can be a game-changer in this regard. Cutting-edge tools like QuickBooks, Xero, and FreshBooks offer robust features that automate the categorization process. These platforms can import bank transactions, automatically categorize them based on user-defined rules, and generate detailed reports. Such automation not only saves time but also minimizes errors, ensuring that every possible deduction is captured. Additionally, these tools often provide real-time insights into cash flow and profitability, empowering self-employed individuals to make informed financial decisions.

To illustrate the practical application of these strategies, consider a scenario in which a freelance writer uses expense tracking software to categorize his business expenses throughout the year. By diligently recording every cost and leveraging the software's automation features, he discovers that he's eligible for several deductions he previously overlooked, such as a portion of his internet bill and a new computer purchased for work. As a result, his taxable income is significantly reduced, leading to substantial tax savings. This example underscores the importance of meticulous expense categorization and the benefits of utilizing advanced tools to streamline the process.

Implementing Advanced Expense Tracking Software

Utilizing advanced expense tracking software can revolutionize the way self-employed individuals manage their finances, significantly enhancing both accuracy and efficiency. These sophisticated tools go beyond mere logging of transactions; they integrate with bank accounts, credit cards, and even invoicing systems to provide a seamless and comprehensive view of one's financial landscape. By automatically categorizing expenses and income, these systems reduce the margin for human error and ensure that all financial activities are meticulously recorded. For instance, platforms like QuickBooks Self-Employed and Xero offer robust features that can automatically sort expenses into IRS-compliant categories, thereby simplifying the preparation for tax filings and optimizing deductions.

Incorporating advanced expense tracking software also allows for real-time financial monitoring, a critical component for proactive financial management. With instant access to up-to-date financial data, self-employed individuals can make informed decisions promptly, avoiding cash flow issues and identifying potential savings opportunities. This real-time insight can be particularly beneficial when planning for quarterly tax payments, as it provides a clear picture of earnings and liabilities. Additionally, many of these tools offer customizable reporting features, enabling users to generate detailed financial reports that can be tailored to specific needs or shared with tax professionals for more precise advice.

The integration of artificial intelligence (AI) and machine learning in expense tracking software represents a significant leap forward in financial management. These technologies can analyze spending patterns, predict future expenses, and even provide personalized financial advice. For example, AI-driven platforms might flag unusual transactions for review or suggest ways to optimize spending based on historical data. By leveraging AI, users can gain deeper insights into their financial habits and identify areas for improvement that might otherwise go unnoticed. This level of analysis not only aids in better financial planning but also helps in maintaining compliance with tax regulations.

Security is another paramount feature of advanced expense tracking software. Given the sensitive nature of financial data, these platforms employ state-of-the-art encryption and security protocols to protect users' information. Multi-factor authentication, secure cloud storage, and regular data backups are standard features that ensure data integrity and privacy. For instance, applications like FreshBooks and Wave adhere to stringent security standards, providing peace of mind that financial data is safeguarded against breaches. This level of security is crucial for self-employed individuals who must protect their financial information from potential cyber threats.

Implementing advanced expense tracking software is not just about adopting new technology; it requires a strategic approach to fully leverage its capabilities. Users should regularly review and update their financial data, set up automatic categorization rules, and utilize the software's full range of features, such as budgeting tools and financial forecasts. Training and familiarization with the chosen platform are essential to maximize its benefits. By dedicating time to understand and configure these tools, self-employed individuals can streamline their financial management processes, ensuring accuracy, compliance, and ultimately, peace of mind.

Using Technology to Simplify Tracking

Imagine waking up one morning to find that managing your finances no longer feels like a burdensome chore but rather a seamless part of your daily routine. With the right technology at your fingertips, this dream can become your reality. In today's fast-paced world, freelancers and independent contractors are increasingly turning to innovative digital tools to simplify the intricate task of tracking income and expenses. Gone are the days of sifting through piles of receipts or scrambling to recall every business expense at tax time. Instead, technology offers a streamlined, efficient, and accurate way to keep your financial records in check, allowing you to focus more on your craft and less on the paperwork.

TRACKING INCOME AND EXPENSES 31

The significance of embracing these technological advancements cannot be overstated. Leveraging mobile apps for real-time expense tracking ensures that every transaction is recorded the moment it happens, reducing the risk of forgotten deductions. Integrating automated accounting software provides a seamless data management experience, minimizing human error and saving precious time. Moreover, utilizing cloud-based solutions offers the dual benefits of multi-device accessibility and heightened security, ensuring that your financial data is both convenient to access and well-protected. As we explore these subtopics in detail, you'll discover how these tools can transform your financial management process, making it not only more efficient but also empowering you with greater control over your financial destiny.

Leveraging Mobile Apps for Real-Time Expense Tracking

Embracing mobile apps for real-time expense tracking can revolutionize the financial management of self-employed individuals. In an era where convenience and efficiency are paramount, mobile applications offer a seamless way to record expenses as they occur, minimizing the risk of forgotten transactions and misplaced receipts. Apps like Expensify, QuickBooks Self-Employed, and Wave have become indispensable tools for freelancers and gig workers, providing intuitive interfaces and functionalities tailored to the unique needs of independent contractors. These apps allow users to capture receipts with their phone cameras, categorize expenses instantly, and sync data across devices, ensuring that no financial detail slips through the cracks.

The ability to track expenses in real-time significantly reduces the administrative burden associated with financial record-keeping. Instead of dedicating hours at the end of each month to manually input data, self-employed individuals can quickly log their expenses on the go. This immediate recording not only saves time but also enhances accuracy, as details are fresh and less prone to error. For instance, a freelancer who travels frequently for work can use a mobile app to record travel expenses the moment they are incurred, ensuring precise and timely documentation. This level of diligence in expense tracking can lead to more accurate financial statements, facilitating better financial decision-making and tax preparation.

Beyond the convenience of real-time tracking, many mobile apps offer advanced features that can provide deeper insights into spending patterns and financial health. For example, some applications analyze transaction data to identify trends, flag unusual expenses, and even offer budget recommendations based on historical data. These insights can empower self-employed individuals to make informed financial decisions, optimize their spending, and identify potential areas for cost-saving. By leveraging these advanced analytics, freelancers can gain a clearer understanding of their financial standing and develop strategies to enhance their financial stability and growth.

Security is another critical aspect where mobile apps excel. Leading expense tracking apps employ robust security measures, including encryption and secure cloud storage, to protect sensitive financial data. This ensures that users' information is safe from unauthorized access and potential breaches. Additionally, the ability to back up data to the cloud means that financial records are not confined to a single device, reducing the risk of data loss due to device malfunction or loss. For self-employed individuals, this level of security and redundancy is crucial in maintaining comprehensive and reliable financial records.

The integration of mobile apps into the financial management toolkit of self-employed individuals represents a significant advancement in how expenses are tracked and managed. By adopting these technologies, freelancers, gig workers, and independent contractors can streamline their financial processes, reduce administrative burdens, and gain valuable insights into their financial health. These tools not only simplify the complexities of expense tracking but also empower users to take control of their financial journey with confidence and ease. As technology continues to evolve, staying abreast of the latest advancements and incorporating them into daily routines will be essential for achieving and maintaining financial freedom.

Integrating Automated Accounting Software for Seamless Data Management

Integrating automated accounting software into your financial toolkit can revolutionize the way you manage data. By automating repetitive tasks, these platforms free up time, allowing you to focus on growing your business instead of getting bogged down by administrative duties. For instance, QuickBooks and Xero are two popular options that offer seamless integration with your bank accounts, automatically categorizing transactions and flagging any irregularities. This automated approach not only reduces the risk of human error but also

TRACKING INCOME AND EXPENSES

ensures that your financial records are always up-to-date, providing you with real-time insights into your financial health.

Beyond basic transaction tracking, advanced accounting software can provide a comprehensive suite of tools that facilitate more sophisticated financial analysis. These platforms often include features like invoicing, payroll management, and detailed financial reporting. Imagine having a dashboard where you can instantly visualize your income streams, expense patterns, and tax obligations. Such detailed, real-time analytics can be crucial for making informed business decisions. For example, the software can help identify which clients are the most profitable, enabling you to allocate resources more effectively or even renegotiate contracts to better serve your financial goals.

The benefits of automated accounting software extend to tax preparation as well. These platforms can generate tax reports that compile all necessary financial data, making it easier to file accurate returns. They also often include tax planning tools that project future tax liabilities based on current earnings, helping you set aside the appropriate funds for quarterly tax payments. This proactive approach can prevent cash flow issues and last-minute scrambles to meet tax deadlines. Additionally, many software solutions are updated regularly to reflect the latest tax laws and regulations, ensuring that your tax planning is always compliant with current standards.

Security and accessibility are also paramount when choosing an automated accounting solution. Cloud-based software offers significant advantages in this regard, providing secure, encrypted storage for your financial data that can be accessed from any device. This multi device accessibility ensures that you can manage your finances on the go, whether you're traveling for business or working from a remote location. The ability to access and update your financial records in real time from multiple devices can be a game-changer, particularly for those who juggle multiple income streams and need to stay organized across different platforms.

The importance of scalability should not be overlooked. As your business grows, so too will your financial management needs. Automated accounting platforms are designed to scale with you, offering additional features and integrations that can handle more complex financial scenarios. For example, you might start with basic expense tracking and invoicing, but as your business expands, you can integrate more advanced functionalities such as multi-currency transactions, inventory management, or even CRM systems. This scalability ensures that your financial management tools can evolve alongside

MASTERING SELF-EMPLOYED TAXES

your business, providing robust support at every stage of your entrepreneurial journey. By integrating automated accounting software, you're not just adopting a tool—you're investing in a comprehensive system that supports long-term financial health and growth. This strategic approach not only simplifies day-to-day financial tasks but also empowers you with the insights needed to drive your business forward confidently.

Utilizing Cloud-Based Solutions for Multi-Device Accessibility and Security

Harnessing the power of cloud-based solutions can revolutionize the way self-employed individuals manage their financial data. These platforms offer the advantage of multi-device accessibility, allowing users to input, review, and update their financial information from any location, at any time. Imagine a freelance graphic designer who travels frequently; with cloud-based accounting tools, they can log expenses incurred during a client visit right from their smartphone, and later review these entries on their laptop. This seamless integration ensures that no piece of financial data is overlooked, promoting meticulous and up-to-date record-keeping.

Beyond convenience, cloud-based solutions provide robust security measures to protect sensitive financial information. Data encryption, automated backups, and secure login protocols are standard features, giving users peace of mind that their information is safeguarded against cyber threats. For instance, a gig worker using a reputable cloud accounting service can rest assured that their financial data is encrypted during transmission and storage, effectively reducing the risk of data breaches. This level of security is crucial for maintaining the integrity and privacy of business records, which is especially important for those handling confidential client information.

Cloud-based accounting platforms often integrate with other financial tools and services, creating a cohesive ecosystem for managing all aspects of a self-employed individual's finances. For example, a software developer might use a cloud-based solution that syncs seamlessly with their invoicing software, bank accounts, and even tax preparation services. This integration reduces the need for manual data entry, minimizes errors, and ensures that all financial activities are accurately recorded and easily accessible. The interconnectedness of these

TRACKING INCOME AND EXPENSES

tools can save significant time and effort, allowing self-employed professionals to focus more on their core business activities.

Staying abreast of the latest advancements in cloud technology can provide a competitive edge. Emerging trends such as artificial intelligence (AI) and machine learning are being integrated into cloud-based accounting systems, offering predictive analytics and automated financial insights. A photographer using a cutting-edge cloud solution might receive AI-generated suggestions on optimizing their expense categories or identifying potential tax deductions. These intelligent features can transform raw financial data into actionable insights, enabling more informed decision-making and strategic financial planning.

To fully leverage the benefits of cloud-based solutions, self-employed individuals should prioritize finding platforms that cater specifically to their unique needs. Conducting thorough research, reading user reviews, and seeking recommendations from peers can help identify the most suitable tools. Additionally, taking advantage of free trials or demos can provide hands-on experience with the platform's features and usability. By choosing the right cloud-based solution, self-employed professionals can enhance their financial management processes, ensuring they remain agile, secure, and well-prepared for any financial challenges that may arise.

As we reflect on the principles laid out in this chapter, the importance of setting up an efficient record-keeping system becomes undeniably clear. A meticulous approach to categorizing business expenses not only ensures compliance with tax regulations but also empowers you to make informed decisions about your financial health. Leveraging technology to simplify tracking transforms what could be a tedious chore into a seamless part of your daily routine, thus saving time and reducing stress. These foundational steps are crucial for establishing a solid financial base from which you can confidently navigate the complexities of self-employed taxes.

Embracing these strategies is more than just a means to an end; it's a proactive stance towards financial independence. By mastering the art of tracking income and expenses, you set the stage for a more organized and less daunting tax season, allowing you to focus on growing your business and achieving your personal goals. As you move forward, consider how these practices can be further refined and adapted to suit your unique needs. Imagine the peace of mind that comes with knowing your financial records are in order, and let that vision motivate you to stay diligent. The journey towards financial freedom is ongoing, and each step you take brings you closer to mastering your self-employed taxes with confidence and ease.

Chapter Three

Claiming Deductions

As we navigate through the labyrinth of self-employed taxes, it becomes clear that claiming deductions is not just a matter of ticking boxes—it's an art form that can significantly impact your financial well-being. Imagine Sam, a freelance graphic designer who started her journey with little understanding of tax deductions. Initially overwhelmed by the myriad of expenses she could potentially write off, Sam felt paralyzed. It wasn't until she met a mentor who guided her through the process that she began to see deductions not as a burden, but as opportunities. Through meticulous record-keeping and strategic planning, Sam transformed her financial outlook, turning potential tax liabilities into savings that fueled her business growth.

Claiming deductions is akin to uncovering hidden treasures within your financial landscape. From common deductions that every freelancer should be aware of, to specific opportunities like the home office deduction, this chapter aims to demystify the process. By maximizing vehicle and travel deductions, you'll learn to turn everyday expenses into valuable tax savings. Each section is crafted to provide practical insights and actionable steps, making you feel empowered rather than overwhelmed.

In the midst of understanding these key concepts, it's essential to grasp their broader significance. Properly claiming deductions can mean the difference between a stressful tax season and a seamless one. More importantly, it serves as a cornerstone of proactive financial management, aligning perfectly with our journey towards financial freedom. By mastering these strategies, you're not just reducing your tax burden; you're investing in your business's future and your

Common Deductions for Freelancers and Contractors

The essence of this topic is unlocking the potential within the tax code to significantly boost your bottom line. Imagine Jane, a graphic designer who recently transitioned from a corporate job to freelancing. Initially, she was overwhelmed by the myriad of tax regulations and uncertain about how to optimize her deductions. However, by understanding and leveraging common deductions available to freelancers and contractors, she not only reduced her tax burden but also reinvested those savings into her growing business. This chapter aims to demystify these deductions, providing you with the tools to maximize your savings and keep more of your hard-earned money.

Navigating the labyrinth of tax deductions can feel daunting, but it's a journey well worth embarking on. Whether it's the home office deduction, the costs of essential equipment and supplies, or even health insurance premiums, each category offers unique opportunities for financial relief. The key lies in comprehending the criteria and maintaining meticulous records, ensuring every eligible expense is claimed. By the end of this section, you'll be equipped with the knowledge to take full advantage of these deductions, transforming what might seem like tedious paperwork into a strategic advantage for your freelance business.

Home Office Deduction and Its Criteria

For freelancers and independent contractors, the home office deduction represents a significant opportunity to reduce taxable income by claiming business expenses associated with their workspace. To qualify, the space must be used exclusively and regularly for business purposes. This means that the area should be a dedicated zone where work activities such as conducting meetings, managing finances, or completing projects take place. The IRS is stringent about this exclusivity criterion—using the same space for personal activities can disqualify the deduction. For instance, a spare bedroom set up as an office that also serves as a guest room wouldn't meet the criteria. Understanding and adhering to these guidelines can ensure that freelancers maximize their allowable deductions without running afoul of IRS regulations.

The two methods to calculate the home office deduction offer flexibility depending on the specific circumstances of the taxpayer. The simplified method allows for a deduction of $5 per square foot of the home used for business, up to 300 square feet, capping the deduction at $1,500. This option is straightforward and requires minimal record-keeping. On the other hand, the regular method involves calculating the actual expenses related to the home office, such as mortgage interest, utilities, insurance, and repairs, prorated based on the percentage of the home devoted to business use. While more complex, this method can potentially yield a larger deduction, particularly in cases where home-related expenses are substantial.

For those opting for the regular method, detailed record-keeping becomes essential. Maintaining meticulous records of all expenses related to the home office is crucial—this includes receipts, bills, and any other documentation that supports the claim. Using accounting software can simplify this process, allowing freelancers to categorize and track expenses consistently. It's also beneficial to keep photographic evidence of the home office setup and its exclusive use, which can serve as valuable documentation in case of an audit. By staying organized and diligent, freelancers can confidently claim their home office deduction and potentially reap significant tax benefits.

Emerging trends in remote work have expanded the possibilities for home office deductions. As more individuals transition to freelancing or remote consulting, the traditional concept of a home office has evolved. Freelancers might now incorporate innovative setups, such as outdoor workspaces or mobile offices within their homes, provided these spaces meet the IRS's criteria for exclusive and regular business use. This trend underscores the importance of staying informed about current IRS guidelines and adapting to changes in work environments. By leveraging these modern workspaces, freelancers can optimize their deductions while maintaining compliance.

Consider the potential pitfalls and plan accordingly. One common mistake is overestimating the percentage of the home used for business, which can raise red flags with the IRS. It's also vital to ensure that the home office deduction is not claimed for periods when the space was not in use for business purposes. Thoughtful planning and a clear understanding of the rules can help avoid these errors. For those uncertain about navigating these complexities, consulting with a tax professional can provide clarity and reassurance, ensuring that deductions

40 MASTERING SELF-EMPLOYED TAXES

are accurately calculated and fully compliant with current tax laws. By mastering these nuances, freelancers can confidently claim their home office deduction and enhance their financial resilience.

Equipment and Supply Expenses

For freelancers and independent contractors, understanding the nuances of equipment and supply expenses is crucial in optimizing tax savings. This category encompasses a broad range of items that are essential for conducting business. These can include computers, software, office furniture, and specialized tools pertinent to one's trade. For example, a graphic designer might invest in high-performance graphic design software and a powerful computer, while a carpenter would likely purchase tools and materials specific to woodworking. Keeping meticulous records of such expenditures not only ensures compliance with tax regulations but also maximizes potential deductions.

One key aspect to consider is the distinction between capital expenses and current expenses. Capital expenses, such as purchasing a new laptop or office furniture, are typically considered long-term investments and may need to be depreciated over several years. On the other hand, current expenses, like printer ink or monthly software subscriptions, are deductible in the year they are incurred. Navigating these distinctions can be complex, but understanding them enables self-employed individuals to strategically plan their purchases and deductions to maximize tax benefits.

Advanced strategies can further enhance the effectiveness of claiming equipment and supply expenses. For instance, Section 179 of the IRS tax code allows businesses to deduct the full purchase price of qualifying equipment and software purchased or financed during the tax year. This provision is particularly beneficial for self-employed individuals looking to make significant investments in their business. Additionally, the concept of "bonus depreciation" can allow for immediate expensing of a large portion of the cost of certain assets, providing substantial upfront tax relief.

Innovation in the workplace has led to new categories of deductible expenses. With the rise of remote work, items like ergonomic office chairs, standing desks, and advanced home networking equipment have become commonplace. These purchases, once considered luxuries, are now essential for maintaining productivity and health in a home office setting. Keeping abreast of current trends and

CLAIMING DEDUCTIONS 41

understanding how they translate into deductible expenses can give freelancers and contractors an edge in managing their finances effectively.

To master the art of claiming equipment and supply expenses, freelancers should adopt a proactive and organized approach. Utilizing accounting software can streamline the process of tracking and categorizing expenses, ensuring nothing is overlooked. Regularly updating one's inventory of business assets and reviewing receipts can prevent last-minute scrambles during tax season. By integrating these practices into their routine, self-employed individuals can navigate the complexities of tax deductions with confidence, ultimately fostering a more financially stable and prosperous business.

Health Insurance Premiums for Self-Employed Individuals

For freelancers and independent contractors, health insurance premiums can be a significant expense, but they also present a valuable tax deduction opportunity. Self-employed individuals who pay for their own health insurance may be eligible to deduct the cost of premiums for medical, dental, and qualified long-term care insurance. This deduction applies not only to the individual but also to their spouse and dependents, providing substantial financial relief. To qualify, one must not be eligible for a health plan through an employer or their spouse's employer. Leveraging this deduction effectively can lead to considerable tax savings, making it an essential component of financial planning for the self-employed.

Understanding the specific criteria for claiming health insurance premiums is crucial. The deduction is available whether you purchase insurance through the Health Insurance Marketplace, directly from an insurance company, or through a professional association. Importantly, the premiums must be paid out-of-pocket and not reimbursed by any other entity. This deduction is taken as an adjustment to income on Form 1040, meaning it can reduce your adjusted gross income (AGI), ultimately lowering your taxable income. However, it's important to note that the deduction cannot exceed the net profit from your self-employment income, ensuring it's tailored proportionately to what you earn.

An often overlooked aspect is the inclusion of premiums for qualified long-term care insurance. This can be particularly beneficial for those planning for future medical needs. The amount you can deduct for long-term care premiums is subject to age-based limits, which increase as you get older. Staying informed about these limits and planning accordingly can lead to optimized tax benefits. Additionally, if you have a Health Savings Account (HSA), you can use it to pay for long-term care insurance premiums and deduct these expenses, further enhancing your tax strategy.

To maximize the benefit of health insurance premium deductions, meticulous record-keeping is indispensable. Maintain organized documentation of premium payments, including invoices, receipts, and bank statements. This practice not only facilitates accurate tax filing but also ensures preparedness in the event of an audit. Consider using accounting software tailored for self-employed individuals, which can automate and streamline the tracking process. This proactive approach to documentation can save time and reduce stress, making the tax season less daunting.

In a broader context, understanding and effectively utilizing health insurance premium deductions can be a stepping stone towards comprehensive financial independence. It exemplifies the importance of being proactive and informed about tax obligations and opportunities. By integrating this knowledge into your overall tax and financial strategy, you can achieve a more secure and prosperous self-employed journey. Engage with financial advisors or tax professionals to explore personalized strategies that align with your specific circumstances, ensuring you're not just compliant but also optimizing your financial outcomes.

Home Office Deduction: What You Need to Know

Picture a world where your home office isn't just a corner of your living room, but a gateway to significant tax savings. Imagine transforming that dedicated workspace into a powerful tool for reducing your tax burden, all while maintaining the freedom and flexibility that comes with being self-employed. This isn't just a dream—it's a very real possibility for freelancers, gig workers, and independent contractors who understand how to effectively leverage the home office deduction. But navigating the maze of IRS rules and regulations can feel overwhelming. That's where this chapter steps in, demystifying the complexities and providing you with a clear roadmap to make the most of this valuable deduction.

One fascinating aspect of the home office deduction is its dual-method approach, offering both a simplified and a regular method to suit different needs. Whether you're a minimalist who prefers straightforward calculations or

CLAIMING DEDUCTIONS

someone who thrives on detailed record-keeping, there's an option that fits your style. But before diving into the numbers, it's crucial to understand the eligibility criteria and the concept of exclusive use. How can you ensure your home office meets IRS standards? And what are the implications of depreciation and recapture rules? As we explore these subtopics, you'll gain the knowledge and confidence to claim your home office deduction with ease, turning a potential headache into a strategic advantage on your path to financial freedom.

Determining Eligibility and Understanding Exclusive Use

For freelancers and independent contractors, the home office deduction can be a valuable tool for reducing taxable income, but it is essential to understand the eligibility criteria and the concept of exclusive use. To qualify for the home office deduction, the space must be used regularly and exclusively for business purposes. This means that the area must be dedicated entirely to your work activities, and not used for personal tasks or leisure. For instance, a corner of your living room where you occasionally check emails would not qualify, but a separate room converted into an office space would. This distinction is crucial as the Internal Revenue Service (IRS) is quite strict about the exclusive use requirement to prevent misuse of the deduction.

Understanding what constitutes exclusive use can sometimes be nuanced. The IRS allows for some leniency in how the space is defined. For example, if you have a dedicated office area within a larger room, it may still qualify as long as it is clearly partitioned and used solely for business purposes. It is also important to document this usage meticulously, as photographic evidence or a detailed floor plan can be invaluable if you are ever audited. Advanced insights suggest maintaining a log of activities conducted in the space to further substantiate your claim. Modern technology, such as time-tracking apps, can help demonstrate the frequency and nature of the business use of your home office.

To determine if you are eligible, consider your work habits and the physical layout of your home. If you are a freelancer who meets clients in a dedicated home office or a graphic designer with a studio space, you are likely eligible. On the other hand, gig workers who operate mainly in the field may find it more challenging to justify a home office deduction unless they perform substantial administrative tasks from home. This eligibility assessment is critical as claiming a deduction without meeting the criteria can result in penalties.

The exclusive use rule also extends to storage spaces and areas used for inventory if you are involved in selling products. For example, a part of your basement used exclusively for storing merchandise can qualify for the deduction. This is particularly relevant for those engaged in e-commerce or home-based retail businesses. It is essential to measure and document the square footage of these storage areas accurately, as this will be needed when calculating the deduction.

Determining eligibility for the home office deduction hinges on understanding and adhering to the exclusive use requirement. By ensuring that your workspace is used solely for business purposes and maintaining thorough documentation, you can confidently claim this valuable deduction. This proactive approach not only maximizes your tax savings but also provides a clear and defensible position should any questions arise. Embracing these practices will help you navigate the complexities of self-employed taxes with greater ease and assurance.

Calculating the Simplified and Regular Methods

Calculating the home office deduction can be a game-changer for freelancers and independent contractors, offering a significant reduction in taxable income. Understanding the two primary methods—the Simplified Method and the Regular Method—is crucial for maximizing this benefit. The Simplified Method is designed to be straightforward, allowing taxpayers to deduct $5 per square foot of home office space, up to a maximum of 300 square feet. This method is particularly beneficial for those who prefer a hassle-free approach without the need to keep meticulous records of home-related expenses. It provides an easy way to claim a deduction while minimizing the administrative burden.

On the other hand, the Regular Method can often yield a more substantial deduction but requires a more detailed accounting of expenses. This method involves calculating the actual expenses related to the home office, such as mortgage interest, rent, utilities, insurance, repairs, and depreciation. To apply this method, taxpayers must determine the percentage of the home used exclusively for business and then allocate the corresponding portion of these expenses to the home office deduction. For instance, if a home office occupies 10% of the total square footage of the home, 10% of the qualifying expenses can be deducted.

Depreciation is a key component of the Regular Method, allowing taxpayers to deduct the gradual wear and tear on their home office over time. This aspect

CLAIMING DEDUCTIONS

can significantly enhance the deduction but also adds complexity, as it requires understanding the useful life of the property and the appropriate depreciation method. Moreover, taxpayers must be aware of the potential for depreciation recapture if they sell their home, as this can result in taxable income in the year of the sale. Thus, while the Regular Method may offer a larger deduction, it necessitates a more thorough understanding of tax laws and diligent record-keeping.

Advanced tax software and consultation with a tax professional can simplify the process of calculating these deductions. Many tax preparation programs are equipped with tools to help taxpayers accurately determine their eligible home office deductions, whether using the Simplified or Regular Method. Additionally, a knowledgeable tax advisor can provide personalized guidance, helping individuals navigate the complexities of depreciation and recapture rules. This professional assistance ensures that taxpayers maximize their deductions while remaining compliant with tax regulations.

Reflecting on the choice between the Simplified and Regular Methods, it's essential to consider both immediate benefits and long-term implications. The Simplified Method offers ease and convenience but may limit the deduction amount. Conversely, the Regular Method, while potentially yielding a higher deduction, demands more effort and a deeper understanding of tax intricacies. By carefully weighing these factors and leveraging available resources, freelancers and contractors can make informed decisions that align with their financial goals, ultimately paving the way toward greater financial freedom.

Navigating Depreciation and Recapture Rules

Understanding the intricacies of depreciation and recapture rules is essential for anyone looking to claim the home office deduction effectively. Depreciation allows self-employed individuals to gradually write off the cost of their home office over time, reflecting the wear and tear or obsolescence of the property used for business purposes. The IRS provides guidelines for calculating depreciation, typically using the Modified Accelerated Cost Recovery System (MACRS) for real property. This method involves spreading the cost of the property over a 39-year period. While this may seem straightforward, it requires precise documentation and calculation to ensure accuracy and compliance.

To begin with, it's crucial to determine the basis of your home office, which generally includes the purchase price of the property, plus any improvements, minus any land value. For example, if your home cost $300,000 and the land is valued at $50,000, the basis for depreciation would be $250,000. If your home office occupies 10% of your home's square footage, you can depreciate 10% of the basis, or $25,000. This amount is then divided by 39 years, resulting in an annual depreciation deduction of approximately $641. Accurate record-keeping is essential here, as the IRS may require detailed evidence of these calculations during an audit.

Depreciation recapture comes into play when you sell your home. Essentially, the IRS requires you to "recapture" the depreciation deductions you've taken, adding them to your taxable income. This can result in a significant tax liability, especially if you've claimed depreciation over many years. For instance, if you've claimed $10,000 in depreciation deductions for your home office and then sell your home, you must report this $10,000 as ordinary income, potentially pushing you into a higher tax bracket. Understanding this can help you plan for future tax obligations and avoid unpleasant surprises.

Advanced strategies can help mitigate the impact of depreciation recapture. One such strategy involves a Section 1031 exchange, which allows you to defer capital gains and depreciation recapture by reinvesting the proceeds from the sale of your property into a similar, like-kind property. This can be particularly advantageous for self-employed individuals planning to continue using a home office in a new location. Another approach is to offset the recaptured depreciation with other business losses or deductions, effectively reducing your taxable income.

Navigating depreciation and recapture rules requires a nuanced understanding of tax laws and strategic financial planning. It's advisable to consult with a tax professional who can provide personalized advice tailored to your specific situation. They can help you develop a comprehensive tax strategy that maximizes your deductions while minimizing potential liabilities. By staying informed and proactive, you can make the most of the home office deduction and secure your financial future.

Maximizing Vehicle and Travel Deductions

What sets this apart is the surprising potential for tax savings hidden within the miles you drive and the trips you take for your business. Imagine this scenario: Alex, a freelance graphic designer, realized he had been leaving money on the table every year by not fully understanding how to claim vehicle and travel deductions. After a bit of research and a commitment to better record-keeping, Alex discovered that his regular drives to meet clients and attend conferences could significantly lower his taxable income. Suddenly, those countless hours spent on the road transformed into tangible financial benefits, allowing Alex to reinvest in his business and fuel his creative endeavors.

To truly understand the power of these deductions, it's essential to grasp the intricacies of mileage rates and the deductibility of travel expenses. Many self-employed individuals miss out on these opportunities simply because they find the rules too complex or daunting. But with the right knowledge and tools, you can turn these often-overlooked aspects of your business into a source of financial empowerment. Whether it's calculating the best method for your mileage deductions, leveraging the costs of business trips, or integrating advanced tools for meticulous record-keeping, each step you take towards mastering these deductions brings you closer to financial freedom. Now, let's dive into the specifics and unlock the potential savings that lie within your everyday business travels.

Understanding Mileage Deduction Methods and Rates

Understanding how to maximize vehicle and travel deductions can substantially impact the overall tax liability for freelancers and independent contractors. One of the most essential components of this strategy is comprehending the mileage deduction methods and rates. The IRS offers two primary methods: the standard mileage rate and the actual expense method. Each has its own intricacies and advantages, making it crucial for self-employed individuals to assess which method aligns best with their unique circumstances.

The standard mileage rate is straightforward and involves multiplying the total business miles driven by the IRS-set rate, which is adjusted annually to reflect changes in operating costs. For instance, in 2023, the standard mileage rate is 65.5 cents per mile. This method is particularly beneficial for those who drive extensively for business purposes, as it simplifies record-keeping and often results in a more substantial deduction than the actual expenses incurred. By maintaining a detailed and accurate mileage log, freelancers can ensure they capture all eligible miles, maximizing their deduction.

On the other hand, the actual expense method requires meticulous tracking of all vehicle-related expenses, including gas, oil, maintenance, repairs, insurance, and depreciation. This method can result in a larger deduction for those with high vehicle operating costs or those who drive less frequently for business purposes. However, it demands more comprehensive record-keeping, as each expense must be documented and categorized correctly. Advanced record-keeping tools, such as mileage tracking apps and accounting software, can streamline this process, reducing the administrative burden and increasing accuracy.

Beyond choosing the appropriate mileage deduction method, self-employed individuals should also be aware of the nuances involved in mixed-use vehicles. When a vehicle is used for both personal and business purposes, only the business portion of the expenses or miles driven can be deducted. It is crucial to maintain clear and precise records to differentiate between personal and business use. This distinction not only ensures compliance with IRS regulations but also maximizes the potential deduction. Utilizing technology, such as GPS-enabled mileage tracking apps, can simplify this process, providing a reliable and defensible log of business travel.

It is also worth exploring how recent changes and trends in tax legislation may affect mileage deductions. For instance, the Tax Cuts and Jobs Act of 2017 introduced significant modifications to vehicle depreciation rules, which can influence the actual expense method calculations. Staying informed about such changes allows freelancers to adapt their strategies accordingly, ensuring they continue to optimize their deductions. Engaging with a knowledgeable tax professional can provide deeper insights into these evolving regulations and offer personalized advice tailored to one's specific tax situation, ultimately contributing to a more robust and effective tax strategy.

Leveraging Travel Expenses for Business Trips and Conferences

Travel expenses for business trips and conferences are not just a necessary part of professional growth and networking; they also offer valuable opportunities for tax deductions. Recognizing the full potential of these deductions can significantly lighten the financial load for self-employed individuals. When planning a trip, it is essential to distinguish between business and personal expenses. While the cost of flights, hotels, and meals related to business activities can be deductible, personal activities during the trip must be meticulously separated and documented to ensure compliance with IRS regulations. For instance, if a freelancer attends a week-long conference but spends a day sightseeing, only the expenses directly associated with the conference are deductible.

CLAIMING DEDUCTIONS

Incorporating travel expenses into your overall tax strategy requires a nuanced understanding of what qualifies as a business trip. Business travel includes trips to meet clients, attend industry conferences, or visit potential partners or suppliers. Beyond the obvious costs like airfare and lodging, there are numerous smaller expenses that can collectively add up, such as baggage fees, internet access, and even dry cleaning. For example, if you're attending a digital marketing conference in another city, your Uber rides to and from the event, the hotel stay, and even the meals consumed during the conference are deductible. However, meticulous record-keeping is critical to substantiate these deductions should the IRS audit your returns.

Advanced record-keeping tools can simplify the tracking of travel expenses. Mobile apps like Expensify or QuickBooks Self-Employed allow freelancers to snap photos of receipts, categorize them, and sync the data with their accounting software. These tools not only streamline the process but also reduce the risk of losing important receipts. Imagine a scenario where a freelance graphic designer travels to a design summit. Using an app, they can instantly record expenses, categorize them under business travel, and even generate detailed reports at tax time. This proactive approach not only ensures compliance but also maximizes potential deductions.

Staying abreast of emerging trends in travel deductions can also enhance your tax strategy. For instance, the rise of remote work and digital nomadism has blurred the lines between business and leisure travel. Recent tax court cases and IRS rulings provide insights into how these trends are being recognized and taxed. If a freelance writer decides to work from a different city for a month, combining work with exploration, understanding how to apportion travel expenses between business and personal use becomes crucial. Leveraging these insights can help you navigate the complexities of modern work travel and optimize your deductions.

To truly leverage travel expenses for maximum benefit, consider engaging in strategic planning. Plan business trips to coincide with industry events or client meetings, thus ensuring the primary purpose of the trip is business-related. Reflect on questions like, "How can I structure my travel to align with business objectives while minimizing personal cost?" By answering such questions, you create a travel itinerary that supports your professional growth and ensures tax efficiency. This strategic approach, combined with advanced record-keeping and a deep understanding of the latest tax rules, will empower you to make the

50 MASTERING SELF-EMPLOYED TAXES

most of your business travel deductions, contributing to your broader goal of financial independence.

Integrating Advanced Record-Keeping Tools for Accurate Tracking

Accurate record-keeping is the linchpin of maximizing vehicle and travel deductions, and integrating advanced tools can transform this often tedious task into an efficient process. In the digital age, numerous applications and software solutions have emerged, designed specifically to cater to the unique needs of the self-employed. Apps like QuickBooks Self-Employed, MileIQ, and Expensify offer robust features for tracking mileage and travel expenses in real-time. These tools utilize GPS technology to automatically log trips, categorize expenses, and even generate reports tailored for tax purposes. The immediacy and precision offered by these platforms ensure that no deductible mile or business-related travel expense is overlooked, thus optimizing potential tax savings.

One of the standout features of these advanced tools is their ability to integrate seamlessly with other financial management software. For instance, linking a mileage tracking app with your primary accounting software can automate the synchronization of data, reducing manual entry and the risk of errors. This interconnected ecosystem allows for a more holistic view of your finances, where every mile driven and expense incurred is accounted for in real-time. By leveraging these integrations, self-employed individuals can maintain up-to-date records with minimal effort, ensuring they are always prepared for tax season with comprehensive and accurate documentation.

Beyond basic tracking, these tools often come equipped with advanced analytics capabilities. They can provide insights into your travel patterns, identify cost-saving opportunities, and even suggest more tax-efficient ways to manage your vehicle and travel expenses. For example, by analyzing your travel data, an app might highlight frequent trips that could be consolidated or suggest alternative routes that are more fuel-efficient. This level of detailed analysis not only enhances your ability to claim deductions accurately but also encourages smarter business travel decisions, contributing to overall financial efficiency.

The adaptability of these tools to evolving tax laws cannot be overstated. Tax regulations regarding vehicle and travel deductions can change, and keeping up with these changes manually can be daunting. Many modern record-keeping tools are regularly updated to reflect the latest tax codes and deduction rates. This ensures that users are not only compliant with current laws but are also optimizing their deductions according to the most recent guidelines. This adaptability provides peace of mind, knowing that your records are always in alignment with the latest tax requirements.

Incorporating advanced record-keeping tools is not just about convenience; it's about strategic financial management. By utilizing these technologies, self-employed individuals can shift their focus from the minutiae of record-keeping to the broader picture of financial planning and growth. Thoughtfully integrating these tools into your routine can free up valuable time and mental energy, allowing you to concentrate on expanding your business and achieving greater financial independence. These tools act as both a shield and a sword: protecting you from potential tax pitfalls while empowering you to maximize your deductions with precision and confidence.

As we wrap up this exploration into the realm of deductions, it's evident that understanding and claiming the right deductions can significantly lighten the tax burden for freelancers and independent contractors. From common deductions that most self-employed individuals can leverage, to the specifics of the home office deduction, and the nuances of maximizing vehicle and travel expenses, these components are crucial in ensuring you keep more of your hard-earned money. Each deduction not only offers financial relief but also underscores the importance of meticulous record-keeping and a proactive approach to managing finances.

Reflecting on these strategies, it becomes clear that the power of deductions lies in their potential to transform your financial landscape, providing the breathing room needed to invest back into your business and personal growth. As we move forward, consider how these insights can be integrated into a broader tax strategy that aligns with your goals. With each step towards mastering these facets of self-employed taxes, you're building a foundation for greater financial freedom and stability. Next, we'll continue to expand on these principles, diving deeper into other essential aspects of financial management that will further empower you on this journey.

Chapter Four

Understanding Quarterly Taxes

Diving deeper, we find ourselves at a critical juncture in the journey to financial freedom: mastering the art of quarterly taxes. For many self-employed individuals, the concept of quarterly tax payments can be as elusive as it is intimidating. Picture this: Sarah, a talented freelance graphic designer, revels in the freedom of setting her own hours and choosing her projects. However, every three months, a shadow looms over her creative sanctuary—the dreaded quarterly tax deadline. This chapter aims to transform that shadow into a beacon of clarity and control, ensuring that you, like Sarah, can navigate these waters with confidence and ease.

Imagine the peace of mind that comes with knowing exactly how much to set aside for taxes each quarter. No more last-minute scrambles, no more surprise penalties—just seamless financial management that allows you to focus on your passion and your work. In this chapter, we'll unravel the mysteries of calculating estimated taxes, guiding you through the process step by step. By the end, you'll understand not only how to determine what you owe, but also how to ensure those figures are as accurate as possible, avoiding the pitfalls of underpayment.

But understanding the numbers is just one part of the equation. Timing is equally crucial. Deadlines for quarterly tax payments are rigid, and missing them can lead to costly penalties that eat into your hard-earned income. We'll explore strategies to help you stay on top of these deadlines, from setting up reminders to automating payments. By integrating these practices into your routine, you'll

UNDERSTANDING QUARTERLY TAXES   53

transform quarterly taxes from a source of stress into a manageable, predictable aspect of your financial life.

Calculating Estimated Taxes

Here's a detailed look at how understanding and calculating estimated taxes can be a game-changer for self-employed individuals. Imagine you're an artist who just landed a lucrative commission or a consultant who signed a new client. Amid the excitement, there's a crucial aspect that often gets overlooked: the tax bill that comes with your newfound income. Misjudging your tax obligations can lead to unpleasant surprises and unnecessary stress. Instead, by grasping how to calculate estimated taxes, you can turn this daunting task into a manageable routine, giving you control over your finances and peace of mind. This proactive approach not only keeps you compliant with tax laws but also helps you avoid penalties and interest, allowing you to focus on what you do best—building your business and enjoying the freedom of self-employment.

But how do you begin? The first step is identifying all your sources of income. This might seem straightforward, but for many freelancers and gig workers, income can come from multiple, sometimes sporadic, channels. Understanding and applying the correct tax brackets for self-employed individuals is the next hurdle. Unlike traditional employees, you bear the responsibility of not only income tax but also self-employment tax, which covers Social Security and Medicare. Finally, refining your tax estimates requires a keen eye on deductions and credits. These adjustments can significantly impact your tax liability, so knowing what you're entitled to claim can save you a substantial amount in taxes.

Identifying Your Total Annual Income Sources

Identifying your total annual income sources is the cornerstone of accurately calculating your estimated taxes as a self-employed individual. This process begins by cataloging every stream of income, which may encompass freelance work, gig economy jobs, consulting fees, and any other self-employed ventures. It's essential to recognize that income isn't limited to cash payments; barter transactions, goods, or services received in exchange for your work also count as income. For example, if you trade your web design services for accounting help, the fair market value of those services must be reported as income. This comprehensive accounting ensures that no income is overlooked, giving you a clear picture of your total earnings.

To facilitate this, maintaining meticulous records is indispensable. Utilize tools like accounting software, spreadsheets, or dedicated apps to log each income source as it comes in. Regularly updating these records can prevent the end-of-year scramble to gather documents and receipts. Consistency in record-keeping not only simplifies tax preparation but also aids in identifying trends in your earnings, which can inform future business decisions. For instance, understanding which months are more profitable can help you plan for periods of lower income, ensuring a steady financial flow throughout the year.

Understanding and applying tax brackets for self-employed individuals is a pivotal next step. Unlike salaried employees, self-employed individuals must account for both income tax and self-employment tax. The self-employment tax covers Social Security and Medicare contributions, which an employer would typically withhold. Being aware of the current tax brackets and how they apply to your total income helps in estimating how much you owe. For example, if your net income places you in the 22% tax bracket, you need to allocate sufficient funds to cover that percentage, plus the self-employment tax rate. This dual calculation is crucial for avoiding underpayment and the associated penalties.

Adjusting for deductions and credits can significantly refine your tax estimates, reducing the amount you owe. Common deductions for self-employed individuals include home office expenses, business supplies, travel costs, and health insurance premiums. It's critical to differentiate between deductions and credits: deductions reduce your taxable income, while credits directly reduce the amount of tax owed. For instance, the Earned Income Tax Credit provides a substantial reduction in your tax bill if you qualify. Keeping abreast of new tax laws and potential deductions can maximize your savings and ensure compliance with IRS regulations.

Proactive financial management involves setting aside a portion of your income regularly to cover your estimated taxes. This practice prevents the last-minute scramble to find funds and the stress of potential penalties for late payments. One effective strategy is to open a separate bank account specifically for tax savings, transferring a percentage of each payment you receive into this account. For example, setting aside 30% of each payment can serve as a general rule of thumb, though this percentage may vary based on your specific tax bracket and deductions. This disciplined approach provides peace of mind,

UNDERSTANDING QUARTERLY TAXES

ensuring you are always prepared for quarterly tax payments and can focus on growing your business with confidence.

Understanding and Applying Tax Brackets for Self-Employed Individuals

Understanding and applying tax brackets for self-employed individuals involves a nuanced approach to ensure accurate tax calculations. Unlike traditional employees, freelancers and independent contractors must navigate the complexities of self-employment tax, which encompasses both income tax and self-employment tax. The self-employment tax includes Social Security and Medicare taxes, typically covered by an employer in a traditional job but now fully the responsibility of the self-employed. To begin, it's essential to identify which tax bracket your total annual income places you in. Tax brackets are progressive, meaning that income is taxed at increasing rates as it rises. For instance, a portion of your income might be taxed at 10%, another portion at 12%, and so on. Understanding where your income falls within these brackets is the first step to accurate tax estimation.

Once your income tax bracket is identified, the next step involves applying these brackets to your self-employment income. This process requires a thorough understanding of the current year's tax rates and brackets, which the IRS updates annually. For example, if your total self-employment income is $80,000, portions of this income will be taxed at different rates based on the progressive tax structure. Staying updated with the latest tax bracket information is crucial as it allows for precise calculation and helps avoid under or overpayment. Resources such as the IRS website or financial news outlets can provide current tax bracket details.

Adjusting for deductions and credits is another critical aspect of refining your tax estimates. Deductions lower your taxable income, while credits reduce the amount of tax you owe. Common deductions for the self-employed include home office expenses, business travel, and health insurance premiums. Utilizing these deductions effectively can significantly impact your taxable income, thereby adjusting your tax bracket and the amount owed. For example, if you earn $80,000 but have $20,000 in deductions, your taxable income reduces to $60,000, potentially placing you in a lower tax bracket for a portion of your earnings.

Tax credits, on the other hand, directly reduce your tax liability and can be particularly beneficial. Credits such as the Earned Income Tax Credit (EITC) or the Child Tax Credit can substantially lower the amount of tax you owe. Understanding and applying these credits requires careful documentation and, often, consultation with a tax professional. These credits can sometimes move you into a lower effective tax bracket, making them a powerful tool for tax planning. For instance, if you qualify for a $2,000 tax credit, your tax liability decreases by this amount, which can make a significant difference in managing your quarterly tax payments.

To bring this all together, consider a scenario where you project an annual self-employment income of $100,000. You would start by identifying the applicable tax brackets for this income. Next, you would apply these brackets to your income, subtracting any eligible deductions and credits to refine your taxable income. This thorough approach ensures that your estimated quarterly tax payments are as accurate as possible, reducing the likelihood of penalties for underpayment. The combination of understanding tax brackets, leveraging deductions, and applying tax credits forms a comprehensive strategy for managing self-employed taxes effectively.

Adjusting for Deductions and Credits to Refine Tax Estimates

Adjusting for deductions and credits is crucial to refining your tax estimates and ensuring accuracy in your quarterly payments. To begin with, self-employed individuals must recognize the variety of deductible expenses available to them. These include, but are not limited to, home office expenses, travel costs, and supplies. Utilizing deductions effectively can significantly reduce taxable income, leading to lower estimated tax payments. For instance, if you work from home, you can deduct a portion of your rent or mortgage, utilities, and internet expenses proportionate to the size of your home office. Such meticulous tracking of eligible deductions can make a substantial difference in your overall tax liability.

Equally important are tax credits, which directly reduce the amount of tax owed, unlike deductions that lower taxable income. Credits such as the Earned Income Tax Credit (EITC) and the Child and Dependent Care Credit can be valuable assets for self-employed individuals. For example, if you qualify for the EITC, it can provide a significant reduction in your tax bill, sometimes even resulting in a refund. Understanding the nuances of these credits and ensuring

UNDERSTANDING QUARTERLY TAXES

eligibility can be a game-changer in managing quarterly taxes. It's essential to stay updated on the latest tax credits available, as tax laws and available credits can change frequently.

Advanced insights into managing deductions and credits also involve forward-thinking and strategic planning. One innovative approach is to project your future income and expenses to determine the most beneficial timing for certain deductions. For example, if you anticipate a higher income next year, it might be advantageous to defer some deductible expenses to that period to offset the increased income. Conversely, if this year's income is higher, accelerating expenses could lower your taxable income more effectively in the current period. This level of strategic planning requires a thorough understanding of your financial landscape and meticulous record-keeping.

Another critical aspect is the integration of digital tools and software to streamline the process of tracking expenses and calculating deductions. Cutting-edge tax software can automatically categorize expenses and identify potential deductions, saving time and reducing the risk of errors. Additionally, these tools often provide real-time updates on tax law changes, ensuring that you are always informed of the latest opportunities for deductions and credits. Leveraging technology can significantly enhance your accuracy and efficiency in managing quarterly tax payments.

To tie it all together, it's essential to regularly review and adjust your tax estimates based on updated income and expense data. As your business evolves, so will your financial situation, necessitating periodic reassessment of your tax obligations. Setting aside time each quarter to revisit your financial records and refine your estimates can prevent surprises at tax time and ensure that you are consistently on track with your payments. This proactive approach not only reduces the risk of penalties but also provides peace of mind, allowing you to focus more on growing your business rather than worrying about tax compliance.

Deadlines and Penalties for Late Payments

To begin, let's consider the excitement of landing a new project or a lucrative gig—moments that spark joy and a sense of accomplishment for any self-employed individual. However, amidst the thrill of new opportunities, the looming specter of quarterly tax deadlines can often feel like an unwelcome intruder,

58 MASTERING SELF-EMPLOYED TAXES

casting a shadow over your financial landscape. Imagine the sinking feeling of realizing you've missed a payment deadline, only to discover that penalties and interest have quietly accumulated, eating into your hard-earned income. It's a scenario that many freelancers and independent contractors face, often due to a lack of awareness or simple oversight.

Understanding the deadlines and penalties associated with quarterly tax payments is not just a matter of compliance; it's a crucial aspect of maintaining financial stability and peace of mind. By mastering these deadlines and the potential repercussions of missing them, you can avoid unnecessary stress and financial setbacks. In the following sections, we will explore the importance of marking your calendar for these critical dates, delve into the consequences of missing payments, and uncover strategies to automate your payment process to ensure you're never caught off guard. This proactive approach will empower you to stay ahead of your tax obligations, allowing you to focus on what you do best—growing your business and enjoying the freedom that comes with being your own boss.

Importance of Marking Calendar Dates for Quarterly Payments

Marking calendar dates for quarterly tax payments is an essential practice for self-employed individuals aiming to maintain financial stability and avoid unnecessary penalties. Unlike traditional employees who have taxes withheld from their paychecks, freelancers and independent contractors must proactively manage their tax obligations. Missing a quarterly payment deadline can result in significant interest and penalties, which can quickly erode hard-earned income. By strategically scheduling these dates, self-employed individuals can ensure they remain compliant with tax regulations and maintain control over their financial health.

Advanced digital tools and applications can significantly assist in this endeavor. For instance, leveraging calendar apps that send automatic reminders for upcoming tax deadlines can help prevent forgetfulness amidst the hustle of managing a business. Additionally, integrating these reminders with financial planning software provides a comprehensive view of one's fiscal obligations. This synergy not only aids in timely payments but also offers insights into cash

UNDERSTANDING QUARTERLY TAXES

flow management, helping individuals allocate funds appropriately throughout the year to meet their tax liabilities without stress.

Beyond digital tools, the psychological benefits of staying organized cannot be overstated. Marking and adhering to quarterly tax payment dates cultivates a disciplined approach to financial management. This discipline can extend to other areas of personal and business finance, instilling a sense of order and predictability. Furthermore, the act of regularly setting aside funds for tax payments can serve as a financial checkpoint, encouraging business owners to review their income and expenses quarterly. This periodic review can reveal trends and patterns that may otherwise go unnoticed, providing valuable insights for future business decisions.

For those seeking innovative approaches, some financial experts recommend establishing a dedicated tax savings account. By transferring estimated tax amounts into this account regularly, self-employed individuals can separate these funds from their general operating expenses. This practice not only ensures that the necessary funds are available when payment dates arrive but also prevents the temptation to use tax money for other purposes. Moreover, earning interest on these saved funds can slightly offset the tax burden, adding an additional layer of financial benefit.

Consider the case of a successful freelance graphic designer who initially struggled with meeting quarterly tax deadlines. By implementing a system of marking calendar dates and setting up automated reminders, she transformed her approach to tax payments. This shift not only eliminated late payment penalties but also provided her with a clearer picture of her financial landscape. As a result, she was able to make more informed decisions about project pricing and business investments. Her story underscores the profound impact that meticulous planning and organization can have on achieving financial peace of mind.

Marking calendar dates for quarterly tax payments is a fundamental strategy that transcends basic compliance. It fosters financial discipline, leverages technology for seamless management, and provides psychological and practical benefits that can enhance overall business performance. By adopting this practice, self-employed individuals can navigate their tax obligations with confidence and clarity, paving the way for sustained financial success.

Consequences of Missing Payment Deadlines and Accruing Interest

Missing quarterly tax payment deadlines can significantly impact a self-employed individual's financial health. When payments are not made on time, the IRS imposes penalties and interest charges, which can accumulate quickly and complicate an already intricate financial landscape. For those unfamiliar with the system, it might be tempting to underestimate the importance of these deadlines. However, understanding the gravity of prompt payments can help prevent costly mistakes. The IRS calculates penalties based on the amount owed and the length of the delay, compounding the financial burden over time. This not only disrupts cash flow but also diverts funds that could be invested back into the business or saved for future needs.

Consider the case of Alex, a freelance graphic designer who missed his quarterly tax payment by two months. Initially, Alex owed $3,000 in estimated taxes. By the time he settled the debt, the penalties and interest had increased his total payment to $3,300. While $300 might not seem exorbitant, it represented a significant amount of money that Alex could have otherwise used to purchase new software or contribute to his retirement fund. Such examples underscore the necessity of adhering to deadlines and the broader implications of financial mismanagement. These consequences are not merely about additional payments; they reflect a deeper disruption to financial planning and stability.

To mitigate these risks, one effective approach is to integrate automated payment systems into your financial routine. Automating your quarterly tax payments ensures that deadlines are consistently met, reducing the likelihood of human error or oversight. Many financial institutions offer services that allow you to schedule payments well in advance, aligning with IRS deadlines. By leveraging these tools, you can maintain a steady cash flow and focus on other aspects of your business without the constant worry of impending tax deadlines. Automation also provides a structured framework, ensuring that your financial obligations are met systematically and efficiently.

Beyond automation, another strategy involves setting aside a specific portion of your income regularly in a separate account designated for tax payments. For instance, allocating 25-30% of your income each month into this account can create a financial buffer, making it easier to meet your quarterly tax obligations.

UNDERSTANDING QUARTERLY TAXES

This disciplined approach fosters better financial habits and ensures that funds are readily available when tax time arrives. Consider it a proactive measure that not only prepares you for tax payments but also instills a sense of financial discipline and foresight.

While the immediate penalties for late payments are a clear deterrent, the long-term effects on your overall financial health are equally critical. Consistent late payments can signal poor financial management, which may affect your creditworthiness and business reputation. Prospective clients or lenders might view your financial instability as a red flag, potentially hindering future opportunities. Therefore, understanding and adhering to quarterly tax payment deadlines is not just about avoiding penalties; it's a crucial aspect of maintaining a robust, professional, and reputable financial profile. By adopting these strategies and fostering a proactive approach to financial management, you can navigate the complexities of self-employed taxes with greater confidence and ease.

Strategies to Avoid Penalties Through Automated Payment Systems

Automated payment systems can be a game-changer for self-employed individuals striving to stay on top of their quarterly tax obligations. By leveraging technology, freelancers and independent contractors can set up automatic deductions, ensuring that payments are made on time without the stress of manually tracking deadlines. For instance, most online banking platforms and financial management tools offer features that allow users to schedule recurring payments directly to the IRS. These automated systems not only save time but also reduce the risk of human error, providing an added layer of security and reliability.

Beyond simple scheduling, advanced financial software can offer predictive analytics and cash flow management features, helping users to anticipate their tax liabilities more accurately. These tools can analyze past income trends, project future earnings, and recommend appropriate quarterly tax payment amounts. Utilizing such sophisticated technology can ensure that self-employed individuals are neither overpaying nor underpaying their taxes, thereby optimizing their cash flow. Moreover, some platforms integrate seamlessly with accounting software, providing a holistic view of one's financial health and tax obligations.

The benefits of automated payment systems extend to compliance as well. Tax regulations can be complex and are subject to frequent changes. Automated systems often come with regular updates that incorporate the latest tax laws, ensuring that payments are in line with current requirements. This proactive approach minimizes the risk of penalties due to outdated information or oversight. For example, cloud-based tax management tools often update their algorithms to reflect changes in tax codes, providing users with peace of mind that their tax payments are compliant with the latest standards.

One practical strategy for avoiding penalties through automation is to set up a dedicated tax savings account. By allocating a specific percentage of income into this account regularly, self-employed individuals can ensure they have sufficient funds to cover their quarterly tax payments. Automated transfers to this account can be scheduled to coincide with income deposits, making the process seamless. This method not only simplifies financial planning but also acts as a safeguard against the temptation to use funds allocated for taxes for other expenses.

Automation can foster a proactive and disciplined financial mindset. Regularly reviewing automated payment schedules and account balances can encourage self-employed individuals to stay engaged with their financial planning. This engagement can lead to better budgeting, more informed business decisions, and ultimately, greater financial independence. By embracing automated systems, freelancers and independent contractors can transform the often daunting task of managing quarterly taxes into a streamlined, efficient process, freeing up time and mental energy to focus on growing their businesses and achieving their financial goals.

Strategies for Managing Quarterly Payments

Let's start by examining an all-too-common scenario: you're knee-deep in a project, deadlines are looming, and the thought of setting aside time to deal with taxes feels nearly impossible. Suddenly, you realize it's time to make another quarterly tax payment. Panic sets in, and you scramble to gather the necessary funds, only to find that you're short. This cycle of stress and financial strain can be avoided with a few strategic approaches to managing your quarterly payments. By establishing a systematic plan, you can transform this daunting task into a manageable routine that seamlessly fits into your financial landscape.

Imagine having a system in place that automatically sets aside a portion of your income for taxes, reducing the last-minute rush and preventing penalties. Picture a tax calendar that keeps you on track with deadlines, ensuring you never miss a payment. Consider the flexibility of adjusting your estimated payments based on your income fluctuations, allowing you to stay aligned with your financial reality. These strategies not only alleviate the burden of quarterly taxes but also empower you to take control of your financial future. As we explore these methods, you'll discover practical steps to integrate them into your routine, making quarterly tax payments a stress-free part of your self-employed journey.

Automate Savings for Quarterly Payments

Automating savings for quarterly tax payments can be a game-changer for self-employed individuals aiming to streamline their financial responsibilities. By setting up automatic transfers from your main income account to a dedicated tax savings account, you can ensure that funds are consistently allocated for your estimated tax payments. This approach minimizes the risk of spending money that should be reserved for taxes and reduces the anxiety of scrambling to gather funds when payments are due. Financial institutions and fintech companies offer various tools to facilitate automated savings, making it easier than ever to set up and maintain these transfers.

Consider using an online banking platform that allows for seamless integration with budgeting software. These platforms can automatically transfer a specified percentage of your income into a separate account earmarked for taxes. For instance, if you estimate that 30% of your income should go toward taxes, an automatic transfer can be set up to move this percentage each time you receive a payment. This strategy not only ensures consistency but also helps you to mentally separate your earnings from your tax liabilities, fostering better financial discipline.

One advanced tactic is to leverage high-yield savings accounts for your tax savings. By doing so, not only are you setting aside money for taxes, but you are also earning interest on those funds. This can slightly offset your tax liability by generating additional income. Some financial experts suggest creating multiple savings accounts—one for each of the four quarterly payments—so you can clearly see how much you have saved for each deadline. This method provides a visual reminder and can help you stay on track with your savings goals throughout the year.

It's also worth exploring the use of financial apps that specialize in tax planning for self-employed individuals. These apps can not only automate savings but also provide real-time analytics on your income and expenses, helping you adjust your savings rate as needed. For example, if your income fluctuates significantly from month to month, these apps can recalibrate the amount transferred to your tax savings account, ensuring you are neither over-saving nor under-saving. This adaptability is crucial in maintaining financial stability and avoiding the penalties associated with underpayment of estimated taxes.

Engaging with a financial advisor who understands the nuances of self-employment can provide personalized insights tailored to your specific situation. Advisors can help you set realistic savings goals based on your income patterns and tax bracket. They might also recommend advanced strategies, such as using tax-advantaged accounts or investing in assets that offer tax benefits. By combining automated savings with professional advice, you can create a robust system that not only meets your tax obligations but also enhances your overall financial health.

Use a Tax Calendar to Track Deadlines

Using a tax calendar to track deadlines is an essential strategy for managing quarterly payments effectively. A tax calendar is more than just a tool; it is the backbone of a well-organized financial strategy. By entering all pertinent dates for estimated tax payments, freelancers can avoid the pitfalls of missed deadlines and the resulting penalties. This proactive approach ensures that tax obligations are met punctually, reducing stress and allowing more focus on business growth. The calendar should include not only the four quarterly due dates but also reminders to assess income and revisit estimated payments, ensuring accuracy and timeliness.

Specific examples highlight the practicality of a tax calendar. Consider a freelance graphic designer who, amidst juggling multiple projects, can easily overlook tax deadlines. By setting up reminders a few weeks before each due date, the designer can prepare funds and submit payments without last-minute scrambles. This method not only fosters financial discipline but also embeds tax payments into the routine business operations, making them less daunting.

UNDERSTANDING QUARTERLY TAXES 65

Additionally, a tax calendar can be synchronized with other financial tools, like budgeting apps or accounting software, to create a seamless financial management system.

The importance of adjusting estimated payments based on income fluctuations cannot be overstated. Freelancers often experience varying income levels throughout the year, making static estimates ineffective. A tax calendar allows for scheduled reviews and adjustments, ensuring that payments align with actual earnings. For instance, a freelance writer who lands a lucrative contract mid-year can immediately update their calendar to reflect increased tax obligations. This adaptability prevents both underpayment and overpayment, optimizing cash flow and avoiding surprises when the tax year ends.

Emerging trends in digital financial tools offer innovative ways to manage a tax calendar. Platforms like QuickBooks Self-Employed or FreshBooks now integrate tax calendars within their ecosystems, providing automated reminders and real-time updates. These tools leverage machine learning to predict tax liabilities based on income patterns, offering freelancers cutting-edge resources to stay ahead of their obligations. The integration of such advanced technologies not only simplifies tax management but also provides valuable insights into financial health, fostering a proactive rather than reactive approach to taxes.

Using a tax calendar is not just about avoiding penalties; it is a cornerstone of financial mastery. By methodically tracking deadlines, freelancers can transform a traditionally stressful task into a manageable routine. This strategic approach allows for better financial planning, more accurate budgeting, and a clearer picture of one's financial landscape. Encouraging the use of a tax calendar empowers freelancers to take control of their tax obligations confidently, paving the way for sustained financial well-being and peace of mind. By embedding this practice into their daily operations, they can focus on what they do best, knowing their tax responsibilities are well in hand.

Adjust Estimated Payments Based on Income Fluctuations

Adjusting estimated payments based on income fluctuations is an essential strategy for managing quarterly taxes effectively. Unlike traditional employees who have a consistent paycheck, self-employed individuals often experience variable income. This variability can make tax planning more challenging but also offers opportunities for optimization. One practical approach is to regularly review your income and expenses to adjust your estimated tax payments accordingly. By doing so, you can avoid the pitfalls of overpayment, which ties up much-needed capital, or underpayment, which could result in penalties and interest. This proactive adjustment ensures that your tax payments are in alignment with your actual earnings, providing a more accurate financial picture.

To navigate these fluctuations, consider implementing a system where you set aside a percentage of each payment you receive into a separate tax savings account. This percentage can be adjusted based on your income trends and projected expenses. For instance, during a high-income period, you might set aside 25-30% of your earnings, while in a slower period, you might reduce this to 15-20%. This method not only ensures you have sufficient funds for your quarterly payments but also reduces the risk of cash flow problems. Financial tools and apps designed for freelancers can automate this process, making it easier to stay on top of your tax obligations.

Advanced forecasting techniques can further refine your estimated payments. Utilizing financial software that offers predictive analytics can provide insights into your income patterns and help you make more informed decisions. These tools often incorporate historical data and can forecast future earnings based on current trends. By integrating such technology into your financial planning, you can create a more dynamic and responsive tax strategy. For example, if your software indicates a likely increase in income for the next quarter, you can preemptively adjust your estimated payments, thus avoiding any last-minute scrambles.

In addition to leveraging technology, it's wise to consult with a tax professional who specializes in self-employed taxes. They can offer personalized advice tailored to your unique financial situation and help you navigate any complexities. For instance, a tax advisor might suggest adjusting your estimated payments quarterly instead of annually, based on your past and projected income. This personalized strategy can be particularly beneficial for those with highly variable income streams, such as seasonal workers or consultants with fluctuating client demands.

The key to managing quarterly payments in light of income fluctuations is ongoing assessment and flexibility. Regularly revisiting your financial records and tax obligations allows you to make timely adjustments, ensuring that you remain compliant and financially healthy. This proactive approach not only mitigates the risk of penalties but also enhances your overall financial stability. By staying adaptable and utilizing both technological tools and professional

UNDERSTANDING QUARTERLY TAXES 67

advice, you can adeptly manage your quarterly tax payments, turning potential pitfalls into opportunities for financial prudence and growth.

Understanding the intricacies of quarterly taxes is a crucial step in the journey towards financial independence for the self-employed. By demystifying the process of calculating estimated taxes, adhering to deadlines, and strategically managing payments, this chapter empowers freelancers, gig workers, and independent contractors to take control of their financial obligations. The knowledge of how to accurately estimate taxes not only mitigates the risk of penalties but also fosters a sense of confidence and preparedness. This proactive approach to managing quarterly taxes ensures that financial surprises are minimized, allowing for smoother cash flow and better financial planning.

As we wrap up this exploration of quarterly taxes, it's evident how pivotal this understanding is within the larger framework of mastering self-employed taxes. Embracing these strategies and insights lays a solid foundation for achieving financial freedom and stability. As you continue to navigate your financial journey, remember that staying informed and proactive is key. Reflect on how these practices can be integrated into your routine, and consider how they can enhance your overall financial strategy. The next steps in this guide will build upon this foundation, providing further tools and insights to help you thrive as a self-employed individual.

Chapter Five

Retirement Planning For The Self Employed

Going deeper, we find ourselves at a crossroads where the present meets the future, a juncture where the choices of today shape the tomorrows of self-employed individuals. Imagine Sarah, a graphic designer who started her freelance journey with dreams of creative freedom and flexible hours. While she's found joy in her work, the notion of retirement often lingers in the back of her mind, wrapped in uncertainty. This chapter offers a beacon of clarity and guidance, illuminating the path to a secure and comfortable retirement.

For those who navigate the self-employment landscape, retirement planning can feel like navigating uncharted waters. Unlike traditional employees who have employer-sponsored plans, the self-employed must take the helm in steering their financial future. Here, we explore retirement account options tailored to the unique needs of freelancers, gig workers, and independent contractors. From SEP IRAs to Solo 401(k)s, each option presents distinct advantages that can significantly impact your long-term financial health. Understanding these choices is the first step in crafting a robust retirement strategy.

The journey doesn't end with selecting the right retirement account. Contributions to these accounts come with valuable tax benefits that can reduce your taxable income, providing immediate financial relief while simultaneously building a nest egg. We will uncover the intricacies of these tax advantages and demonstrate how proactive contributions today can pave the way for a stress-free retirement. By creating a comprehensive long-term strategy, you can ensure that your golden years are not only financially secure but also filled with the same sense of freedom and independence that defines your self-employed career.

Exploring Retirement Account Options

In recent years, we've seen a surge in the number of self-employed individuals taking control of their financial futures. It's a thrilling yet daunting journey, marked by the freedom to carve your own path but also the responsibility to lay down a solid financial foundation. Among the critical aspects of this foundation is planning for retirement—a task that often feels like navigating a labyrinth without a map. Imagine, for a moment, setting up a sturdy tent in the wilderness, knowing you'll eventually need it for shelter. Just as you'd want the best materials and the most reliable design, so too should you seek out the optimal retirement accounts tailored for your unique situation. What sets this apart is the plethora of retirement options available specifically for self-employed individuals, each with its distinct advantages and nuances.

Consider the Solo 401(k), an ideal solution for high earners looking to maximize their contributions, or the SEP and SIMPLE IRAs, which offer flexible contribution options to match fluctuating incomes. Then there's the Roth IRA, which provides the enticing prospect of tax-free withdrawals in retirement. These aren't just accounts; they're powerful tools in your financial toolkit, designed to help you build a comfortable and secure future. As we explore these options, we'll uncover how they can transform your retirement planning from a perplexing challenge into a manageable and even exciting endeavor. This chapter will guide you through the maze, spotlighting the benefits and strategies that can make all the difference in achieving your long-term financial goals.

Understanding the Solo 401(k) and Its Benefits for High Earners

The Solo 401(k) stands as a powerful retirement savings vehicle tailored specifically for self-employed individuals and small business owners with no full-time employees other than a spouse. This plan serves as a boon for high earners, offering significant contribution limits that outshine many other retirement accounts. In 2023, for instance, individuals can contribute up to $22,500 as an employee, with an additional $7,500 catch-up contribution if they are 50 or older. Moreover, as an employer, they can contribute up to 25% of their net self-employment income, with total contributions not exceeding $66,000 (or $73,500 for those 50 and older). This dual contribution structure allows self-employed high earners to maximize their retirement savings, thus offering a robust avenue for securing financial independence in their later years.

One of the compelling benefits of a Solo 401(k) is the ability to make both pre-tax and Roth contributions, providing flexibility in tax planning. Pre-tax contributions reduce taxable income for the year they are made, offering immediate tax savings, which can be particularly advantageous for individuals in higher tax brackets. On the other hand, Roth contributions are made with after-tax dollars, allowing for tax-free withdrawals in retirement. This dual option enables high earners to strategically balance their tax liabilities between their working years and retirement, optimizing their overall tax efficiency.

Another noteworthy aspect is the loan provision embedded within the Solo 401(k) plan. Participants can borrow up to 50% of their account balance, with a maximum loan limit of $50,000, whichever is lesser. This feature can serve as a financial safety net, providing liquidity during unforeseen circumstances without incurring penalties or taxes typically associated with early withdrawals. While it is crucial to approach retirement loans cautiously, this flexibility can offer peace of mind and financial agility, making the Solo 401(k) a versatile tool for comprehensive retirement planning.

High earners can also capitalize on the Solo 401(k) to perform a Roth conversion strategy, particularly in years when their taxable income is lower. By converting pre-tax funds to Roth within the Solo 401(k), individuals can take advantage of lower tax rates and benefit from tax-free growth and distributions in retirement. This strategy, while complex, can significantly enhance the tax efficiency of retirement savings, especially for those anticipating higher tax rates in the future. It underscores the importance of an informed and proactive approach to retirement planning, leveraging the unique features of the Solo 401(k).

In the evolving landscape of retirement planning, the Solo 401(k) remains a formidable option for self-employed high earners. Its high contribution limits, tax flexibility, loan provisions, and potential for Roth conversions make it an indispensable component of a well-rounded retirement strategy. As you nav-

RETIREMENT PLANNING FOR THE SELF EMPLOYED 71

igate your financial journey, consider how the Solo 401(k) can be integrated into your broader retirement plan, providing a solid foundation for long-term financial security. Engaging with a financial advisor or tax professional can further illuminate personalized strategies to maximize the benefits of this powerful retirement tool, ensuring you are well-prepared to enjoy a financially secure and fulfilling retirement.

Comparing SEP IRAs and SIMPLE IRAs for Flexible Contribution Options

When evaluating SEP IRAs and SIMPLE IRAs for flexible contribution options, it's essential to understand the unique characteristics and advantages each account offers, catering to the diverse needs of self-employed individuals. A Simplified Employee Pension (SEP) IRA stands out for its higher contribution limits, making it an attractive choice for those who anticipate fluctuating income or wish to maximize their retirement savings during profitable years. In 2023, SEP IRAs allow contributions up to the lesser of 25% of net earnings or $66,000, providing significant room for tax-deferred growth. This feature is particularly beneficial for high-income earners who seek to reduce their taxable income while securing a robust retirement fund.

In contrast, a Savings Incentive Match Plan for Employees (SIMPLE) IRA offers more straightforward setup and administration, making it an appealing option for those who prioritize ease of use. With a SIMPLE IRA, self-employed individuals can contribute both as an employer and an employee, allowing for contributions up to $15,500 in 2023, with an additional catch-up contribution of $3,500 for those aged 50 or older. This dual contribution capability provides a practical balance between flexibility and simplicity, especially for those with modest earnings who still wish to take advantage of tax-deferred savings.

While both SEP IRAs and SIMPLE IRAs offer tax-deferred growth, their suitability often depends on individual business structures and financial goals. For instance, a freelance consultant with variable income might lean towards a SEP IRA to capitalize on high-earning years, while a small business owner with steady, moderate income might find the consistent contribution structure of a SIMPLE IRA more manageable. Understanding these nuances can help self-employed individuals select the retirement plan that best aligns with their financial trajectory and retirement aspirations.

Recent research and trends in retirement planning for the self-employed highlight the increasing popularity of diversifying retirement savings across multiple accounts. Some self-employed professionals are opting to maintain both a SEP IRA and a SIMPLE IRA, leveraging the higher contribution limits of the SEP IRA during peak earning years and the steady, manageable contributions of a SIMPLE IRA during leaner times. This dual-account strategy offers a dynamic approach to retirement savings, ensuring that individuals can adapt their contributions in response to their financial circumstances while maximizing their tax advantages.

To make an informed decision, it's crucial for self-employed individuals to consider their long-term financial strategy and consult with a financial advisor. By weighing the pros and cons of each retirement account and understanding their unique benefits, self-employed professionals can craft a tailored retirement plan that supports their financial independence and peace of mind. Ultimately, proactive planning and strategic contributions to SEP IRAs and SIMPLE IRAs can pave the way for a secure and fulfilling retirement, empowering individuals to take control of their financial future with confidence.

Exploring Roth IRAs for Tax-Free Withdrawals in Retirement

Roth IRAs offer an enticing option for self-employed individuals seeking tax-free withdrawals in retirement. Unlike traditional IRAs, contributions to a Roth IRA are made with after-tax dollars, meaning you won't receive an immediate tax deduction. However, the long-term benefits can be substantial. Once you hit retirement age and have met the five-year holding requirement, withdrawals of both contributions and earnings are entirely tax-free. This can be a game-changer for those anticipating higher tax rates in the future, providing a tax-efficient stream of income when it may be needed most.

For self-employed professionals, Roth IRAs also offer a unique level of flexibility. Contributions can be made at any time and in any amount up to the annual limit, which in 2023 is $6,500 for those under 50 and $7,500 for those 50 and older. This flexibility is particularly beneficial for freelancers and gig workers, whose income can fluctuate significantly from year to year. In years when income is lower, contributing to a Roth IRA can be a strategic move to maximize retirement savings without the immediate tax implications tied to traditional retirement accounts.

RETIREMENT PLANNING FOR THE SELF EMPLOYED 73

Additionally, Roth IRAs have no required minimum distributions (RMDs) during the account holder's lifetime, unlike traditional IRAs and 401(k)s. This feature allows self-employed individuals to let their investments grow tax-free for as long as they wish, providing greater control over their financial future. This can be particularly advantageous for those who do not need to draw on their retirement savings immediately upon reaching retirement age, allowing for potentially more significant growth of the retirement nest egg.

Recent research highlights the growing appeal of Roth IRAs among self-employed individuals. Trends indicate an increasing number of younger professionals opting for Roth IRAs, capitalizing on the potential for decades of tax-free growth. Financial planners often recommend Roth IRAs for those who anticipate being in a higher tax bracket in retirement, making it a forward-thinking choice for long-term financial planning. Moreover, the ability to withdraw contributions (but not the earnings) from a Roth IRA without penalties or taxes at any time can serve as a financial safety net, adding an extra layer of security for the self-employed.

To fully leverage the benefits of a Roth IRA, self-employed individuals should consider integrating it into a comprehensive retirement strategy. This involves regular reviews of income projections, tax planning, and investment performance to ensure that contributions are optimized and aligned with long-term goals. Engaging with a financial advisor who understands the nuances of self-employment can provide invaluable insights and help tailor a retirement plan that maximizes the benefits of Roth IRAs. By making informed decisions and staying proactive, self-employed individuals can harness the full potential of Roth IRAs to secure a financially stable and tax-efficient retirement.

Tax Benefits of Retirement Contributions

Let's dive into the heart of what makes retirement planning not just a future aspiration but a present-day advantage for self-employed individuals. Imagine this: you're sitting at your desk, juggling client work and invoices, and the thought of retirement feels like a distant shore. Yet, what if I told you that every dollar you set aside for your golden years could also lighten your tax load today? This dual benefit transforms the act of saving into a strategic move that serves your present and future self. By understanding how retirement contributions lower your taxable income now, you're essentially giving yourself a tax break while securing financial stability for later.

Consider the story of Jane, a freelance graphic designer who discovered the magic of tax-deferred growth on her investments. She realized that not only was she building a nest egg, but she was also allowing her money to grow unhindered by immediate taxes. This epiphany led her to leverage catch-up contributions, enabling her to save more aggressively as she approached her retirement years. Jane's journey illustrates the profound impact of these tax benefits, encouraging you to view retirement contributions as a powerful tool in your financial toolkit. As we explore these subtopics, you'll see how lowering your taxable income today, enjoying tax-deferred growth, and making the most of catch-up contributions can set you on a path to financial freedom.

Lowering Your Taxable Income Today

For self-employed individuals, contributing to a retirement account isn't just about securing your future; it's also a powerful strategy to reduce your taxable income today. By directing a portion of your earnings into retirement accounts such as a Simplified Employee Pension (SEP) IRA, Solo 401(k), or a Savings Incentive Match Plan for Employees (SIMPLE) IRA, you can effectively lower your adjusted gross income (AGI). This reduction in AGI not only decreases the amount of income subject to federal taxes but can also reduce your state tax liability, depending on where you live. For instance, if you contribute $10,000 to a SEP IRA, your taxable income for the year decreases by that amount, potentially saving you thousands in taxes.

Consider the impact of these contributions on different tax brackets. For a freelancer earning $80,000 annually, a $10,000 contribution could move a portion of their income from a higher tax bracket into a lower one, resulting in significant tax savings. This immediate reduction in taxable income is particularly beneficial for those in higher tax brackets, where the savings can be substantial. Additionally, lowering your AGI can also make you eligible for other tax credits and deductions that have income limits, such as the Child Tax Credit or education-related credits. This multi-layered approach to tax savings underscores the strategic importance of retirement contributions.

Beyond the direct tax savings, these contributions offer a compound benefit through tax-deferred growth. This means that the money within your retirement account grows without being subject to annual taxes on dividends, interest, or capital gains, allowing the investments to compound more efficiently over time. This tax deferral can significantly boost your retirement savings, particularly when you start early and contribute consistently. For example, a $10,000 contribution growing at an average annual rate of 7% can become over $76,000 in 30 years, all without the drag of annual taxes on the growth.

The ability to make catch-up contributions provides an additional layer of tax advantages, especially for those aged 50 and above. These catch-up contributions allow older self-employed individuals to contribute beyond the standard limits, offering a valuable opportunity to accelerate retirement savings while further reducing taxable income. For example, in 2023, individuals over 50 can contribute an additional $6,500 to their Solo 401(k), on top of the $22,500 standard contribution limit. This not only amplifies retirement savings but also enhances the immediate tax benefits.

To maximize these benefits, it's essential to integrate retirement contributions into a broader financial strategy. This involves balancing current cash flow needs with long-term retirement goals, ensuring that contributions are sustainable and aligned with overall financial health. Employing tools like financial planning software or consulting with a tax professional can provide personalized insights, helping you determine the optimal contribution levels and account types for your specific situation. By thoughtfully incorporating retirement contributions into your financial plan, you not only pave the way for a secure future but also enjoy tangible tax benefits today, creating a win-win scenario for your financial well-being.

Enjoying Tax-Deferred Growth on Investments

Investing in retirement accounts offers a unique advantage through tax-deferred growth, a powerful tool for self-employed individuals striving to secure their financial futures. By opting for tax-deferred accounts, such as a Traditional IRA, SEP IRA, or Solo 401(k), individuals can allow their investments to grow without the immediate burden of taxes. This deferred taxation means that the earnings on investments—whether from interest, dividends, or capital gains—are not taxed until funds are withdrawn, typically during retirement. This strategy enables the invested funds to compound more significantly over time, accelerating the growth of the retirement nest egg.

Consider a scenario where a freelancer contributes $10,000 annually to a tax-deferred retirement account with an average annual return of 7%. Over 20 years, the tax-deferred growth can significantly outpace a taxable account. In a taxable account, the freelancer would need to pay taxes on the gains every year, diminishing the compounding effect. In contrast, the tax-deferred account allows the full 7% return to compound annually without interruption, culminating in a substantially larger balance by retirement. This compounding effect is a cornerstone of retirement planning, highlighting the importance of starting contributions early and consistently.

Tax-deferred growth also provides flexibility in tax planning. Since taxes on the earnings are postponed until withdrawal, self-employed individuals can strategically manage their tax brackets in retirement. For instance, if they anticipate being in a lower tax bracket upon retirement, they can withdraw funds at a lower tax rate, effectively reducing their overall tax liability. This preemptive planning can be particularly advantageous, allowing individuals to optimize their tax situations over the long term and free up more resources for other financial goals during their working years.

Tax-deferred accounts often come with additional benefits, such as the ability to make catch-up contributions if you're over 50. This provision is especially beneficial for those who may have started saving for retirement later in life or who wish to bolster their retirement savings as they approach retirement age. The extra contributions not only enhance the retirement fund but also further leverage the tax-deferred growth, maximizing the potential benefits. Understanding and utilizing these provisions can make a substantial difference in the financial stability and comfort of one's retirement years.

It's essential to remain informed about the latest developments in tax laws and retirement account regulations. Changes in legislation can impact contribution limits, tax treatment, and withdrawal rules, which in turn can influence your retirement planning strategy. Staying abreast of these changes ensures that self-employed individuals can adapt their plans accordingly, maintaining the tax-deferred growth advantage. Engaging with financial advisors or tax professionals who specialize in self-employment can provide valuable insights and help navigate the complexities of retirement planning, ultimately leading to a more secure and prosperous retirement.

Leveraging Catch-Up Contributions for Greater Savings

For self-employed individuals nearing the age of 50, catch-up contributions offer a unique opportunity to bolster retirement savings significantly. These

RETIREMENT PLANNING FOR THE SELF EMPLOYED 77

additional contributions, permitted by the IRS, allow individuals to exceed the standard limits set for retirement accounts, providing a means to accelerate their savings as they approach retirement. For example, in 2023, those aged 50 and over can contribute an extra $6,500 to their 401(k) and an additional $1,000 to their IRA. This is not just a mechanism for increasing retirement funds but also a strategic tool for optimizing tax benefits, making it an essential consideration for savvy financial planning.

Catch-up contributions can substantially lower taxable income in the present year, which is particularly beneficial for high earners. By directing more income into retirement accounts, self-employed individuals can reduce their Adjusted Gross Income (AGI), potentially qualifying for additional tax credits and deductions. For instance, a freelancer who maximizes their catch-up contributions to a SEP IRA could see a significant reduction in their AGI, thereby possibly qualifying for the Qualified Business Income Deduction (QBI) or even reducing their tax bracket. This dual benefit of increasing retirement savings and lowering current tax liabilities makes catch-up contributions a powerful strategy.

The advantage of tax-deferred growth should not be underestimated. Contributions made to retirement accounts like 401(k)s, IRAs, or SEP IRAs grow tax-deferred, meaning the earnings on these investments are not taxed until withdrawal. This allows the investments to compound more efficiently over time. For those taking advantage of catch-up contributions, the accelerated growth can be even more pronounced. A self-employed consultant who contributes the maximum allowable amount, including catch-up contributions, to their Solo 401(k) can amass a significantly larger nest egg due to the compounded tax-deferred growth.

For those who have started saving for retirement later in life, catch-up contributions provide a crucial second chance. It's never too late to begin, and these additional contributions can help make up for lost time. Consider a self-employed graphic designer who begins contributing to their retirement accounts at age 50. By maximizing catch-up contributions each year, they can significantly enhance their retirement fund over a decade or more, potentially closing the gap caused by years of lower savings. This illustrates the transformative potential of catch-up contributions for late starters.

Incorporating catch-up contributions into a retirement strategy involves careful planning and discipline. Self-employed individuals should regularly review their financial statements and retirement plans, adjusting contributions as necessary to ensure they are on track to meet their retirement goals. Utilizing financial planning tools and consulting with a tax professional can provide valuable guidance in maximizing these contributions. By integrating catch-up contributions into their overall financial strategy, self-employed individuals can not only achieve greater savings but also ensure a more secure and comfortable retirement.

Creating a Long-Term Retirement Strategy

At the intersection of theory and practice, we find the art of crafting a long-term retirement strategy tailor-made for the self-employed. Imagine for a moment standing at the edge of a vast, uncharted territory. Just as an explorer maps out a route through unknown lands, so too must the self-employed chart a course towards a financially secure retirement. It's a journey filled with unique challenges and unparalleled opportunities, demanding a blend of foresight, creativity, and disciplined planning. This isn't just about stashing away money for the future—it's about building a robust, diversified strategy that grows and adapts with you over time.

Consider Sarah, a freelance graphic designer who, after years of focusing solely on her immediate income, realized she needed a solid plan for her retirement. She began by establishing a diverse investment portfolio, understanding that relying on a single income source would be akin to venturing into the wilderness with only one tool. She calculated her projected retirement expenses and income, treating it as her personal financial compass. By incorporating tax-advantaged retirement accounts and strategies, she not only secured her future but also optimized her tax savings in the present. Sarah's journey illustrates the importance of a meticulous, multifaceted approach to retirement planning, one that ensures financial stability while embracing the freedom and flexibility that come with self-employment.

Establishing a Diverse Investment Portfolio

Crafting a diverse investment portfolio is a cornerstone of a robust retirement plan for the self-employed, providing not only a cushion against market volatility but also a pathway to sustainable financial growth. A well-rounded portfolio typically encompasses a blend of asset classes, including stocks, bonds, real estate, and alternative investments such as commodities or cryptocurrencies. This mix ensures that the portfolio is not overly reliant on any single asset type, thereby mitigating risk. For instance, while stocks offer high potential returns, they can also be volatile. Bonds, on the other hand, provide more stable returns and can offset the fluctuations in the stock market. By strategically balancing these elements, self-employed individuals can safeguard their retirement savings against unforeseen economic shifts.

Recent research underscores the importance of diversification within asset classes as well. For example, within the stock component of a portfolio, it's prudent to invest in both domestic and international markets, spanning various industries and sectors. This approach not only spreads risk but also taps into different economic cycles and growth opportunities. Emerging markets can offer higher growth potential, while established markets provide stability. Similarly, within the bond portion, one might include a mix of government, municipal, and corporate bonds with varying maturities. This layered strategy ensures that the portfolio can endure different interest rate environments, offering both short-term liquidity and long-term growth.

Incorporating alternative investments into a retirement portfolio can further enhance diversification. These non-traditional assets, such as private equity, hedge funds, or even precious metals, often have low correlation with traditional asset classes like stocks and bonds. This means they can perform well even when the stock market is down, providing an additional layer of protection. For example, during periods of economic downturn, commodities like gold often retain or even increase in value, serving as a hedge against inflation and market instability. However, it's essential to approach alternative investments with caution, considering their complexity and potential for higher fees.

The role of technology in portfolio management cannot be overstated, particularly with the advent of robo-advisors and advanced financial planning software. These tools use algorithms to create and manage a diversified portfolio tailored to individual risk tolerance, financial goals, and time horizon. They can automatically rebalance the portfolio, ensuring that it remains aligned with the investor's objectives. For the self-employed, who may not have the time or expertise to manage their investments actively, these technological solutions offer an efficient and cost-effective way to maintain a diversified portfolio. Additionally, they provide access to a broad range of investment options that might not be readily available through traditional financial advisors.

It's vital to regularly review and adjust the portfolio to reflect changing financial circumstances and market conditions. Life events such as marriage, the birth of a child, or significant changes in income can all impact one's financial goals and risk tolerance. Periodic reassessment ensures that the portfolio remains in line with these evolving needs. Moreover, staying informed about market trends and economic forecasts can help in making informed decisions about when to adjust the asset allocation. For instance, if economic indicators suggest a period of prolonged inflation, it might be wise to increase holdings in assets that typically perform well in such environments, like real estate or commodities.

Calculating Projected Retirement Expenses and Income

Calculating projected retirement expenses and income is a crucial step in crafting a robust long-term retirement strategy for the self-employed. This endeavor begins with understanding the unique financial landscape of freelancers and independent contractors, who often experience variable income streams and lack employer-sponsored retirement benefits. To address these challenges, one must first assess their current financial situation, including all sources of income, ongoing expenses, and savings. This assessment forms the foundation for projecting future needs and helps identify any gaps that need to be addressed.

A practical approach to estimating retirement expenses involves categorizing and breaking down costs into essential and discretionary spending. Essential expenses include housing, utilities, healthcare, and food, while discretionary expenses cover travel, hobbies, and entertainment. Factoring in inflation is critical, as it erodes purchasing power over time. Utilizing financial planning tools or consulting with a financial advisor can provide more precise estimates, taking into account historical inflation rates and personal spending habits. These projections help create a clearer picture of the amount of money required to maintain one's desired lifestyle during retirement.

On the income side, self-employed individuals should consider all potential sources of retirement income, such as Social Security benefits, retirement account withdrawals, and any passive income streams like rental properties or investments. It's essential to understand the rules governing Social Security benefits, particularly how early or delayed retirement affects monthly payments. Additionally, knowing the withdrawal rules and tax implications of different retirement accounts, such as IRAs and 401(k)s, ensures that retirees can maximize their income while minimizing tax liabilities. Diversifying income sources can provide a safety net and reduce the risk associated with relying on a single income stream.

Incorporating advanced financial planning techniques can further enhance retirement readiness. Scenario analysis, for instance, allows individuals to model various financial situations, such as market downturns or unexpected expenses, and assess their impact on retirement plans. This proactive approach helps identify potential risks and develop contingency plans. Another sophisticated strategy involves the use of tax-efficient withdrawal sequences, where retirees draw from taxable accounts before tapping into tax-advantaged accounts, thereby optimizing tax outcomes and prolonging the life of their savings.

It's important to keep abreast of emerging trends and research in retirement planning. For example, the concept of "safe withdrawal rates" has evolved, with recent studies suggesting more flexible approaches compared to the traditional 4% rule. Staying informed about such developments can provide self-employed individuals with innovative strategies to refine their retirement plans. By regularly reviewing and adjusting projections based on the latest insights and personal circumstances, one can maintain a resilient and adaptable retirement strategy, ensuring financial security and peace of mind in the later years.

Incorporating Tax-Advantaged Retirement Accounts and Strategies

Choosing the right tax-advantaged retirement accounts and strategies is pivotal for self-employed individuals aiming to secure a financially stable future. A wide array of options exists beyond the traditional IRA and 401(k) accounts, each offering distinct benefits tailored to various financial goals and circumstances. For instance, a Simplified Employee Pension (SEP) IRA allows for substantial contributions, up to 25% of net earnings from self-employment, with a maximum limit that adjusts for inflation annually. This can be particularly advantageous for those experiencing fluctuating incomes, as contributions can be scaled up or down depending on the year's financial performance. Additionally, the Solo 401(k), designed for business owners without employees, offers both employee and employer contribution options, providing a dual advantage in maximizing retirement savings while reducing taxable income.

The tax benefits of these accounts are significant. Contributions to a SEP IRA or Solo 401(k) are tax-deductible, reducing the overall taxable income for the year in which they are made. This not only lowers the immediate tax burden but also allows the investment to grow tax-deferred, meaning taxes on gains are not paid until the funds are withdrawn, typically during retirement when one's tax rate may be lower. Roth IRAs, while not tax-deductible, offer tax-free growth and tax-free withdrawals in retirement, which can be a strategic component of a well-rounded retirement plan. Balancing contributions between these different account types can optimize both current tax savings and future tax liabilities, providing a comprehensive approach to long-term financial planning.

Incorporating advanced strategies such as the "Backdoor Roth IRA" can further enhance retirement planning. This strategy involves contributing to a traditional IRA and then converting those funds to a Roth IRA, thereby circumventing income limits that typically restrict direct Roth IRA contributions. This approach requires careful planning and awareness of potential tax implications during the conversion process, but it can be an effective way to maximize tax-advantaged retirement savings for high-income earners. Additionally, Health Savings Accounts (HSAs) can play a dual role. Contributions are tax-deductible, the funds grow tax-free, and withdrawals for qualified medical expenses are also tax-free. Post-65, HSA funds can be used for non-medical expenses without penalty, though subject to income tax, making them a versatile tool in retirement planning.

Emerging trends in financial technology also offer innovative solutions for managing tax-advantaged accounts. Robo-advisors, for example, can automate the investment process, ensuring optimal asset allocation and rebalancing to maintain the desired risk profile. These platforms often include tax-loss harvesting features, which can offset capital gains with losses, further enhancing tax efficiency. Additionally, blockchain technology and cryptocurrencies are beginning to find their way into retirement accounts, offering new avenues for diversification. While these options come with higher volatility and regulatory considerations, they present an opportunity for those willing to explore cutting-edge investment strategies.

To effectively incorporate these strategies, it's crucial to regularly revisit and adjust the retirement plan. Projected retirement expenses and income should be recalculated periodically to reflect changes in lifestyle, health, and financial markets. Utilizing tax-advantaged accounts requires ongoing education and adaptation to new laws and regulations.

As we wrap up our exploration of retirement planning for the self-employed, it's essential to recognize the profound impact these strategies can have on your

RETIREMENT PLANNING FOR THE SELF EMPLOYED   83

financial future. By exploring various retirement account options such as SEP IRAs, Solo 401(k)s, and SIMPLE IRAs, you gain the flexibility and control needed to tailor your retirement plan to your unique needs. The tax benefits associated with these contributions not only reduce your taxable income today but also set you on a path to a more secure and comfortable retirement. Crafting a long-term retirement strategy is about more than just saving money; it's about ensuring that you can maintain your desired lifestyle and achieve financial independence even after you've stopped working.

Embracing proactive retirement planning underscores the broader message of this book: taking control of your finances is both empowering and essential for achieving peace of mind. As you move forward, remember that each step you take towards understanding and managing your taxes and retirement planning brings you closer to financial freedom. Reflect on your goals, stay motivated, and continue to seek out knowledge and resources that will support your journey. This chapter has equipped you with the tools to make informed decisions about your retirement, setting the stage for the next phase of your financial journey. Stay committed to your financial well-being, and let the lessons learned here inspire you to build a robust strategy that will serve you well into the future.

Chapter Six

Healthcare Options For The Self Employed

Journey with us as we explore the intricate and often overwhelming world of healthcare options for the self-employed. Picture this: Sarah, a thriving freelance graphic designer, has just landed a major client. She's on cloud nine until she realizes she no longer has the safety net of her previous employer's health insurance. Like many self-employed individuals, Sarah finds herself navigating a labyrinth of choices, from health insurance marketplaces to healthcare sharing plans. The anxiety of making the wrong choice can be paralyzing, but it doesn't have to be. This chapter aims to transform that anxiety into empowerment, guiding you through the myriad of options available to ensure you make informed decisions about your health and well-being.

Healthcare is a cornerstone of financial stability, and understanding your options is crucial to achieving true financial freedom. We'll delve into the mechanics of health insurance marketplaces, demystifying the process of finding a plan that fits both your needs and your budget. The self-employed health insurance deduction is another powerful tool in your financial arsenal, and we'll break down how to maximize this benefit to keep more of your hard-earned money. For those exploring alternatives, healthcare sharing plans offer a community-driven approach to managing medical costs, and we'll examine their pros and cons to help you determine if this path aligns with your values and financial goals.

As we traverse these topics, remember that each decision you make is a step toward greater control over your financial destiny. The goal is not only to provide you with the knowledge to navigate your healthcare options but also to inspire confidence in your ability to make choices that support both your health and your financial well-being. By the end of this chapter, you'll have a clearer understanding of the landscape and be better equipped to select the healthcare options that best serve your journey to financial independence.

Navigating Health Insurance Marketplaces

A crucial element in this discussion is understanding the labyrinthine world of health insurance marketplaces. Imagine stepping into a bustling marketplace filled with a myriad of stalls, each one offering a different kind of protection for your most valuable asset—your health. For the self-employed, the stakes are even higher. Without the safety net of employer-provided insurance, navigating this marketplace becomes not just a necessity, but a critical component of your overall financial strategy. The decisions you make here can significantly impact both your financial well-being and peace of mind.

Let's dive into the heart of this marketplace, starting with understanding the various plan categories and coverage levels. Think of it as decoding a treasure map where each clue—each plan detail—brings you closer to finding the right balance between cost and comprehensive coverage. Next, we'll explore how to evaluate the cost versus benefits of different insurance options, ensuring you get the most value for every dollar spent. Finally, we'll uncover the secrets of leveraging subsidies and tax credits to reduce your premiums, turning what seems like an overwhelming expense into a manageable and even advantageous part of your financial plan. This journey through the health insurance marketplaces is not just about ticking off a box on your to-do list; it's about empowering yourself with the knowledge to make informed, confident decisions that safeguard your health and your wallet.

Understanding Plan Categories and Coverage Levels

Health insurance marketplaces can initially seem daunting, but understanding the various plan categories and coverage levels can simplify the process significantly. These marketplaces typically offer four main categories of plans: Bronze, Silver, Gold, and Platinum. Each category corresponds to a different level of coverage and cost-sharing between the insurer and the insured. Bronze plans generally have the lowest monthly premiums but the highest out-of-pocket costs when care is needed. Conversely, Platinum plans come with the highest premiums but offer the lowest costs for medical services. Understanding these categories is crucial for self-employed individuals, as it allows them to align their health insurance choices with both their financial capabilities and healthcare needs.

The distinctions between these plan categories are not just about cost but also about the extent and quality of coverage. For instance, Bronze plans may be suitable for those who are relatively healthy and expect minimal medical expenses, while Gold or Platinum plans might be more appropriate for individuals with ongoing health conditions that require frequent medical attention. Evaluating these plans through the lens of personal healthcare requirements can lead to more informed and effective decisions. Moreover, some plans within these categories may offer additional benefits such as dental and vision coverage, which can be a significant consideration for those relying on a comprehensive healthcare solution.

Beyond coverage levels, it's essential to consider the network of healthcare providers associated with each plan. Health insurance plans often come in different types such as Health Maintenance Organizations (HMOs), Preferred Provider Organizations (PPOs), and Exclusive Provider Organizations (EPOs). HMOs usually require members to choose a primary care physician and get referrals for specialist care, making them a cost-effective option for those willing to navigate their care within a specific network. PPOs and EPOs, on the other hand, offer more flexibility in choosing healthcare providers but usually come with higher premiums and out-of-pocket costs. Understanding these intricacies helps self-employed individuals select a plan that not only fits their budget but also meets their personal and professional healthcare needs.

Subsidies and tax credits available through the healthcare marketplaces can significantly reduce the cost of premiums, making higher-tier plans more accessible. The Affordable Care Act (ACA) provides income-based subsidies that can lower monthly premiums and out-of-pocket costs, making it crucial for self-employed individuals to accurately estimate their annual income to maximize these benefits. For example, individuals earning between 100% and 400% of the federal poverty level may qualify for premium tax credits, which can be applied directly to reduce the cost of premiums. Additionally, the Cost-Sharing Reduction (CSR) subsidies available for Silver plans can further diminish out-of-pocket costs, making them an attractive option for those who qualify.

In selecting the most appropriate health insurance plan, it's imperative to consider both current healthcare needs and potential future scenarios. Self-employed individuals should factor in their business growth projections, potential increases in income, and any anticipated changes in healthcare needs. For instance, someone planning to expand their business might foreseeably have a higher income next year and thus may not qualify for the same level of subsidies, affecting their choice of plan.

Evaluating Cost vs. Benefits for Different Insurance Options

Evaluating the cost versus benefits of different insurance options is a crucial step for the self-employed seeking optimal healthcare coverage. In the vast landscape of health insurance, plans are typically categorized into metal tiers: Bronze, Silver, Gold, and Platinum. Each tier reflects a different balance between monthly premiums and out-of-pocket expenses, with Bronze plans generally offering lower premiums but higher costs when care is needed, and Platinum plans featuring higher premiums but minimal out-of-pocket expenses. Understanding these categories helps individuals align their health needs and financial capabilities. For instance, a healthy freelancer with minimal healthcare needs might lean towards a Bronze plan, while someone with chronic conditions might find a Gold or Platinum plan more cost-effective in the long run.

To evaluate the true cost-effectiveness of a health plan, one must consider more than just the premiums. Deductibles, co-pays, co-insurance, and out-of-pocket maximums all play significant roles in the overall expense. For example, a plan with a lower premium but a high deductible might seem attractive initially, but if frequent doctor visits or medications are needed, the out-of-pocket costs can quickly add up. Conversely, a higher premium plan with a low deductible and comprehensive coverage might result in lower total annual healthcare expenditure. Therefore, it's vital to project potential healthcare needs

88   MASTERING SELF-EMPLOYED TAXES

and expenses realistically when comparing plans. Tools such as cost calculators provided by insurance marketplaces can be invaluable in this analysis.

Subsidies and tax credits can significantly affect the affordability of health insurance for the self-employed. The Premium Tax Credit, available through the Health Insurance Marketplace, can lower monthly premiums based on income and household size. Advanced Premium Tax Credits (APTCs) are particularly beneficial as they can be applied directly to lower monthly premium payments. It's essential to accurately estimate annual income to maximize these benefits without incurring repayment obligations at tax time. For example, if a freelancer's income fluctuates widely, it may be prudent to use a conservative income estimate to avoid the risk of overestimating and having to repay credits.

Healthcare sharing plans, though not traditional insurance, offer an alternative that some self-employed individuals find appealing. These plans involve a group of people who share healthcare costs, often rooted in a common ethical or religious background. While typically less expensive than conventional insurance, these plans come with limitations and risks, such as exclusions for pre-existing conditions and a lack of regulatory protections. Evaluating these plans requires a thorough understanding of their structure, the scope of coverage, and potential out-of-pocket expenses. For instance, a healthcare sharing plan might work well for someone with minimal healthcare needs and a strong alignment with the group's principles.

In assessing different insurance options, it's also important to consider emerging trends and innovations in the healthcare sector. Telehealth services, for example, have become increasingly integrated into insurance plans, offering convenience and potentially lower costs for routine care. Moreover, some insurance providers now offer wellness incentives, such as discounts for maintaining a healthy lifestyle or participating in preventive care programs. These additional benefits can enhance the overall value of a plan. For instance, a policy that includes comprehensive telehealth services and wellness incentives might offer substantial savings and convenience, making it a superior choice for the tech-savvy, health-conscious freelancer.

Leveraging Subsidies and Tax Credits to Reduce Premiums

Navigating the complex landscape of health insurance marketplaces can be daunting, but understanding how to leverage subsidies and tax credits can significantly reduce premiums for the self-employed. These financial aids are designed to make health insurance more accessible and affordable, particularly for individuals who may not have the safety net of employer-provided plans. By strategically utilizing these subsidies and credits, self-employed professionals can mitigate one of the largest financial burdens they face, ensuring more of their income can be directed towards growth and savings.

One of the key tools available is the Premium Tax Credit (PTC), which lowers the cost of premiums for plans purchased through the Health Insurance Marketplace. Eligibility for the PTC depends on your income level relative to the federal poverty line, with those earning between 100% and 400% of the federal poverty level qualifying. This sliding scale ensures that those who need the most assistance receive the highest subsidies. For instance, a freelancer earning 200% of the federal poverty level can receive a substantial reduction in their monthly premium, making a higher-tier plan more affordable and providing better coverage.

Another critical aspect of leveraging subsidies is understanding how to estimate your annual income accurately. Underestimating or overestimating your income can lead to financial complications at tax time. An accurate projection not only maximizes your subsidies but also prevents owing money back. Tools like income calculators and detailed bookkeeping can help in making precise estimates. For example, a graphic designer with fluctuating monthly income might use a conservative estimate to ensure they stay within the eligibility bracket while avoiding surprises during tax filing.

Self-employed individuals should consider the Advanced Premium Tax Credit (APTC), which allows them to apply the tax credit to their monthly insurance premium payments in advance. This option can significantly reduce out-of-pocket costs each month, rather than waiting for a lump sum credit at the end of the year. A case in point would be a freelance writer who opts for the APTC to lower their monthly premium, thereby freeing up cash flow for business expenses or personal savings.

It's also vital to stay informed about policy changes and updates to the Health Insurance Marketplace, as these can impact the availability and amount of subsidies and credits. Engaging with recent research and trends, such as legislative adjustments or shifts in poverty level thresholds, can provide an edge in making the most cost-effective decisions. For instance, recent expansions in eligibility criteria or increases in subsidy amounts can change the calculus of which plans offer the best value. By staying proactive and informed, self-employed professionals can continuously optimize their health insurance strategy, ensuring long-term financial stability and peace of mind.

Leveraging subsidies and tax credits effectively requires a blend of accurate income estimation, strategic use of available tools, and staying updated with policy changes. For the self-employed, this proactive approach can transform health insurance from a daunting expense into a manageable, even advantageous, aspect of their financial plan. By mastering these elements, they can ensure they are not only covered but also positioned for financial growth and stability.

Understanding the Self-Employed Health Insurance Deduction

One fascinating aspect of being self-employed is the unique opportunity to tailor one's financial strategies to maximize benefits, and one such advantage is the self-employed health insurance deduction. Imagine, for a moment, navigating the labyrinth of tax regulations and discovering a hidden door that leads directly to a significant reduction in your taxable income—this door is the health insurance deduction. It's a game-changer, allowing freelancers, gig workers, and independent contractors to deduct the premiums paid for medical, dental, and even long-term care insurance. Not only does this deduction offer immediate financial relief, but it also underscores the importance of strategic planning in achieving financial freedom.

Understanding how to leverage this deduction can make a substantial difference in your overall tax liability, and it begins with knowing the eligibility requirements and income limitations. By accurately calculating your deduction, you can ensure that you are not leaving money on the table. Furthermore, this deduction directly impacts your adjusted gross income (AGI) and taxable income, which in turn, influences your entire tax strategy. As we delve into the specifics, you'll gain the clarity needed to confidently navigate this aspect of your financial journey, ensuring that every dollar you spend on health insurance works as hard for you as possible.

Eligibility Requirements and Income Limitations

Eligibility for the self-employed health insurance deduction hinges on specific criteria that must be met to qualify, making it essential for self-employed individuals to understand these requirements thoroughly. To be eligible, one must not have access to a subsidized health plan from either their own employer or a spouse's employer. This stipulation ensures that the deduction is reserved for those genuinely shouldering the burden of their health insurance costs independently. Additionally, the insurance must be established under the self-employed individual's business, signifying that the policy is directly tied to their self-employment income. This connection underscores the importance of accurate record-keeping, as it links the insurance expenses to the business operations, thereby qualifying them for the deduction.

Income limitations play a crucial role in determining the extent to which the self-employed health insurance deduction can be claimed. Specifically, the deduction cannot exceed the amount of earned income from the business under which the insurance plan is established. This limitation means that if the business has a net loss or minimal profit, the deductible amount for health insurance premiums may be substantially reduced or even eliminated. For instance, a freelancer with a net profit of $20,000 from their business can only deduct up to that amount for health insurance premiums, even if the actual premium costs are higher. Understanding this connection between business income and deduction limits is vital for effective financial planning.

Accurately calculating the self-employed health insurance deduction requires a nuanced understanding of the interplay between various factors, including total income, business expenses, and other deductions. The deduction is taken above-the-line, which means it reduces adjusted gross income (AGI) and can potentially lower overall tax liability. However, the calculation must be precise, considering any changes in income or business expenses throughout the year. Utilizing tax software or consulting with a tax professional can ensure that all relevant factors are considered, and the deduction is maximized within the legal framework. This meticulous approach can lead to significant tax savings, directly impacting the financial health of a self-employed individual.

The impact of the self-employed health insurance deduction on adjusted gross income and taxable income is profound, as it directly lowers AGI, which is the benchmark for many other tax credits and deductions. By reducing AGI, self-employed individuals may become eligible for additional tax benefits that are otherwise phased out at higher income levels. For example, a lower AGI could make one eligible for the Child Tax Credit or Education Credits, providing further financial relief. This cascading effect highlights the strategic importance of the self-employed health insurance deduction, not just as a standalone benefit but as a gateway to other financial advantages within the tax code.

Navigating the self-employed health insurance deduction requires staying abreast of current regulations and potential changes in the tax landscape. Recent legislative changes and emerging trends in healthcare and taxation can influence eligibility criteria and deduction limits. For instance, shifts in healthcare policy or tax reform efforts can alter the parameters of what constitutes a deductible expense. Staying informed through reputable sources, engaging with financial advisors, and leveraging advanced tax planning tools can equip self-employed individuals to adapt to these changes proactively. This forward-thinking approach ensures that they not only comply with current regulations but also strategically position themselves to maximize their financial benefits in an evolving environment.

Calculating Your Deduction Accurately

Calculating your self-employed health insurance deduction with precision requires a nuanced understanding of various factors that influence the final amount. This deduction, designed to alleviate the financial burden of health insurance premiums for self-employed individuals, allows for the deduction of premiums paid for medical, dental, and qualified long-term care insurance for yourself, your spouse, and dependents. To calculate this deduction accurately, start by gathering all relevant documentation, including premium payment receipts and policy information. These records will form the basis of your calculations, ensuring you claim the maximum allowable deduction.

One critical aspect to consider is the interplay between your net profit and the deduction itself. Your net profit, as reported on your Schedule C or Schedule F, directly influences the amount you can deduct. Specifically, the deduction cannot exceed your net profit from self-employment. Therefore, it's essential to have a precise calculation of your net earnings, accounting for all business income and expenses. This step not only ensures compliance with IRS guidelines but also maximizes your potential deduction. For instance, if your net profit is

$30,000 and you paid $5,000 in health insurance premiums, you can deduct the full $5,000, provided other conditions are met.

Incorporating advanced considerations, such as the coordination with other deductions and credits, can optimize your tax strategy. The self-employed health insurance deduction is an above-the-line deduction, meaning it reduces your adjusted gross income (AGI). This reduction can have cascading benefits, potentially qualifying you for additional deductions or credits that have AGI thresholds, such as the Earned Income Tax Credit or education credits. By lowering your AGI, you may unlock further tax savings, amplifying the impact of this deduction. It is crucial to approach this calculation holistically, considering how it integrates with your overall tax planning.

Emerging trends and recent research in the field of tax strategy highlight the importance of proactive planning and regular review. Staying abreast of legislative changes, such as alterations in tax law or adjustments to deduction limits, ensures your calculations remain current and compliant. Utilizing tax software or consulting with a tax professional can provide advanced insights and updates tailored to your specific situation. These tools and experts can help identify potential errors and opportunities, ensuring that your deduction calculation is both accurate and advantageous.

To bring these concepts into practical application, consider a scenario where a self-employed graphic designer, earning a net profit of $45,000, pays $8,000 in health insurance premiums. By accurately documenting and calculating the deduction, the designer reduces their AGI by $8,000, lowering their taxable income to $37,000. This reduction could potentially place them in a lower tax bracket, offering significant tax savings. Thought-provoking questions arise: How might this deduction interact with other business expenses? What strategies can be employed to balance premium payments and net profit? Addressing these questions encourages a deeper understanding and application of tax strategies, empowering self-employed individuals to manage their finances proactively.

Impact on Adjusted Gross Income and Taxable Income

The self-employed health insurance deduction can significantly influence both adjusted gross income (AGI) and taxable income, offering a powerful tool for financial optimization. By deducting premiums for medical, dental, and long-term care insurance, self-employed individuals can effectively lower their

AGI, which in turn reduces their overall tax liability. This reduction in AGI is particularly beneficial as it may enhance eligibility for other tax credits and deductions that have income thresholds. For instance, a lower AGI can mean greater eligibility for the Earned Income Tax Credit (EITC) or the Child Tax Credit, providing additional financial relief.

Accurately calculating the self-employed health insurance deduction requires a thorough understanding of its impact on taxable income. This deduction is classified as an "above-the-line" deduction, meaning it is subtracted from total income to arrive at the AGI. This is crucial because AGI is a key determinant in various tax calculations and thresholds. By reducing AGI, self-employed individuals not only lower their taxable income but also potentially decrease their marginal tax rate. For example, if a freelancer's AGI dips below a certain threshold due to the health insurance deduction, they might fall into a lower tax bracket, resulting in significant tax savings.

Understanding the interplay between AGI and taxable income can help self-employed individuals make more informed financial decisions. For example, a lower AGI can positively affect the calculation of student loan interest deductions, IRA contribution limits, and even the phase-out of itemized deductions. Additionally, reducing AGI through health insurance deductions can impact eligibility for certain education tax benefits, such as the American Opportunity Tax Credit or the Lifetime Learning Credit. This nuanced understanding allows self-employed individuals to strategically plan their finances, maximizing tax efficiency and long-term savings.

Incorporating recent insights and emerging trends can further enhance the utility of the self-employed health insurance deduction. With the rise of telemedicine and alternative healthcare options, self-employed individuals might explore incorporating these into their health plans, potentially maximizing their deductions. Additionally, understanding the evolving landscape of health insurance marketplaces can provide opportunities to select plans that not only meet healthcare needs but also offer optimal tax benefits. Keeping abreast of legislative changes and trends in healthcare can provide a strategic advantage, ensuring that self-employed individuals continue to reap the maximum tax benefits available.

To apply these insights practically, self-employed individuals should consider proactive strategies such as consulting with a tax professional to ensure accurate deduction calculations. Utilizing tax software with robust support for self-employed deductions can also streamline the process, reducing the risk of errors.

HEALTHCARE OPTIONS FOR THE SELF EMPLOYED   95

Regularly reviewing and adjusting health insurance plans to align with both healthcare needs and financial goals can ensure sustained tax benefits. By maintaining meticulous records of health insurance premiums and related expenses, self-employed individuals can confidently claim their deductions, ultimately enhancing their financial stability and paving the way for long-term success.

Evaluating Healthcare Sharing Plans

Think about a scenario where you're sitting at your kitchen table, surrounded by stacks of paperwork, trying to figure out how to secure affordable healthcare as a self-employed individual. You've heard whispers about healthcare sharing plans—those intriguing alternatives to traditional health insurance—but you're not quite sure what they entail. The idea of joining a community where members share healthcare costs sounds promising, especially if it means lower premiums and a more personalized approach to coverage. But before diving in, it's essential to understand the nuances that set these plans apart from conventional insurance.

A closer examination shows that healthcare sharing plans can indeed offer substantial benefits, but they come with their own set of complexities. Understanding the cost and coverage differences is crucial; these plans often have lower monthly contributions but may not cover all medical expenses. Assessing the network and member requirements is another vital step, as these plans usually have specific rules about who can join and what types of care are covered. Additionally, evaluating the risk-sharing models and limitations will help you gauge whether a healthcare sharing plan aligns with your financial and health needs. By peeling back the layers and examining these aspects, you'll be better equipped to make an informed decision that supports your path to financial freedom and peace of mind.

Understanding the Cost and Coverage Differences

Healthcare sharing plans, often referred to as health share programs, present a compelling alternative to traditional health insurance for self-employed individuals. These plans operate on a model of collective responsibility, where members contribute monthly premiums into a communal pool. This pool is then used to cover eligible medical expenses for the community, offering a unique way of managing healthcare costs. Unlike conventional insurance plans, which are governed by state and federal regulations, healthcare sharing plans are typically managed by non-profit organizations with a set of guidelines that members must adhere to. This structure can lead to cost savings, but it also introduces variability in terms of coverage and reimbursement processes.

One of the primary distinctions between healthcare sharing plans and traditional insurance is the cost structure. Monthly contributions to sharing plans are often significantly lower than insurance premiums, making them an attractive option for those with limited budgets. However, these reduced costs come with trade-offs. For instance, sharing plans may not cover pre-existing conditions immediately, often requiring a waiting period before such conditions are eligible for sharing. Additionally, the scope of coverage can vary widely, with some plans excluding certain types of care, such as mental health services or preventive care, which are typically covered by traditional insurance policies. Understanding these nuances is crucial for self-employed individuals to ensure they are not caught off guard by unexpected medical expenses.

Coverage differences are another critical factor to consider when evaluating healthcare sharing plans. Traditional insurance plans are bound by the Affordable Care Act (ACA) to cover a comprehensive list of essential health benefits, including hospitalization, maternity care, and prescription drugs. In contrast, healthcare sharing plans are not subject to these regulations, providing them with the flexibility to tailor their coverage offerings. While this can lead to more personalized plans that cater to specific needs, it also means that members must carefully review the terms of coverage to understand what is and isn't included. For instance, some plans may have caps on the amount they will pay for certain services or may require members to share a higher portion of the costs for specific treatments.

The flexibility of healthcare sharing plans also extends to their operational models. Some plans operate on a reimbursement basis, where members pay for their medical expenses upfront and then submit claims for reimbursement from the communal pool. Others may negotiate directly with healthcare providers to secure discounted rates for their members. This variability in operational models can impact the ease and speed with which members receive support for their medical expenses. It is essential for self-employed individuals to assess how these differences align with their financial capabilities and healthcare needs. For example, those who prefer to avoid out-of-pocket expenses may favor plans that negotiate directly with providers.

Innovative perspectives on healthcare sharing plans suggest that they are evolving to become more inclusive and comprehensive. Some newer plans are beginning to incorporate aspects of traditional insurance, such as wellness programs and preventive care incentives, to attract a broader member base. Additionally, advancements in telemedicine and digital health platforms are being integrated into these plans, providing members with more accessible and cost-effective healthcare solutions. These trends indicate a growing recognition of the need to balance cost savings with adequate coverage, making healthcare sharing plans a viable option for a wider range of self-employed individuals.

Assessing the Network and Member Requirements

Healthcare sharing plans offer a unique alternative to traditional health insurance, particularly appealing to the self-employed seeking flexible and often more affordable coverage options. However, understanding the nuances of these plans is essential to making an informed decision. One key factor is the network and member requirements. Unlike conventional insurance, healthcare sharing plans often operate through a network of members who share healthcare costs among themselves. This community-based approach can be both a boon and a challenge, depending on the specifics of the network and the individual's healthcare needs.

Members of healthcare sharing plans typically must adhere to certain lifestyle and medical practices, as these plans are often rooted in shared values or religious beliefs. This means that potential members need to carefully assess whether their personal lifestyle and healthcare choices align with the plan's requirements. For instance, some plans might exclude coverage for services related to lifestyle choices such as smoking or excessive alcohol consumption. Additionally, pre-existing conditions may not be covered, or there might be a waiting period before such conditions are eligible for cost-sharing. These stipulations can significantly impact the overall utility of the plan for some individuals.

Another critical aspect to evaluate is the geographical reach and provider network of the healthcare sharing plan. Traditional insurance plans typically have extensive networks of doctors and hospitals, making it relatively easy to find in-network care. In contrast, healthcare sharing plan networks can be more limited, potentially requiring members to travel further or compromise on their choice of healthcare providers. Prospective members should thoroughly inves-

98   MASTERING SELF-EMPLOYED TAXES

tigate the list of participating providers to ensure that their preferred healthcare professionals and facilities are included.

The administrative processes and member requirements of healthcare sharing plans can differ considerably from those of traditional insurance. Members often need to be proactive in managing their healthcare expenses, including submitting medical bills for reimbursement rather than having providers bill the plan directly. This added layer of responsibility necessitates a higher level of organization and financial management from the member. Understanding these administrative nuances beforehand can help avoid surprises and ensure a smoother experience when accessing healthcare services.

Evaluating member testimonials and reviews can provide valuable insights into the practicalities of a healthcare sharing plan. Feedback from current and past members can highlight common issues, strengths, and areas for improvement, offering a realistic picture of what to expect. Additionally, engaging with online forums and communities dedicated to healthcare sharing plans can provide a wealth of information and support, helping prospective members make a well-rounded and informed decision. By thoroughly assessing these network and member requirements, self-employed individuals can better determine if a healthcare sharing plan aligns with their needs and preferences.

Evaluating the Risk-Sharing Models and Limitations

Healthcare sharing plans have gained traction as an alternative to traditional health insurance, particularly among self-employed individuals seeking cost-effective solutions. These plans operate on a risk-sharing model, where members contribute a monthly share amount into a collective pool managed by the organization. When a member faces medical expenses, they can submit a request for sharing, and the collective pool covers the costs, subject to the plan's guidelines. Understanding the nuances of these models is crucial to determine if this approach aligns with one's healthcare needs and financial goals.

One key aspect to evaluate is the cost and coverage differences between healthcare sharing plans and traditional insurance. Typically, healthcare sharing plans have lower monthly contributions compared to insurance premiums. However, they may also come with higher out-of-pocket costs, as they often do not cover routine care or preventative services. Additionally, these plans might have limitations on coverage for pre-existing conditions, which can be a significant consideration for those with ongoing health issues. It's essential to carefully compare the total potential out-of-pocket expenses in various scenarios to truly understand the financial impact.

Another critical factor is the network and member requirements imposed by healthcare sharing organizations. Unlike traditional insurance networks that include a wide range of healthcare providers, sharing plans may have restrictions on which providers members can visit. Some plans require members to adhere to specific lifestyle guidelines or participate in certain community activities, reflecting the organization's values or religious affiliations. Assessing these requirements against personal values and lifestyle choices is essential to ensure compatibility and avoid unexpected limitations.

The risk-sharing model itself also comes with its set of limitations that need to be carefully considered. Unlike traditional insurance, healthcare sharing plans are not regulated by the Affordable Care Act (ACA), meaning they are not obligated to cover essential health benefits or maintain the same level of consumer protections. This lack of regulation can lead to significant variability in how claims are handled and what costs are covered. Prospective members should scrutinize the plan's guidelines on what constitutes a shareable expense and the process for submitting claims to avoid surprises during critical times of need.

Despite these limitations, healthcare sharing plans can offer a viable solution for many self-employed individuals, especially those seeking lower monthly costs and who are comfortable with the risk-sharing concept. Recent trends indicate a growing number of these plans incorporating telemedicine services and wellness programs, aiming to enhance value while controlling costs. Potential members should look for plans that embrace such innovations, as they can offer additional benefits and improve overall healthcare accessibility.

The decision to join a healthcare sharing plan should be based on a thorough understanding of its risk-sharing model and limitations. Engaging with current members, reading reviews, and consulting with a financial advisor or healthcare expert can provide deeper insights into the plan's practicalities. By weighing the pros and cons and considering personal health needs and financial circumstances, self-employed individuals can make informed choices that align with their pursuit of financial freedom and well-being.

Reflecting on the core concepts discussed, it's evident that navigating healthcare as a self-employed individual requires a proactive and informed approach. The journey through health insurance marketplaces unveils a plethora of options tailored to diverse needs and budgets, empowering you to make choices that align with your financial and wellness goals. The self-employed health insurance deduction emerges as a powerful tool, offering significant tax relief while underscoring the importance of meticulous record-keeping. Evaluating healthcare sharing plans adds another layer of consideration, presenting an alternative path that might resonate with those seeking community-based support and lower costs.

As you forge ahead on your path to financial independence, the understanding and strategic management of healthcare options play a vital role in your overall financial health. This chapter equips you with the knowledge to make informed decisions, ensuring that your healthcare choices bolster rather than hinder your journey. Embrace the insights gained here as a cornerstone of your broader financial strategy, recognizing that proactive planning in healthcare is as crucial as any other aspect of your financial life. As we transition to the next chapter, consider how these healthcare strategies can be integrated with other facets of your financial planning, continually moving you closer to the peace of mind and security that comes with true financial freedom.

Chapter Seven

Legal Considerations And Business Structures

Have you ever considered the intricate dance between choosing the right business entity and the financial freedom you aspire to achieve? Picture this: Maria, a successful graphic designer, started her freelancing journey with boundless enthusiasm but quickly found herself lost in a maze of legal jargon and tax implications. It wasn't until she took a step back to understand the importance of her business structure that she truly began to thrive. Her story isn't unique. Like many self-employed individuals, the path to financial freedom is often paved with legal considerations that can either propel you forward or hold you back.

Unveiling the layers of business structures reveals a world of opportunities and responsibilities. From sole proprietorships to LLCs and corporations, each entity carries its own set of legal protections, liabilities, and tax responsibilities. Understanding these nuances is not just about compliance; it's about strategically positioning yourself for growth and stability. Imagine the peace of mind that comes with knowing your personal assets are protected, or the satisfaction of optimizing your tax strategy to keep more of your hard-earned money. These decisions are the foundation upon which your financial future is built, and they deserve careful consideration.

By exploring the impact of your business structure on taxes, you'll begin to see how proactive planning can transform your financial landscape. This chapter will guide you through the essential considerations, helping you make informed choices that align with your goals and aspirations. Whether you're just starting out or looking to restructure for better efficiency, understanding these elements is crucial. As you turn the page, prepare to gain insights that will not only demystify the complexities but also empower you to take control of your financial destiny, just as Maria did.

Choosing the Right Business Entity

Experts have long debated the optimal business entity for self-employed individuals, each structure presenting a unique blend of benefits and challenges. Imagine Sarah, a graphic designer who recently transitioned from a corporate job to full-time freelancing. Excited by her newfound freedom, she initially registered as a sole proprietor. However, as her client base grew, so did her concerns about liability and tax obligations. Sarah's story isn't unique. Many freelancers and independent contractors grapple with the same questions: Should I remain a sole proprietor, or would forming an LLC offer better protection and tax advantages? Is an S Corporation too complex for my needs, or could it save me money in the long run? These questions are not merely academic; they can significantly impact your financial health and peace of mind.

Understanding the intricacies of business entities is crucial for anyone aiming to master self-employed taxes. Each structure—from sole proprietorships to LLCs and S Corporations—affects not only how you file taxes but also your legal liabilities and potential for growth. This section will guide you through the maze of options, providing clear insights and practical advice. We'll start by examining the simplest form of business structure, the sole proprietorship, and its tax implications. Then, we'll explore the advantages and drawbacks of Limited Liability Companies (LLCs) for self-employed individuals. Finally, we'll navigate the complexities of S Corporations and partnerships, helping you make informed decisions that align with your financial goals.

LEGAL CONSIDERATIONS AND BUSINESS STRUCTURES   103

Understanding Sole Proprietorships and Their Tax Implications

Sole proprietorships represent the most straightforward business structure for self-employed individuals, offering simplicity and ease of operation. As the default configuration for most freelancers and independent contractors, a sole proprietorship requires no formal registration with state authorities, making it an attractive option for those eager to start their venture without a labyrinth of bureaucracy. However, this simplicity comes with its own set of tax implications that must be meticulously understood to optimize financial outcomes. As the owner, you are personally responsible for all business debts and obligations, and this liability extends to your personal assets. This characteristic underscores the importance of comprehending how income from a sole proprietorship is reported on your personal tax return, specifically using Schedule C (Form 1040).

One of the primary tax implications of a sole proprietorship is the treatment of business income. All profits generated by the business are considered personal income and are subject to self-employment tax. This includes both Social Security and Medicare taxes, which can be significant but are necessary to fund your future benefits. To accurately calculate these taxes, it's crucial to maintain diligent records of all income and allowable expenses, as this will directly influence your taxable income. Tools such as accounting software or even a dedicated business bank account can simplify this process, ensuring that you capture every deductible expense, from office supplies to business travel. By leveraging these deductions, you can significantly reduce your overall tax liability, highlighting the need for a proactive approach to financial management.

Another critical aspect to consider is the quarterly estimated tax payments required for sole proprietors. Unlike traditional employees who have taxes withheld from their paychecks, sole proprietors must estimate their tax liability and make payments to the IRS four times a year. This system necessitates a keen understanding of your expected income and expenses throughout the year, as failing to make adequate payments can result in penalties and interest charges. Many new business owners find this aspect daunting, but with careful planning and regular financial reviews, it becomes a manageable task. Setting aside a portion of your earnings each month specifically for these payments can help mitigate the financial strain and ensure you remain compliant with IRS requirements.

While sole proprietorships offer unmatched simplicity, they also present unique challenges, particularly in terms of risk and liability. Because there is no legal distinction between the owner and the business, personal assets such as your home, car, and savings are potentially at risk if the business incurs debt or is sued. This vulnerability makes it imperative to consider additional protective measures, such as acquiring appropriate business insurance or even revisiting your business structure as the enterprise grows. While the sole proprietorship may be ideal for starting out, evolving into a limited liability company (LLC) or another structure may provide the necessary legal protections and tax benefits as your business expands.

Despite these challenges, a sole proprietorship can offer unparalleled flexibility and control over your business operations. It allows for a direct correlation between effort and reward, with all profits flowing directly to you without the need for complex corporate formalities or profit-sharing arrangements. This direct approach can be particularly empowering for those who value autonomy and have a clear vision for their business. Understanding the tax implications and proactively managing your financial responsibilities can transform potential pitfalls into opportunities for growth and stability.

Evaluating the Benefits and Drawbacks of LLCs for Self-Employed Individuals

For self-employed individuals, forming a Limited Liability Company (LLC) can offer a range of advantages. One of the most appealing benefits is the personal liability protection it provides. Unlike a sole proprietorship, where personal assets are at risk if the business incurs debt or legal issues, an LLC separates personal and business finances, safeguarding personal wealth. This protection can be crucial for freelancers or contractors who may face contractual disputes or financial uncertainties. It's a safety net that allows business owners to take calculated risks without jeopardizing their personal financial stability.

Another significant benefit of an LLC is the potential for tax flexibility. LLCs can choose how they wish to be taxed, either as a sole proprietorship, partnership, S Corporation, or even a C Corporation, depending on the specific needs and goals of the business. For instance, an LLC can opt for pass-through

LEGAL CONSIDERATIONS AND BUSINESS STRUCTURES   105

taxation, where business income is reported on the owner's personal tax return, avoiding the double taxation that corporations face. This can result in substantial tax savings, particularly for those with high earnings. Additionally, LLC owners can take advantage of various tax deductions and credits, reducing the overall tax burden.

The advantages of LLCs come with certain complexities that must be navigated. Setting up an LLC involves more paperwork and higher initial costs compared to a sole proprietorship. There are state-specific filing fees and annual reporting requirements that can vary significantly, adding to the administrative workload. Moreover, LLCs are often subject to self-employment taxes on net earnings, which can be a considerable expense. These factors necessitate a thorough evaluation of the cost-benefit ratio before deciding to form an LLC.

The operational structure of an LLC also demands careful consideration. While it provides flexibility, it requires a well-drafted operating agreement to outline the management and financial arrangements among members. This document is crucial for preventing disputes and ensuring smooth operations. For solo entrepreneurs, it may seem redundant, but it serves to clarify roles, responsibilities, and profit-sharing mechanisms, which can be vital as the business grows or if new members are added. This foresight can prevent future legal and operational complications, making the LLC a more sustainable business structure in the long run.

In weighing the benefits and drawbacks of an LLC, self-employed individuals must consider their specific business needs, financial goals, and risk tolerance. Consulting with legal and tax professionals can provide tailored advice and help navigate the complexities of forming and operating an LLC. This proactive approach ensures that the decision to establish an LLC aligns with both short-term needs and long-term aspirations, paving the way for sustainable business growth and financial security. By understanding the intricacies of LLCs, self-employed professionals can make informed choices that enhance their business resilience and tax efficiency.

Navigating the Tax Complexities of S Corporations and Partnerships

Navigating the tax intricacies of S Corporations and partnerships can be a nuanced yet rewarding endeavor for self-employed individuals seeking to optimize their financial strategies. S Corporations, often referred to as S Corps, offer a unique blend of advantages, particularly when it comes to tax savings. Unlike sole proprietorships and traditional corporations, S Corps allow income to pass through directly to shareholders, avoiding the double taxation that typically plagues C Corporations. This pass-through taxation means that profits are taxed only once at the individual level, potentially resulting in significant tax savings. Additionally, S Corp owners can classify a portion of their income as salary and another as distribution, which may reduce self-employment taxes, provided the salary is deemed "reasonable" by the IRS.

Partnerships, on the other hand, offer flexibility and collaborative potential that can be especially appealing for self-employed individuals looking to pool resources or expertise. Similar to S Corps, partnerships benefit from pass-through taxation, where income is reported on individual partners' tax returns, thus avoiding double taxation. However, partnerships introduce a level of complexity in terms of profit-sharing and tax reporting. Each partner must account for their share of the profits or losses, and this can be influenced by the partnership agreement, which dictates the distribution of income, deductions, and credits. This agreement becomes crucial in ensuring all partners are aligned on financial expectations and responsibilities, thus minimizing conflicts and potential legal disputes.

One of the key considerations when choosing between these business structures is understanding how they impact self-employment taxes. In an S Corp, shareholders who actively work in the business are considered employees, which means they are subject to payroll taxes on their salary but not on distributions. This can result in substantial tax savings, particularly for high-income earners. Partnerships, conversely, do not offer this distinction; all earnings are subject to self-employment tax, which can be a drawback for individuals seeking to minimize their taxable income. However, partnerships often provide greater ease of management and fewer administrative burdens compared to S Corps, which require more formalities such as issuing stock and maintaining corporate minutes.

Recent developments in tax law and regulations have added layers of complexity and opportunity to these structures. For instance, the Tax Cuts and Jobs Act (TCJA) of 2017 introduced a 20% Qualified Business Income (QBI) deduction for pass-through entities, including S Corps and partnerships. This deduction can significantly reduce taxable income, but it comes with stringent qualifying criteria and limitations based on income levels and business types.

LEGAL CONSIDERATIONS AND BUSINESS STRUCTURES 107

Keeping abreast of these changes and seeking expert advice can help self-employed individuals maximize their benefits while remaining compliant. Furthermore, innovative accounting software and tax planning tools have made it easier to manage these complexities, providing real-time insights and projections that can guide strategic decision-making.

To leverage the benefits of S Corporations and partnerships, self-employed individuals must adopt a proactive and informed approach. This includes regular consultations with tax professionals, ongoing education about tax laws, and strategic financial planning. By understanding the specific tax implications and operational requirements of these business structures, self-employed individuals can make informed decisions that align with their long-term financial goals.

Legal Protections and Liability

The essence of this topic is the pivotal role legal protections and liability play in your journey as a self-employed professional. Imagine you're a freelance graphic designer, excited about a lucrative project with a new client. You've poured countless hours into perfecting your designs, only to find out that the client refuses to pay, and worse yet, they've started using your designs without permission. This scenario can be a nightmare, but understanding legal protections and liability can be your shield against such predicaments. It's not just about shielding yourself from potential pitfalls; it's about empowering you to operate confidently, knowing you have the legal backing to safeguard your hard-earned work and reputation.

As we navigate through the intricacies of legal protections and liability, we'll explore how choosing the right business entity can fortify your defenses against personal liability. We'll delve into the importance of understanding contractual obligations and how you can mitigate risks with airtight agreements. Additionally, we'll touch on the often-overlooked realm of intellectual property rights and how to handle legal disputes if they arise. Each of these elements is a cornerstone in building a robust legal foundation for your business, ensuring that you're not just surviving but thriving in the self-employed landscape.

Choosing the Right Business Entity for Liability Protection

Selecting the appropriate business entity is paramount for self-employed professionals aiming to shield themselves from liability and optimize their tax situation. The choice of entity—whether it's a sole proprietorship, partnership, limited liability company (LLC), S corporation, or C corporation—has far-reaching implications. For instance, while a sole proprietorship is the simplest to set up, it offers no personal liability protection. In contrast, an LLC or corporation provides a legal buffer, separating personal assets from business obligations. This distinction is critical for freelancers and contractors who want to protect their homes, savings, and other personal assets from potential business-related lawsuits or debts.

Understanding the nuances of each business structure can be a game-changer. An LLC, for instance, combines the flexibility of a sole proprietorship with the liability protection of a corporation. This makes it a popular choice among small business owners and freelancers. On the other hand, S corporations can offer tax advantages by allowing business income to pass through to the owners' personal tax returns, thereby avoiding double taxation. However, they come with more stringent requirements and administrative overhead. It's essential to evaluate not only the immediate benefits but also the long-term implications of each structure, considering factors like potential growth, funding needs, and the complexity of compliance.

Contractual obligations and risk mitigation are also integral to choosing the right business entity. An LLC or corporation can simplify contractual relationships by providing a clear legal entity separate from the individual. This separation can enhance credibility with clients and partners, facilitating smoother negotiations and more robust contracts. Moreover, these entities can provide a framework for risk management, enabling business owners to delineate responsibilities, establish protocols for dispute resolution, and implement safeguards against potential legal issues. This proactive approach to risk mitigation is crucial for maintaining business continuity and fostering a trustworthy professional reputation.

Intellectual property (IP) rights are another critical consideration when selecting a business entity. Freelancers and independent contractors often create unique content, designs, or products that require legal protection. Establishing an LLC or corporation can simplify the process of registering and defending in-

LEGAL CONSIDERATIONS AND BUSINESS STRUCTURES   109

tellectual property by providing a clear ownership structure. Additionally, these entities can offer better avenues for enforcing IP rights and resolving disputes, ensuring that creative assets are adequately safeguarded. Understanding how different business structures impact IP management can help self-employed individuals make informed decisions that protect their innovations and enhance their competitive edge.

Navigating legal disputes is an inevitable part of running a business, and the choice of entity plays a significant role in this process. An LLC or corporation can provide a more structured approach to dispute resolution, including formal mechanisms for arbitration and mediation. These entities can also limit personal liability in case of litigation, ensuring that only business assets are at risk. For self-employed professionals, this can mean the difference between a manageable legal challenge and a catastrophic financial loss. By carefully selecting and structuring their business entity, freelancers and gig workers can build a resilient foundation that supports sustainable growth and financial stability.

Understanding Contractual Obligations and Risk Mitigation

Navigating contractual obligations is a cornerstone of risk mitigation for self-employed individuals. Whether you're a freelancer, independent contractor, or gig worker, understanding the intricacies of contracts is essential to protect your interests and ensure smooth business operations. A well-drafted contract not only outlines the scope of work but also clarifies payment terms, deadlines, and deliverables, minimizing the potential for disputes. For instance, clearly specifying the payment schedule can prevent cash flow issues and provide a safety net in case of non-payment. By setting clear expectations from the outset, you create a foundation of trust and professionalism that benefits both parties involved.

Risk mitigation in contracts goes beyond just clear terms; it involves anticipating potential issues and incorporating clauses that address them. One effective strategy is to include a force majeure clause, which outlines what happens if unforeseen events, such as natural disasters or pandemics, prevent either party from fulfilling their obligations. Another critical element is the indemnity clause, which specifies which party is responsible for certain damages or losses. By proactively addressing these scenarios, you safeguard your business from unexpected legal and financial repercussions. For example, if a client defaults on payment, a well-drafted contract with an indemnity clause can help you recover legal fees and other associated costs.

Intellectual property (IP) concerns are another vital aspect of contractual obligations. As a self-employed professional, your creations—whether they are designs, written content, or software—are your most valuable assets. Ensuring that your contract includes clauses that clearly define IP ownership and usage rights can prevent future disputes and unauthorized use of your work. A common approach is to retain ownership of your IP while granting the client a license to use it for specific purposes. This not only protects your creative rights but also opens up opportunities for you to repurpose and monetize your work in other ways, maximizing its value.

In addition to these protective measures, staying informed about the latest legal developments and trends is crucial for effective risk mitigation. For instance, emerging technologies like blockchain are revolutionizing contract enforcement through smart contracts, which automatically execute and enforce terms when predefined conditions are met. Staying abreast of such innovations can provide you with advanced tools to enhance your contractual security. Furthermore, subscribing to industry-specific legal updates or joining professional associations can keep you informed about changes in regulations that may impact your contractual obligations.

The goal of understanding contractual obligations and risk mitigation is to create a robust framework that allows you to focus on your core business activities with confidence. By meticulously drafting contracts, incorporating essential clauses, protecting your intellectual property, and staying updated with legal trends, you minimize the risk of legal disputes and financial losses. This proactive approach not only enhances your professional credibility but also contributes significantly to your journey towards financial independence and stability. Engaging with these concepts critically and practically ensures that you are not just reacting to issues but strategically preventing them, thus fostering a more resilient and successful business.

Navigating Intellectual Property Rights and Legal Disputes

Navigating intellectual property rights and legal disputes is a crucial aspect of managing a self-employed business, particularly in a world where ideas and creative work hold significant value. Understanding the basics of intellectual property (IP) can shield freelancers and independent contractors from potential legal pitfalls. Intellectual property encompasses trademarks, copyrights, patents, and trade secrets—each offering different forms of protection. For instance, a graphic designer might need to secure copyrights for their original artwork, while a tech consultant might rely on trade secrets to protect proprietary methodologies. By comprehending the nuances of these protections, self-employed individuals can safeguard their creations against unauthorized use and ensure they retain full control over their work.

One of the most effective ways to navigate intellectual property rights is through proactive registration and documentation. Registering trademarks or copyrights with appropriate government bodies provides legal recognition and a stronger foundation for enforcing rights if infringements occur. For example, a writer who registers the copyright of their manuscript gains an official record that can serve as evidence in legal disputes. Additionally, maintaining meticulous records of the creation process, including drafts, sketches, and emails, can substantiate claims of original ownership. This approach not only fortifies legal standing but also instills confidence in clients and collaborators about the legitimacy and professionalism of the business.

Legal disputes over intellectual property can be daunting, but understanding the avenues for resolution can mitigate the stress. Mediation and arbitration are alternative dispute resolution methods that offer a less adversarial and often more cost-effective option than litigation. For instance, a freelance software developer who faces a dispute over code ownership might opt for mediation to reach a mutually agreeable solution without the prolonged expense of court proceedings. In cases where litigation becomes unavoidable, having a clear, documented history of the IP and its usage can significantly bolster the case. Knowledge of these processes empowers self-employed professionals to approach disputes with a clear strategy and a focus on resolution.

Staying abreast of emerging trends and technologies in intellectual property law is equally vital. The rapid pace of innovation means that new forms of IP and corresponding legal frameworks are constantly evolving. For instance, the rise of digital art and NFTs (non-fungible tokens) has introduced novel challenges and opportunities for protecting creative works. Self-employed individuals should actively seek out continuing education opportunities, such as workshops and webinars, to stay informed about these developments. Engaging with professional networks and legal experts who specialize in IP can provide valuable insights and support, ensuring that one's approach to intellectual property remains current and effective.

Fostering a proactive mindset towards intellectual property can transform potential risks into opportunities for growth and differentiation. By strategically managing IP, self-employed individuals not only protect their assets but also enhance their market position. For instance, a consultant who develops a proprietary framework and trademarks it can leverage this IP to build a unique brand identity and command higher fees. Encouraging innovation and actively seeking to understand and utilize IP protections can thus become a cornerstone of a successful, resilient business strategy. Embracing this mindset encourages a forward-thinking approach, turning the complexities of intellectual property into a powerful tool for achieving long-term success and financial independence.

The Impact of Business Structure on Taxes

Visualize a future where your business flourishes, and your tax strategy is not just a necessity but a powerful tool driving your success. Imagine the confidence you'll feel when you know that every financial decision you make is optimized for the greatest benefit, not only for today but for years to come. This isn't a distant dream; it's entirely within your grasp, and the key lies in understanding how your choice of business structure impacts your taxes. Each type of business entity—whether a sole proprietorship, a limited liability company (LLC), or an S corporation—comes with its own set of tax implications that can either enhance your financial health or become a hidden drain on your resources.

Consider Sarah, a freelance graphic designer who started as a sole proprietor. She enjoyed the simplicity of her setup until she realized she was paying more in self-employment taxes than necessary. After consulting with a tax professional, she switched to an LLC and later elected S corporation status, significantly reducing her tax burden and enhancing her savings. Her journey highlights the critical importance of choosing the right business entity. As we delve into the specifics of sole proprietorships, LLCs, and S corporations, you'll discover how each structure affects your taxes and how you can make informed decisions to maximize your financial freedom. Let's embark on this exploration, ensuring that your business structure not only supports your entrepreneurial spirit but also serves as a robust foundation for your financial goals.

Sole Proprietorships and Pass-Through Taxation

Understanding the tax implications of operating as a sole proprietorship is pivotal for self-employed individuals. Sole proprietorships are the most straightforward business structure and, as such, are favored by many freelancers and gig workers. This structure involves a single owner who is personally responsible for all business liabilities and debts. Significantly, sole proprietorships utilize pass-through taxation, meaning the business itself is not taxed separately. Instead, the income generated by the business is reported on the owner's personal tax return. This can simplify tax filing and reduce the administrative burden for those just starting out.

Pass-through taxation means that the business's profits and losses are directly transferred to the owner's personal income tax return, specifically on Schedule C. This method streamlines the tax process and can be advantageous for those who want to avoid the complexities associated with other business structures. For example, a freelance graphic designer earning $80,000 a year would report this income on their individual tax return, thus avoiding the need for a separate corporate tax filing. However, it's crucial for sole proprietors to meticulously track all business-related income and expenses, as this will directly impact their taxable income and potential deductions.

One significant consideration for sole proprietors is the requirement to pay self-employment taxes, which cover Social Security and Medicare contributions. Unlike traditional employees, sole proprietors must pay both the employer and employee portions of these taxes, which can amount to approximately 15.3% of net earnings. While this can seem daunting, there are strategies to mitigate the impact. For instance, sole proprietors can deduct half of their self-employment tax when calculating their adjusted gross income. This deduction can provide some relief and should be factored into comprehensive tax planning.

Beyond the basics, it's essential to recognize the evolving landscape of tax regulations and potential legislative changes that may affect sole proprietors. Keeping abreast of these changes is vital for maintaining compliance and optimizing tax outcomes. Recent trends indicate a growing emphasis on digital record-keeping and the use of software to streamline tax preparations. Tools like QuickBooks and TurboTax Self-Employed can significantly ease the process of tracking expenses and preparing for tax season. By leveraging these technologies, sole proprietors can ensure they are capturing all allowable deductions, thereby reducing their overall tax liability.

The simplicity of a sole proprietorship offers both benefits and challenges. While the ease of setup and transparent pass-through taxation are appealing, the responsibility of self-employment taxes and personal liability requires diligent financial management. Sole proprietors should continually educate themselves on tax strategies, seek professional advice when necessary, and utilize modern tools to stay organized. In doing so, they can navigate the tax landscape with confidence and ensure they are making the most of their financial opportunities.

Limited Liability Companies and Tax Flexibility

Limited Liability Companies (LLCs) offer a unique blend of flexibility and protection for self-employed individuals, making them an attractive option for many. One of the standout features of an LLC is the ability to choose how it is taxed. By default, a single-member LLC is treated as a sole proprietorship for tax purposes, while a multi-member LLC is taxed as a partnership. However, LLCs have the option to elect corporate taxation, either as a C corporation or an S corporation, offering a level of adaptability that can be tailored to fit various financial strategies and long-term goals. This tax flexibility allows entrepreneurs to select the structure that optimizes their tax liabilities and aligns with their business objectives.

Consider a freelance graphic designer who has established a single-member LLC. By default, the designer's income is reported on Schedule C of their personal tax return, similar to a sole proprietorship. This simplicity can be beneficial for those just starting out or who prefer straightforward bookkeeping. Yet, as the business grows, the designer might choose to have the LLC taxed as an S corporation to potentially reduce self-employment taxes on a portion of their income. This strategic shift can lead to significant tax savings, demonstrating the inherent adaptability of the LLC structure.

The taxation of LLCs also provides opportunities for advanced tax planning. With the ability to be taxed as a corporation, LLCs can take advantage of corporate tax rates and benefits, such as fringe benefits and retirement plans that are typically more favorable than those available to sole proprietors. For instance, an LLC taxed as a C corporation can offer its members health insurance and other benefits as tax-deductible business expenses. This can be particularly

LEGAL CONSIDERATIONS AND BUSINESS STRUCTURES   115

advantageous for businesses with multiple owners or those planning to reinvest profits back into the company.

LLCs benefit from the pass-through taxation model, which can simplify tax obligations by eliminating the double taxation that traditional corporations face. In a pass-through entity, business profits and losses are reported on the owners' personal tax returns, allowing for the offset of other personal income with business losses. This can be a powerful tool for new businesses that might experience initial losses, providing a means to reduce overall taxable income and improve cash flow during the critical early stages of growth.

To illustrate the real-world impact, consider a tech startup with three co-founders. By forming an LLC, they can initially take advantage of pass-through taxation to manage their personal tax liabilities while reinvesting in the business. As the startup scales, they might transition to being taxed as an S corporation to better manage self-employment taxes. This flexibility ensures that as their business evolves, their tax strategy can evolve in tandem, aligning with their financial needs and objectives. The ability to adapt and optimize tax obligations through the LLC structure not only offers immediate financial benefits but also positions the business for sustainable growth and success.

S Corporations and Self-Employment Tax Savings

S Corporations, often abbreviated as S Corps, present a compelling option for self-employed individuals seeking to optimize their tax liabilities. Unlike sole proprietorships and standard LLCs, S Corps offer unique mechanisms to reduce self-employment taxes, which can significantly impact overall financial health. At the heart of this advantage is the ability to distinguish between salary and distributions. Owners of S Corps must pay themselves a reasonable salary, subject to payroll taxes, but the remaining profits can be distributed as dividends, which are typically exempt from self-employment taxes. This strategic allocation can result in substantial tax savings, allowing more capital to be reinvested into the business or saved for future endeavors.

The concept of a "reasonable salary" is pivotal to the tax benefits of an S Corporation. The IRS mandates that S Corp owners pay themselves a fair market wage for the work they perform. This requirement is designed to prevent abuse of the tax system by underpaying salaries to minimize payroll taxes. Determining what constitutes a "reasonable salary" can be complex, involving factors such as industry standards, the complexity of the work, and the time commitment of the owner. Seeking guidance from tax professionals or utilizing salary benchmarking tools can help ensure compliance while maximizing tax efficiency.

In addition to tax savings, S Corporations offer other financial advantages that can bolster the overall health of a business. For instance, S Corps allow for the deduction of certain fringe benefits, such as health insurance premiums for employees, including the owner, which can further reduce taxable income. Additionally, S Corp status can enhance credibility with clients and investors, as it demonstrates a level of sophistication and commitment to structured financial practices. This perception can be particularly beneficial for freelancers and gig workers looking to expand their client base or attract investment.

While the benefits of S Corporations are clear, the process of electing S Corp status requires careful consideration and adherence to specific procedures. Business owners must file Form 2553 with the IRS to elect S Corporation status, and this election must be made timely, typically within the first two and a half months of the tax year in which the election is to take effect. Furthermore, maintaining S Corp status involves ongoing compliance with various regulations, such as holding annual meetings and keeping detailed corporate minutes. These requirements, while manageable, necessitate a commitment to organizational discipline and record-keeping.

The decision to operate as an S Corporation should be informed by a comprehensive analysis of one's business model, income levels, and long-term financial goals. Engaging with a knowledgeable tax advisor can provide invaluable insights tailored to individual circumstances, ensuring that the benefits of S Corp status are fully realized. By thoughtfully navigating the complexities of S Corporations, self-employed individuals can leverage this business structure to achieve significant tax savings, enhance their professional standing, and move closer to their goal of financial independence.

Choosing the right business structure and understanding the associated legal considerations are pivotal steps in your journey to financial independence. The decisions you make in this area will not only influence your tax obligations but also determine the level of legal protection and personal liability you face. Recognizing the impact of these choices can empower you to build a solid foundation for your business, ensuring that you are well-protected and optimized for tax efficiency. By carefully weighing the pros and cons of each business entity—be it a sole proprietorship, LLC, S-Corp, or another structure—you can align your business goals with the most advantageous legal and tax frameworks.

LEGAL CONSIDERATIONS AND BUSINESS STRUCTURES   117

As you move forward, consider how these foundational decisions integrate with your broader financial strategy. Reflect on the importance of proactively managing your legal and tax responsibilities, and think about seeking professional advice to tailor your choices to your unique circumstances. This chapter is not just an end, but a stepping stone toward greater financial literacy and stability. Embrace these insights as you continue to navigate the complexities of self-employment, and prepare to delve into the next aspects of your financial journey with confidence and a clear vision for your future.

Chapter Eight

Avoiding Common Tax Mistakes

Venturing into the realm of self-employment is like stepping onto a vibrant and unpredictable stage. The freedom and flexibility it offers can be exhilarating, yet the responsibilities, particularly when it comes to taxes, can quickly become overwhelming. Picture Sarah, a graphic designer who left her corporate job to pursue freelance work. Initially, the thrill of being her own boss overshadowed the complexities of managing her finances. It wasn't until tax season arrived that she realized the landscape was dotted with potential pitfalls. Sarah's story is far from unique, but it serves as a vivid reminder of the importance of navigating this terrain with care.

One might wonder, how can something as seemingly straightforward as taxes become so fraught with pitfalls? The answer lies in the myriad of details that self-employed individuals must juggle. From categorizing income and expenses correctly to staying on top of deadlines and maximizing deductions, the responsibilities are numerous and nuanced. Each misstep can lead to penalties, missed opportunities, or even audits. This chapter will shine a light on these common tax mistakes, not to intimidate, but to empower you with the knowledge needed to avoid them.

Understanding and sidestepping these errors is paramount on your journey to financial freedom. By giving these topics the attention they deserve, you'll not only protect your hard-earned income but also position yourself for long-term success. This chapter will explore the intricacies of correctly classifying income and expenses, the critical importance of meeting deadlines, and

AVOIDING COMMON TAX MISTAKES

the often-overlooked deductions and credits that can significantly impact your bottom line. Armed with this information, you'll be better equipped to make informed decisions and maintain peace of mind as you navigate the complexities of self-employed taxes.

Misclassifying Income and Expenses

To begin, let's consider the story of Sarah, a talented graphic designer who decided to leave her corporate job and pursue freelancing full-time. With her newfound freedom, she was excited to take on diverse projects and work with a variety of clients. However, as tax season approached, Sarah found herself overwhelmed by the sheer volume of her financial records. She had been mixing personal and business expenses, incorrectly categorizing her mixed-use assets, and struggling to allocate her income from multiple revenue streams accurately. This scenario is all too common among self-employed individuals, but it doesn't have to be a nightmare.

Imagine a future where you navigate your finances with the precision and confidence of a seasoned entrepreneur. By mastering the art of distinguishing between business and personal expenses, correctly categorizing mixed-use assets, and accurately allocating your income, you can avoid costly mistakes and keep more of your hard-earned money. This chapter will guide you through the intricacies of these crucial tasks, empowering you to take control of your financial destiny. As you continue, you'll uncover practical strategies and insights that will transform your approach to managing income and expenses, setting the stage for a smoother, more prosperous financial journey.

Differentiating Business and Personal Expenses

Understanding the distinction between business and personal expenses is pivotal for anyone navigating the realm of self-employed taxes. Misclassification can lead to audits, penalties, and lost deductions, making a clear demarcation not only necessary but also financially advantageous. Business expenses are those directly related to the operation of your enterprise, such as office supplies, software subscriptions, or professional services. Conversely, personal expenses are those incurred for individual benefit, like personal groceries or household utilities. The challenge arises when an expense could potentially fall into both categories, like a cell phone used for both personal and business purposes. Keeping meticulous records and, when in doubt, consulting a tax professional can help ensure that expenses are correctly classified.

A nuanced understanding of mixed-use assets is essential to avoid pitfalls in tax reporting. Mixed-use assets—those utilized for both business and personal reasons—require careful allocation to ensure compliance with tax regulations. For example, if you use your personal vehicle for client meetings, only the mileage driven for business purposes is deductible. The IRS provides specific guidelines on how to calculate these deductions accurately, often involving prorated calculations based on the percentage of business use. Utilizing tools like mileage tracking apps or dedicated accounting software can simplify this process, ensuring that you capture every business mile and expense accurately.

Accurately allocating income between multiple revenue streams is another critical aspect of managing self-employed taxes. Freelancers and independent contractors often juggle various projects and clients, making it essential to track each revenue stream meticulously. Whether you're earning from freelance writing, consulting, or selling products online, each income source must be documented separately. This not only aids in precise tax reporting but also provides valuable insights into which revenue streams are most profitable. Advanced financial management tools can help automate income tracking, offering a streamlined way to categorize and allocate earnings from diverse sources.

Emerging trends in tax technology are revolutionizing how self-employed individuals handle these complexities. Machine learning algorithms and artificial intelligence are increasingly being integrated into tax software, offering predictive analytics and real-time error detection. These advancements can help identify potential misclassifications before they become problematic, providing a proactive approach to tax management. Staying abreast of these technological developments can give freelancers a significant edge, turning tax season from a stressful ordeal into a manageable, even straightforward, task.

Engaging in critical thinking about expense classification can also lead to more strategic financial planning. Consider hypothetical scenarios: What if you invest in a home office renovation? How should you allocate those expenses? By rigorously analyzing and questioning such situations, you can better prepare for real-life occurrences. This proactive mindset not only helps in accurate tax reporting but also in making informed business decisions that optimize your financial health. For instance, understanding that a portion of your home office expenses can be deducted might incentivize you to improve your workspace,

AVOIDING COMMON TAX MISTAKES   121

thereby enhancing productivity and potentially increasing your income. By adopting these advanced strategies and leveraging cutting-edge tools, self-employed individuals can navigate the complex landscape of tax obligations with confidence and precision. The goal is not just to comply with tax laws but to use this knowledge to empower your financial journey, transforming potential pitfalls into stepping stones towards financial freedom.

Properly Categorizing Mixed-Use Assets

Navigating the proper categorization of mixed-use assets is crucial for self-employed individuals aiming to optimize their tax strategy. Mixed-use assets, such as a vehicle used for both personal and business purposes or a home office that doubles as a guest bedroom, present unique challenges when it comes to accurate expense reporting. A clear understanding of how to delineate the business portion from the personal use is imperative, not only for compliance but also for maximizing allowable deductions. For instance, meticulously tracking the mileage used for client meetings versus personal errands can significantly impact the deductible amount on your tax return. This practice requires diligent record-keeping and an honest assessment of usage patterns.

One practical approach to managing mixed-use assets is to adopt a systematic tracking method, such as using apps or software designed for expense logging. These tools can automatically differentiate between personal and business expenses based on predefined categories. For example, a mileage tracking app can log trips made for business purposes separately from personal travel, ensuring accuracy and ease during tax season. This separation is vital because the IRS scrutinizes mixed-use assets closely, and any discrepancies can lead to audits or penalties. By leveraging technology, self-employed individuals can maintain precise records and substantiate their claims with confidence.

When it comes to home office deductions, the IRS provides specific guidelines to determine the portion of your home used exclusively for business. This includes calculating the square footage of the dedicated office space relative to the total area of your home. However, it's essential to remember that the space must be used regularly and exclusively for business purposes to qualify. A room that serves multiple functions, like a guest bedroom, may not meet the criteria unless the business use is clearly delineated. Adopting a consistent method for measuring and documenting the business use percentage can help substantiate your claims if questioned.

In addition to physical assets, digital tools and software used for both personal and business activities also fall under the category of mixed-use assets. Subscriptions to software services like cloud storage, design programs, or productivity tools often blur the lines between personal and professional use. To navigate this, it's beneficial to allocate costs based on usage patterns. For example, if a graphic designer uses a design software 70% of the time for client projects and 30% for personal art, then 70% of the subscription cost can be claimed as a business expense. Detailed usage logs and clear documentation will support these allocations and ensure compliance.

It's worth exploring the evolving landscape of tax regulations and best practices related to mixed-use assets. Recent developments, such as the increasing prevalence of remote work and flexible workspaces, have prompted new considerations for home office deductions and mixed-use asset categorization. Keeping abreast of these changes through reliable resources and consultations with tax professionals can provide self-employed individuals with the latest insights and strategies. By staying informed and proactive, you can navigate the complexities of mixed-use assets with greater precision and confidence, ultimately enhancing your financial management and tax efficiency.

Accurately Allocating Income Between Multiple Revenue Streams

Navigating the labyrinth of income allocation among various revenue streams is a critical skill for self-employed professionals. Accurate income allocation ensures not only compliance with tax regulations but also a clearer picture of financial health. Missteps in this area can lead to significant tax discrepancies, making it imperative to differentiate between primary and secondary income sources. For instance, a freelance graphic designer might earn from direct client work, online courses, and royalties from digital assets. Each of these streams must be meticulously recorded and categorized to avoid conflating distinct income types. This segregation aids in precise tax reporting and enables more strategic financial planning.

To accurately allocate income, it is essential to establish a robust system for tracking revenue. This might involve using accounting software that can handle multiple income categories, ensuring that each dollar earned is attributed correctly. Advanced tools like QuickBooks or Xero offer features that auto-

AVOIDING COMMON TAX MISTAKES

matically categorize income based on preset rules. Additionally, maintaining separate bank accounts for different income streams can simplify this process. For example, a writer with income from book sales, speaking engagements, and freelance articles might use individual accounts to track these revenue streams distinctly, facilitating easier reconciliation and reporting.

Understanding the tax implications of each revenue stream is another crucial aspect. Different types of income can be subject to varying tax treatments. Passive income, such as royalties, might be taxed differently from active income like consulting fees. Being aware of these distinctions allows for more accurate tax planning and potentially reduces taxable income through strategic deductions. For example, a musician earning from live performances and streaming royalties must recognize the differing tax responsibilities and potentially leverage deductions specific to each type of income, such as travel expenses for live gigs and home office deductions for online streaming work.

Advanced concepts such as income splitting and deferral can further optimize tax obligations. Income splitting involves distributing income among family members in lower tax brackets, legally reducing the overall tax burden. This strategy can be particularly advantageous for family-run businesses where spouses or children contribute to the work. Income deferral, on the other hand, involves delaying income receipt to a future tax period, which can be beneficial in years where additional income might push one into a higher tax bracket. For instance, a consultant might defer the receipt of a large project payment to the following fiscal year if it's more tax advantageous.

It's vital to stay informed about the latest tax regulations and emerging trends in income allocation. Legislative changes can significantly impact how income should be reported and taxed. Engaging with a knowledgeable tax professional can provide personalized insights and ensure compliance with the latest rules. Regularly reviewing IRS guidelines and participating in tax-related webinars or workshops can also keep self-employed professionals ahead of the curve. By staying proactive and informed, freelancers and independent contractors can confidently navigate the complexities of income allocation, avoiding pitfalls and maximizing their financial well-being.

Ignoring Deadlines and Penalties

Throughout history, the concept of time has been both a friend and a foe to humanity. For the self-employed, time can be particularly treacherous when it comes to tax deadlines. Picture this: you're diligently working on a project, immersed in the creativity and grind that define your freelance career. Days blur into weeks, and before you know it, a crucial tax deadline has passed. It's a familiar tale for many independent workers, but one that brings with it a cascade of stress, penalties, and financial setbacks. The reality is that ignoring deadlines isn't just a minor oversight—it can be a costly mistake that disrupts your financial stability and peace of mind.

But here's the good news: navigating deadlines and avoiding penalties is entirely within your grasp. Imagine having a system in place that ensures you never miss a due date, turning what was once a source of anxiety into a seamless part of your routine. By understanding the consequences of missing tax deadlines, employing strategies for timely filings and payments, and leveraging technology for deadline management, you can transform this potential pitfall into a strength. In doing so, you'll not only safeguard your finances but also build confidence in your ability to manage your business with precision and foresight. Let's explore how you can make this transition, starting with the critical importance of meeting those all-important deadlines.

Understanding the Consequences of Missing Tax Deadlines

Missing tax deadlines can have far-reaching consequences, extending beyond the immediate financial penalties. The Internal Revenue Service (IRS) imposes both failure-to-file and failure-to-pay penalties, which can quickly accumulate and create significant financial strain. For independent contractors and freelancers, these penalties can disrupt cash flow, making it challenging to manage other business expenses. For instance, the failure-to-file penalty is typically 5% of the unpaid taxes for each month or part of a month that a tax return is late, up to a maximum of 25% of the unpaid taxes. This can add up rapidly, particularly for those with substantial tax liabilities. In addition to financial penalties, missing deadlines can also trigger audits, increasing the burden of compliance and potentially leading to further complications.

AVOIDING COMMON TAX MISTAKES

Beyond the immediate financial repercussions, missing tax deadlines can also affect your credit score. Although the IRS does not directly report tax debts to credit bureaus, unpaid taxes can result in a tax lien. A tax lien is a legal claim against your property due to unpaid taxes, and it can significantly impact your creditworthiness. This can make obtaining loans or credit lines more difficult and expensive, further hindering your financial freedom. Awareness of these broader impacts underscores the importance of timely tax filing and payment, encouraging a more proactive approach to tax management.

One of the less obvious consequences of missing tax deadlines is the potential loss of benefits and opportunities. For example, filing taxes late can disqualify you from claiming certain tax credits or deductions that have specific deadlines. The Earned Income Tax Credit (EITC) is one such benefit that requires timely filing. Missing out on these credits can result in a higher tax liability than necessary, reducing your net income. Additionally, late filing can delay your eligibility for government programs or financial aid, which often rely on up-to-date tax information.

To mitigate these risks, developing a robust strategy for timely tax filing and payment is essential. This involves setting clear deadlines and reminders well ahead of the official IRS deadlines. Utilizing tax software can streamline this process, offering automated reminders and easy-to-follow steps for submission. Software solutions like QuickBooks Self-Employed or TurboTax can be invaluable tools for managing deadlines. These platforms often include features that calculate estimated taxes, track due dates, and even allow for electronic filing, reducing the likelihood of oversight.

Leveraging technology for deadline management is not just about using software; it also involves integrating multiple tools to create a cohesive system. Calendar applications, such as Google Calendar or Outlook, can be synchronized with tax software to ensure that all tax-related deadlines are visible and prioritized. Setting multiple reminders, including one several weeks before the due date and another a few days before, can help ensure that deadlines are not missed. Additionally, exploring mobile apps that offer push notifications can provide real-time updates and alerts, making it easier to stay on top of tax obligations. This multi-faceted approach not only minimizes the risk of missing deadlines but also fosters a disciplined and organized approach to financial management.

Strategies for Timely Tax Filing and Payment

When it comes to timely tax filing and payment, the first step is understanding the critical nature of organization. Maintaining a well-organized financial system is paramount. This means diligently keeping track of all income sources, receipts, and expenses throughout the year, rather than scrambling at the last minute. Utilizing digital tools like accounting software can significantly streamline this process. These platforms not only help in categorizing and storing financial data but also often come with features that remind you of upcoming deadlines. For instance, software like QuickBooks or FreshBooks integrates with your bank accounts, providing real-time financial tracking and deadline alerts. This proactive approach minimizes the risk of missing crucial filing dates and ensures that you are always prepared when tax season arrives.

Another vital strategy is setting aside funds for taxes regularly. Unlike traditional employees whose taxes are deducted from their paychecks, self-employed individuals must manage their tax payments themselves. A common rule of thumb is to set aside approximately 25-30% of your income for taxes. This can be done by creating a separate savings account specifically for tax purposes. Each time you receive payment for your services, transfer the estimated tax portion into this account. This practice not only helps in avoiding any shortfall when tax payments are due but also mitigates the stress of large, lump-sum payments. By breaking down tax savings into smaller, manageable amounts, the financial burden becomes less daunting.

Leveraging the expertise of a tax professional can also be a game-changer. Tax laws and regulations are continually evolving, and staying updated can be challenging for a busy self-employed individual. A certified public accountant (CPA) or a tax advisor who specializes in self-employed taxes can provide invaluable guidance. They can help you navigate the complexities of tax code changes, identify eligible deductions, and ensure that all your filings are accurate and timely. Regular consultations with a tax professional can also uncover potential tax-saving opportunities that you might not be aware of, further enhancing your financial efficiency.

Another innovative approach is to utilize automated tax filing services, which have gained popularity in recent years. Companies like TurboTax Self-Employed and H&R Block offer tailored solutions for freelancers and independent contractors. These services guide you through the tax filing process step-by-step,

AVOIDING COMMON TAX MISTAKES   127

ensuring that you don't miss any crucial details. They also offer options to e-file your taxes, which is faster and often more secure than traditional paper filing. Additionally, many of these platforms offer audit support, giving you peace of mind in the event of an IRS inquiry.

Staying informed about emerging trends and legislative changes in tax laws is essential. Subscribing to newsletters from reputable financial and tax advisory firms, attending webinars, and participating in relevant online forums can keep you updated on the latest developments. For example, recent changes in tax laws regarding deductible expenses for home offices or new tax credits for self-employed health insurance premiums can have significant implications for your tax strategy. By staying informed, you can adapt your financial planning to maximize tax benefits and avoid potential penalties. This proactive approach not only ensures compliance but also empowers you to make informed decisions that align with your long-term financial goals.

Leveraging Technology for Deadline Management and Penalty Avoidance

Harnessing the power of technology can significantly streamline tax management for self-employed individuals, transforming what often feels like a burden into a manageable task. Modern software solutions, such as QuickBooks and Xero, offer automated features that track income and expenses in real-time, reducing the risk of human error. These platforms often include reminders for upcoming tax deadlines, ensuring that critical dates are not overlooked. By integrating these tools into daily financial practices, freelancers and independent contractors can maintain a proactive approach, mitigating the risk of incurring penalties due to missed deadlines. Incorporating AI-driven insights, such as predictive analytics, can further enhance these platforms, offering advanced forecasting capabilities that help users plan ahead and allocate funds for tax payments more effectively.

Beyond traditional accounting software, a plethora of mobile apps like Expensify and FreshBooks cater specifically to the needs of self-employed individuals. These apps allow users to capture receipts, categorize expenses, and generate comprehensive financial reports from their smartphones. The convenience of mobile access ensures that no deductible expense is forgotten, and financial data remains up-to-date. This constant connectivity supports a more dynamic and responsive approach to tax management, making it easier to adhere to filing requirements and avoid late fees. Furthermore, these apps often sync with cloud storage, providing a secure backup of all financial records, which is essential for both tax preparation and potential audits.

Calendar and reminder applications, such as Google Calendar or Microsoft Outlook, are invaluable for managing tax deadlines. Users can set recurring alerts for quarterly tax payments, annual filings, and other critical dates. These reminders can be customized to provide ample notice, allowing sufficient time to gather necessary documents and complete filings without the last-minute rush. For those who prefer a more integrated approach, some accounting software solutions offer built-in calendar functionalities that automatically populate with important tax deadlines based on user-specific criteria. This seamless integration ensures that deadlines are consistently visible and top-of-mind.

Emerging trends in fintech are pushing the envelope further with smart contracts and blockchain technology, promising even more robust solutions for tax compliance. Blockchain's immutable ledger can provide an unalterable record of transactions, ensuring accuracy and transparency in financial reporting. Smart contracts can automate tax payments and filings based on predefined criteria, reducing the manual effort involved and minimizing the risk of errors. As these technologies continue to evolve, they offer exciting potential for revolutionizing tax management, making it more efficient and less prone to human oversight.

Leveraging technology for deadline management and penalty avoidance isn't just about utilizing the latest tools; it's about cultivating a mindset of continuous improvement and adaptability. Staying informed about new software updates, app features, and fintech innovations can provide self-employed individuals with a competitive edge in their financial management practices. Engaging in online forums, subscribing to industry newsletters, and participating in webinars can offer additional insights and practical tips from peers and experts alike. By embracing these technological advancements and fostering a proactive approach, self-employed individuals can navigate their tax obligations with greater confidence and ease, paving the way towards sustained financial success.

Overlooking Deductions and Credits

Try to imagine walking into a room filled with unclaimed treasure, each item representing a potential deduction or credit that could significantly reduce your tax burden. Yet, many self-employed individuals leave these treasures untouched, simply because they are unaware of their existence or unsure of how to claim them. This scenario is more common than you might think, and it can cost you thousands of dollars every year. Embracing the art of identifying and claiming all available deductions and credits isn't just about saving money—it's about empowering yourself to take control of your financial destiny.

A crucial element in this discussion is understanding how seemingly mundane aspects of your work life can translate into substantial tax savings. From the cozy corner of your home office to the premiums you pay for health insurance, there are numerous opportunities to ease your tax burden if you know where to look. Take the example of advanced education expenses: many freelancers and independent contractors invest in courses or certifications to hone their skills, yet fail to realize these costs can often be written off. By being proactive and informed, you can transform everyday expenses into powerful financial tools, ensuring that you keep more of what you earn.

Maximizing Home Office Deductions

For self-employed individuals, the home office deduction is one of the most valuable yet often overlooked tax benefits. It's essential to understand that this deduction isn't merely about having a designated workspace; it's about maximizing the potential savings it offers. To qualify, the space must be used exclusively and regularly for business purposes, which means no mixing it with personal activities. This exclusivity might seem restrictive, but the financial rewards can be substantial. For example, calculating the deduction can be done using two methods: the simplified option, which allows a standard deduction of $5 per square foot up to 300 square feet, or the regular method, which involves calculating actual expenses such as mortgage interest, utilities, and repairs. Choosing the right method can significantly impact your tax savings, making it crucial to understand the nuances of each.

Beyond the basic eligibility, the intricacies of what constitutes a deductible expense can further enhance your tax strategy. For instance, if you use the regular method, you can deduct a portion of your home-related expenses proportional to the percentage of your home used for business. This includes not only the obvious costs like rent or mortgage interest but also more nuanced expenses such as depreciation, insurance, and even home improvements that benefit your office. Savvy freelancers might also consider indirect expenses—like security systems or landscaping—that, while not directly related to the office space, can still be partially deducted if they contribute to the overall business environment.

Recent developments in remote work trends have also influenced how home office deductions are perceived and utilized. With the rise in telecommuting and virtual businesses, the IRS has clarified guidelines to ensure taxpayers can legitimately claim these deductions without fear of audits or penalties. This shift reflects a broader recognition of the evolving nature of workspaces, allowing more individuals to benefit from deductions that previously seemed reserved for traditional home offices. Staying informed about these changes ensures you can take full advantage of the opportunities available, adapting your tax strategy to align with current regulations and best practices.

Incorporating advanced concepts like the depreciation of home office improvements can further maximize your deductions. For example, if you invest in energy-efficient windows or a new HVAC system that benefits your home office, you can depreciate these improvements over several years, spreading out their tax benefits. This approach not only reduces your immediate tax burden but also creates a long-term strategy for managing business expenses. Understanding the lifecycle of these assets and their impact on your overall tax plan requires a more sophisticated grasp of tax laws, but the payoff can be considerable.

To make the most of home office deductions, consider working with a tax professional who can offer personalized advice based on your unique situation. They can help you navigate the complexities of IRS regulations, ensuring your deductions are both maximized and compliant. Additionally, leveraging software tools that track and categorize expenses can simplify the process, providing you with a clear and organized record to present during tax season. By combining professional guidance with efficient tools, you can confidently claim home office deductions, ultimately contributing to your financial independence and peace of mind.

Leveraging Health Insurance Premium Credits

Navigating the intricacies of health insurance premium credits can be a game-changer for the self-employed. One of the most impactful provisions is the Self-Employed Health Insurance Deduction, which allows eligible freelancers and independent contractors to deduct the cost of health insurance premiums paid for themselves, their spouses, and their dependents directly from their gross income. This deduction can significantly lower taxable income, resulting in substantial tax savings. It's essential to understand that this benefit applies only to premiums paid for coverage under a qualifying plan. Therefore, maintaining meticulous records and ensuring the selected insurance meets the criteria are vital steps toward maximizing this opportunity.

Beyond the foundational deduction, the Affordable Care Act (ACA) introduced the Premium Tax Credit (PTC), which offers additional financial relief. The PTC is designed to assist those purchasing health insurance through the Health Insurance Marketplace by lowering the premiums based on income levels. For self-employed individuals, accurately estimating annual income is crucial, as the credit amount is determined by this estimate. A higher-than-expected income may result in needing to repay some or all of the credits received, while a lower income could mean an increased credit. This dynamic requires a proactive approach, with periodic income assessments and adjustments to stay aligned with eligibility criteria.

A nuanced yet powerful strategy involves leveraging the interplay between the Self-Employed Health Insurance Deduction and the Premium Tax Credit. While the deduction directly reduces taxable income, lowering the Adjusted Gross Income (AGI) can, in turn, increase eligibility for a higher PTC. This dual benefit creates a synergistic effect, maximizing overall savings. However, it demands a sophisticated understanding of tax regulations and a meticulous approach to income and expense tracking. Consulting with a tax professional can provide the necessary expertise to navigate these complexities, ensuring optimal utilization of both benefits.

Recent developments and emerging trends in health insurance premiums also offer new avenues for tax savings. For instance, Health Reimbursement Arrangements (HRAs) have gained traction, allowing self-employed individuals to reimburse themselves for medical expenses, including premiums, on a pre-tax basis. This arrangement can be particularly advantageous for those with fluctuating incomes, providing a flexible and tax-efficient method to manage health care costs. Keeping abreast of such innovations and adapting one's strategy accordingly can provide a competitive edge, ensuring that no potential savings are overlooked.

To engage more deeply with the material, consider the following scenario: Imagine a self-employed graphic designer who meticulously tracks her income and expenses. She uses the Self-Employed Health Insurance Deduction to lower her AGI, subsequently increasing her eligibility for a higher Premium Tax Credit. By periodically reassessing her income projections and adjusting her financial strategy, she not only maximizes her tax savings but also ensures stable and affordable health coverage. This proactive, informed approach exemplifies the power of leveraging health insurance premium credits to achieve financial stability and peace of mind.

Exploring Advanced Education Expense Write-offs

Self-employed individuals often miss out on advanced education expense write-offs, a valuable opportunity to reduce taxable income while investing in their professional growth. Understanding these deductions begins with recognizing what qualifies as an education expense. Generally, expenses for courses that maintain or improve skills required in your current trade or business are deductible. For instance, if you're a freelance graphic designer, enrolling in advanced design courses or software training can be considered a legitimate write-off. This not only reduces your tax burden but also enhances your skill set, making you more competitive in the marketplace.

To maximize these deductions, it's crucial to keep meticulous records of all related expenses. This includes tuition, books, supplies, and any other necessary fees. Utilizing accounting software can simplify this process, allowing you to categorize and track expenses accurately. Moreover, staying updated on IRS guidelines is essential, as tax laws and eligible deductions can evolve. Subscribing to IRS updates or consulting with a tax professional can ensure you're leveraging the most current information to your benefit.

An often-overlooked aspect is the potential for travel expenses to be deductible if they are directly related to educational pursuits. Suppose you need to attend a workshop or seminar that requires travel. In that case, costs such as airfare, lodging, and meals might qualify as deductible expenses. However, the trip must be primarily for business purposes, and personal activities should

AVOIDING COMMON TAX MISTAKES

be minimal. Documenting the business purpose of the travel and maintaining receipts will help substantiate these deductions if questioned.

Beyond traditional courses, consider unconventional education opportunities that may also be deductible. Online courses, webinars, and even certain certifications can qualify if they are directly related to your business. For instance, if you're an independent consultant, a certification in a niche area of your field can not only be tax-deductible but also position you as an expert, potentially leading to higher earnings. This approach aligns with the broader goal of financial independence by strategically investing in your education to enhance your income potential.

Engaging with a tax advisor who specializes in self-employed tax issues can provide tailored advice on maximizing education expense write-offs. They can help identify less obvious deductions and ensure compliance with tax regulations. Additionally, exploring tax-saving strategies such as the Lifetime Learning Credit or the American Opportunity Credit can further reduce your taxable income. These credits can be particularly beneficial, as they directly reduce the amount of tax owed, offering substantial savings. By proactively managing your education expenses and leveraging available tax benefits, you can achieve a more favorable financial outcome while continuously advancing your professional skills.

As we bring this chapter to a close, it's clear that the journey to financial freedom is paved with careful attention to detail and a proactive approach to tax management. Misclassifying income and expenses can lead to significant issues down the line, so taking the time to understand the nuances of what constitutes business versus personal expenses is crucial. Ignoring deadlines and penalties can quickly erode your hard-earned income, but staying organized and setting reminders can mitigate these risks. Overlooking deductions and credits is like leaving money on the table; knowing which deductions apply to your situation can provide substantial financial benefits. Each of these common mistakes has the potential to disrupt your path to financial stability, yet each is easily avoidable with the right knowledge and tools.

Reflecting on these points, it's evident that mastering self-employed taxes isn't just about avoiding pitfalls—it's about empowering yourself with the knowledge to make informed decisions that support your financial goals. This chapter underscores the importance of accuracy, timeliness, and awareness in managing your tax responsibilities. As we move forward, consider how these lessons integrate into the broader picture of your financial journey. Equipped with this understanding, you're better prepared to tackle the complexities of self-employment with confidence and clarity. What steps will you take today to ensure your financial future is secure and prosperous?

Chapter Nine

Working With Tax Professionals

D ive into the complexities of working with tax professionals, where the right guidance can mean the difference between financial chaos and clarity. Imagine this: Jane, a freelance graphic designer, was drowning in a sea of receipts, invoices, and tax forms. She spent countless hours trying to navigate the labyrinth of self-employed taxes, only to find herself more confused than ever. It wasn't until she enlisted the help of a seasoned tax professional that she finally felt the weight lift off her shoulders. This chapter explores how you, too, can find that relief and focus on what you do best—running your business.

As your business grows, so do your responsibilities, and managing your taxes can quickly become overwhelming. This chapter will guide you through the pivotal moments when hiring an accountant is not just beneficial but essential. We will walk you through the process of finding a tax advisor who understands your unique needs and can offer tailored advice to optimize your financial strategies. The goal is to empower you to make informed decisions that align with your journey toward financial independence.

Collaborating effectively with a tax professional is more than just handing over a stack of documents; it's about building a partnership based on trust and mutual understanding. This chapter delves into the nuances of maintaining a productive relationship with your accountant, ensuring that you are both on the same page throughout the year. By the end, you'll have a clear roadmap for leveraging expert advice to streamline your tax obligations, ultimately paving the way for a more organized and stress-free financial life.

When to Hire an Accountant

Picture a world where tax season isn't synonymous with stress and frustration but is instead a seamless part of your financial journey—an opportunity rather than an obligation. Imagine sitting in a cozy office, sipping coffee, as a knowledgeable professional sifts through your financial records with the precision of a seasoned detective. This scenario isn't a fantasy but a potential reality when you consider the immense benefits of hiring an accountant. Many self-employed individuals often grapple with the complexities of tax codes and the ever-changing landscape of financial regulations. The right accountant can transform this daunting task into a manageable, even enlightening, experience, ensuring you're not only compliant but also strategically positioned for financial growth.

Reflect on a time when you felt overwhelmed by the myriad of tax forms, deductions, and credits. Perhaps you missed out on potential savings simply because you didn't know they existed, or maybe you found yourself entangled in a complex audit. These situations underscore the pivotal role an accountant can play. By navigating complex tax scenarios, maximizing your deductions, and providing strategic financial insights, a skilled tax professional becomes an invaluable ally. They bring a wealth of knowledge and experience, ensuring you make informed decisions that benefit your financial health in the long run. As you explore the nuances of when to hire an accountant, consider the profound impact this decision can have on your journey to financial freedom and peace of mind.

Navigating Complex Tax Situations and Audits

Navigating complex tax situations and potential audits can be a daunting aspect of self-employment, often necessitating the expertise of a seasoned accountant. When your tax circumstances transcend the straightforward, the value of professional guidance becomes indispensable. Complex tax situations can arise from various sources, including but not limited to, multiple income streams, substantial investment portfolios, or international earnings. An experienced accountant can decipher intricate tax codes and regulations, ensuring compliance while maximizing benefits. They can also help in preemptively identifying red

WORKING WITH TAX PROFESSIONALS

flags that might trigger audits, thus mitigating risks before they escalate into serious issues.

Consider a scenario where a freelancer simultaneously runs a consultancy and invests in rental properties. The interplay of various income types—earned, passive, and potentially capital gains—creates a labyrinthine tax situation. An accountant can streamline this complexity, applying their knowledge to optimize tax outcomes. For instance, they might utilize advanced strategies such as income splitting or asset depreciation to lower taxable income. These nuanced approaches are often overlooked by those without specialized training, underscoring the importance of professional intervention.

In the unfortunate event of an audit, having an accountant on your side can be a game-changer. Audits are not only stressful but also time-consuming and detail-oriented. An accountant can act as an intermediary between you and the tax authorities, presenting your case in the most favorable light. They can help gather and organize required documentation, ensuring every piece of information is accurate and complete. Their expertise can also be pivotal in negotiating settlements, potentially reducing the financial impact of any discrepancies uncovered during the audit process.

Accountants stay abreast of the latest changes in tax laws and regulations, an area where self-employed individuals often struggle to keep pace. For instance, recent developments in tax legislation could introduce new opportunities for deductions or require adjustments to existing financial strategies. An accountant's ongoing education and familiarity with these changes enable them to adapt your tax strategy dynamically, ensuring you remain compliant while capitalizing on new benefits. This proactive approach can result in significant tax savings over time, contributing to your long-term financial stability.

The value of a tax professional extends beyond mere compliance and immediate tax savings. They can offer strategic financial planning advice that aligns with your broader financial goals. This could involve setting up retirement accounts, advising on the tax implications of major financial decisions, or even planning for eventual business succession. By incorporating an accountant into your financial team, you leverage their expertise not just for current tax needs but as part of a holistic approach to building and preserving wealth, ultimately guiding you toward financial independence with confidence and security.

Maximizing Deductions and Credits for Higher Savings

Maximizing deductions and credits is a cornerstone of effective tax strategy for self-employed individuals. Engaging a tax professional can significantly enhance your ability to identify and capitalize on these opportunities, ensuring you keep more of your hard-earned money. One critical area where an accountant can provide immense value is in their ability to stay updated with the ever-evolving tax code. With frequent changes in legislation, having an expert who can navigate the nuances, interpret new laws, and apply them to your specific situation can lead to substantial savings. For instance, recent modifications to the home office deduction rules or the expanded provisions under the CARES Act might offer benefits you've overlooked.

A tax advisor's expertise goes beyond just knowing the rules; they can also strategize and implement long-term tax-saving plans tailored to your business model. Consider the Qualified Business Income (QBI) deduction, which allows eligible self-employed individuals to deduct up to 20% of their qualified business income. This deduction is fraught with conditions and limitations, and a seasoned accountant can guide you through the complexities, ensuring you meet all the criteria without inadvertently triggering disqualifying factors. By structuring your income and expenses appropriately, they can help you maximize this and other similar deductions.

Professionals can also uncover less obvious deductions and credits that you might not be aware of. For example, if you're involved in a specific industry, such as software development or manufacturing, there may be sector-specific credits available. Research and development (R&D) tax credits, often underutilized by small businesses, can offset significant amounts of taxable income when properly documented and claimed. An accountant familiar with your industry can identify these niche opportunities and guide you through the application process, ensuring compliance and maximizing benefits.

Tax professionals can also offer strategic advice on timing your expenses and income to optimize your tax position. For instance, they might recommend accelerating certain expenses into the current tax year or deferring income to the next, depending on your financial projections and the anticipated changes in tax laws. By manipulating the timing of transactions, you can manage your taxable income more effectively, smooth out cash flow, and reduce your overall tax liability. This level of strategic planning can be challenging to achieve without professional insight and experience.

Working with an accountant can provide peace of mind by ensuring that your claims are well-documented and substantiated, reducing the risk of triggering an audit. Should an audit occur, having a professional who is well-versed in your financial history and the intricacies of your tax returns can be invaluable. They can represent you, communicate effectively with tax authorities, and provide the necessary documentation to support your deductions and credits, thereby mitigating stress and potential penalties. This proactive approach not only safeguards your current financial health but also sets a solid foundation for future growth and stability.

Strategizing for Long-Term Financial Planning and Growth

Strategizing for long-term financial planning and growth is an essential consideration for self-employed individuals. Engaging a tax professional can be a game-changer in this respect, as they bring a wealth of expertise that transcends basic tax filing. A proficient accountant doesn't merely prepare your taxes; they can help orchestrate a comprehensive financial strategy that aligns with your personal and professional aspirations. For example, they can assist in setting up retirement accounts such as SEP-IRAs or Solo 401(k)s, ensuring that you are not only compliant but also optimizing your contributions to secure a comfortable future. This proactive approach can result in substantial tax savings and a more robust financial foundation.

Consider the intricacies involved in tax-efficient investing. A seasoned tax advisor can guide you through the labyrinth of capital gains taxes, passive income sources, and other investment-related tax implications. For instance, while many self-employed individuals might focus solely on their immediate income streams, an accountant can highlight the benefits of diversifying your portfolio to include tax-advantaged investments. This could involve real estate ventures or municipal bonds, which offer specific tax benefits. By understanding and leveraging these opportunities, you can significantly enhance your long-term financial stability and growth.

Tax professionals are well-versed in the latest legislation and emerging trends that could impact your financial trajectory. They can provide insights into new tax credits, deductions, and regulatory changes that you might not be aware of. For instance, recent updates in tax laws might offer new opportunities

140 MASTERING SELF-EMPLOYED TAXES

for deductions related to home office expenses or health insurance premiums. Staying abreast of these changes can be daunting without expert guidance. A knowledgeable advisor ensures that you are not only compliant but also making the most of every available benefit, helping you to keep more of what you earn and invest it wisely.

It's also important to consider the role of tax professionals in risk management and audit preparedness. While no one likes to think about being audited, it's a reality that must be faced, especially for self-employed individuals who often have more complex tax situations. An experienced accountant can help you establish and maintain meticulous records, ensuring that you have the necessary documentation to support your claims. They can also represent you in dealings with the IRS, providing a layer of protection and peace of mind that is invaluable. This proactive approach to risk management can prevent costly penalties and safeguard your financial health.

The relationship with a tax advisor is not one of mere transaction but of ongoing collaboration. By regularly reviewing your financial status and goals with an expert, you can continuously adapt your strategies to changing circumstances. Life events such as marriage, the birth of a child, or the purchase of a new home all have significant tax implications. A tax professional can help you navigate these changes smoothly, ensuring that your long-term financial plan remains on track. This continuous, adaptive planning is crucial for achieving sustained growth and financial independence, empowering you to focus on your passion and career with confidence.

Finding the Right Tax Advisor

Picture a world where your tax obligations are no longer a source of stress, but a well-managed aspect of your thriving business. Imagine having a trusted advisor by your side, someone who not only understands the intricacies of self-employed taxes but also knows the nuances of your specific industry. This could be your reality when you find the right tax advisor. Navigating the labyrinth of self-employment taxes can be daunting, but with the right professional guidance, it becomes a manageable and even insightful journey. The key lies in choosing a tax advisor who aligns with your needs, values, and business goals.

WORKING WITH TAX PROFESSIONALS

Finding the right tax advisor is more than just a transactional relationship; it's about establishing a partnership that can significantly impact your financial health and peace of mind. Evaluating credentials and experience is the first step in this process, ensuring that your advisor has the necessary expertise. But it doesn't stop there. Compatibility and communication style play a crucial role in how effectively you can work together, while specialization and industry knowledge can make a world of difference in optimizing your tax strategy. As we delve into these subtopics, you'll gain the tools to identify and collaborate with a tax advisor who can help you navigate your financial journey with confidence and ease.

Evaluating Credentials and Experience

Choosing the right tax advisor is crucial for self-employed individuals aiming for financial freedom. Evaluating credentials and experience is the first step in this process. A tax advisor's qualifications can provide insight into their expertise and reliability. Look for certifications such as CPA (Certified Public Accountant), EA (Enrolled Agent), or a tax attorney with a JD (Juris Doctor). These designations indicate a high level of formal education and adherence to ethical standards in the field. Beyond credentials, years of experience handling tax matters for self-employed clients can significantly impact the quality of advice and services provided. Consider advisors who have a proven track record in managing complex tax situations similar to your own.

Experience goes beyond the number of years in practice; it also encompasses the types of clients and tax issues an advisor has dealt with. For instance, a tax professional who has worked extensively with freelancers, gig workers, and independent contractors will be better equipped to navigate the unique challenges these groups face. This specialized experience means they are familiar with industry-specific deductions, regulatory requirements, and the latest tax laws affecting self-employed individuals. When evaluating potential advisors, ask detailed questions about their experience with clients in similar fields and how they have helped them optimize their tax situations.

In addition to formal qualifications and experience, it's important to assess the practical outcomes an advisor has achieved for their clients. Look for testimonials, case studies, or client references that highlight how the advisor has successfully minimized tax liabilities, maximized deductions, and navigated audits or disputes with tax authorities. These real-world examples provide a clearer picture of the advisor's effectiveness and problem-solving abilities. Advanced insights into how an advisor stays current with tax law changes and their approach to continuing education can also be telling. Advisors who regularly attend industry conferences, complete advanced training, and participate in professional networks are likely to be more knowledgeable about cutting-edge tax strategies.

Understanding the methodologies and tools an advisor uses is also essential. Inquire about the software and analytical tools they employ to manage and optimize tax returns. Advanced tax software can streamline the preparation process, ensuring accuracy and compliance while uncovering potential savings opportunities. Advisors who utilize data analytics and forecasting tools can offer more strategic advice, helping clients plan for future tax obligations and financial milestones. This technology-savvy approach often indicates a forward-thinking advisor who prioritizes efficiency and precision in their work.

Consider the advisor's approach to collaboration and communication. Effective tax planning is an ongoing process that requires clear, consistent, and proactive communication. Advisors who take the time to explain complex tax concepts in understandable terms can empower you to make informed financial decisions. Regular updates and check-ins throughout the year—not just during tax season—are indicative of an advisor committed to your long-term financial success. By evaluating these factors, you can find a tax advisor who not only has the credentials and experience but also the practical skills and communication style that align with your financial goals.

Assessing Compatibility and Communication Style

Selecting a tax advisor who aligns with your business ethos and communication preferences is paramount in fostering a productive and long-term professional relationship. This harmony ensures that both parties are on the same wavelength, facilitating smoother interactions and more effective tax planning. Compatibility is not merely about liking the advisor on a personal level; it's about ensuring their approach to financial management dovetails seamlessly with your own business goals and operational style. For instance, if you prefer a proactive approach to financial planning, your tax advisor should be someone who anticipates and strategizes for future financial scenarios rather than merely reacting to immediate issues.

WORKING WITH TAX PROFESSIONALS

Communication style plays a crucial role in this dynamic. A tax advisor who can translate complex tax jargon into understandable, actionable advice is worth their weight in gold. Consider how they explain intricate tax laws and financial strategies during your initial consultations. Are they patient and thorough, or do they rush through explanations? An advisor who can break down complicated concepts into digestible information empowers you to make informed decisions about your financial health. For example, an advisor who efficiently uses visual aids or software tools to illustrate tax strategies can significantly enhance your understanding and comfort level.

It's also essential to gauge how responsive and accessible the tax advisor is. In the fast-paced world of self-employment, timely advice can make a significant difference. Ask potential advisors about their availability and preferred communication channels. Do they respond promptly to emails and phone calls? Can they schedule urgent consultations if needed? Understanding their responsiveness helps set realistic expectations and ensures that help is available when you need it most. An advisor who is consistently hard to reach may not be the best fit, especially during critical tax seasons or financial emergencies.

The advisor's ability to listen actively and understand your unique business circumstances is invaluable. They should be genuinely interested in learning about your business model, challenges, and long-term objectives. This depth of understanding allows them to offer tailored advice rather than generic solutions. For instance, a freelancer with fluctuating income streams will have different tax planning needs compared to a gig worker with more consistent earnings. An advisor attuned to these nuances can provide more relevant and effective guidance, ensuring your tax strategy aligns with your specific financial landscape.

Consider the advisor's approach to ongoing education and staying updated with the latest tax laws and financial trends. The tax landscape is continually evolving, and an advisor who is committed to professional development will be better equipped to navigate these changes. Inquire about their participation in professional organizations, attendance at industry conferences, or subscription to tax-related publications. This commitment to staying informed not only enhances their expertise but also reflects their dedication to providing the best possible service to their clients. A tax advisor who prioritizes continuous learning can offer innovative solutions and cutting-edge strategies, ensuring your business remains compliant and optimized for financial success.

Investigating Specialization and Industry Knowledge

Selecting a tax advisor with specialization and industry knowledge is crucial for maximizing the benefits of professional guidance. Not all tax advisors are created equal, and their areas of expertise can significantly impact the quality of service you receive. For instance, an advisor well-versed in the nuances of self-employment tax regulations will be better equipped to navigate the complexities of your financial situation. They can identify unique opportunities for deductions and credits that a generalist might overlook. By seeking out a specialist who understands the specific challenges and opportunities within your industry, you can ensure that your tax strategy is optimized for your unique needs.

To identify a tax advisor with the right specialization, start by examining their credentials and professional background. Look for certifications such as Certified Public Accountant (CPA) or Enrolled Agent (EA), along with any additional training or coursework related to self-employment or your specific industry. A tax advisor who has taken the time to deepen their knowledge in these areas demonstrates a commitment to staying current with tax laws and best practices. Additionally, consider their years of experience and client portfolio. An advisor who has consistently worked with self-employed individuals or within your industry will have a more nuanced understanding of the potential pitfalls and opportunities you might face.

Another critical factor is the advisor's familiarity with the latest trends and legislative changes that affect self-employed taxes. Tax laws are constantly evolving, and staying abreast of these changes is essential for effective financial planning. For example, recent changes in healthcare regulations or retirement planning options can have significant tax implications. A well-informed advisor will not only help you comply with current laws but also leverage new opportunities to your advantage. Regularly engaging in continuing education and being an active member of professional organizations are good indicators that an advisor is committed to maintaining their expertise.

Equally important is the advisor's ability to communicate complex tax concepts in an accessible manner. A tax advisor who can translate intricate tax jargon into clear, actionable advice is invaluable. This skill ensures you fully understand your tax situation and can make informed decisions. Effective communication also fosters a collaborative relationship, where you feel comfortable

WORKING WITH TAX PROFESSIONALS   145

asking questions and discussing your financial goals. Compatibility in communication style can make a significant difference in how well you work together and, ultimately, in the effectiveness of your tax strategy.

Consider seeking out testimonials or reviews from other self-employed individuals within your industry. Personal recommendations can provide insight into an advisor's reliability, professionalism, and ability to deliver results. Don't hesitate to ask potential advisors for references or case studies that demonstrate their expertise in handling similar tax situations. By thoroughly vetting potential tax advisors and prioritizing specialization and industry knowledge, you can build a strong partnership that supports your financial success and peace of mind.

Collaborating Effectively with Your Accountant

Consider the possibility that your financial future hinges not just on your ability to earn, but on how effectively you collaborate with the experts who can help you manage and optimize those earnings. Imagine your accountant as a co-pilot on your journey to financial freedom—someone who can navigate the complexities of tax laws and financial planning while you focus on what you do best. It's not merely about handing over receipts and hoping for the best; it's about establishing a partnership built on clear communication, regular updates, and strategic planning. This collaboration could be the key to unlocking peace of mind and ensuring that you're making the most of your hard-earned money.

Effective collaboration with your accountant begins with establishing clear communication channels and expectations. It's essential to share comprehensive financial records and documentation regularly, allowing your accountant to provide you with the most accurate and beneficial advice. Scheduling periodic review meetings to assess and adjust your financial strategies ensures that you're always on the right track and making informed decisions. By taking these steps, you transform your accountant from a distant advisor into an integral part of your financial team, empowering you to navigate the intricacies of self-employment taxes with confidence and clarity.

Establish Clear Communication Channels and Expectations

Establishing clear communication channels and expectations with your accountant is a cornerstone of effective collaboration. This begins with defining how and when you will communicate. Will you primarily use email, phone calls, or a secure messaging app? Setting these parameters from the outset helps prevent misunderstandings and ensures that both parties are on the same page. For instance, agreeing to a response time for emails—say, within 24 hours—can foster a sense of reliability and trust. Additionally, clarify what types of issues warrant immediate attention versus those that can wait for a scheduled meeting. This level of detail not only streamlines interactions but also ensures that critical matters are addressed in a timely manner.

A robust communication strategy also involves setting mutual expectations regarding the scope of services. Are you seeking comprehensive tax planning, or do you primarily need assistance with filing annual returns? Articulating your needs clearly allows your accountant to tailor their services effectively. This is particularly crucial for self-employed individuals whose financial situations can be more complex than those of traditional employees. For example, if you have multiple income streams from freelance work, gig economy jobs, and investments, your accountant needs to be aware of these nuances to provide accurate advice. A well-defined scope prevents any gaps in service that could lead to costly errors or missed opportunities.

Regular and transparent communication also fosters a proactive approach to tax planning. Instead of merely reacting to tax obligations as they arise, an ongoing dialogue with your accountant allows for strategic planning throughout the year. Consider setting up a quarterly check-in to discuss upcoming tax liabilities, potential deductions, and any changes in your financial situation. For instance, if you anticipate a significant increase in income, your accountant can help you adjust your estimated tax payments accordingly. This proactive stance not only reduces the risk of underpayment penalties but also enhances your overall financial stability.

To further enhance collaboration, leverage technology to streamline communication and document sharing. Tools like cloud-based accounting software can provide real-time access to financial data, making it easier for both you and your accountant to stay informed. These platforms often come with features that allow for secure document sharing and instant messaging, thereby reducing the time spent on administrative tasks. For example, you can upload receipts and invoices directly to the software, where your accountant can access and categorize them without the need for cumbersome email attachments. This not only saves time but also ensures that all financial records are well-organized and easily accessible.

Don't underestimate the power of a personalized approach. While technology can significantly enhance efficiency, it's essential to maintain a human touch in your interactions. Regularly express your goals, concerns, and any changes in your business or personal life that might impact your financial situation. For example, if you're planning to purchase a home or expand your business, sharing these plans with your accountant allows for more tailored advice. By fostering an environment of open and honest communication, you create a partnership that is not just transactional but genuinely supportive of your long-term financial well-being.

Share Comprehensive Financial Records and Documentation Regularly

Maintaining a comprehensive and up-to-date compilation of your financial records and documentation is paramount when collaborating effectively with your accountant. By ensuring that all financial documents, including income statements, expense receipts, invoices, and bank statements, are meticulously organized and readily accessible, you facilitate a smoother and more efficient accounting process. This proactive approach not only minimizes the risk of errors but also allows your accountant to provide more accurate and insightful advice tailored to your unique financial situation. Consider using digital tools and cloud-based platforms to streamline the sharing process, ensuring that both you and your accountant have real-time access to the necessary documents.

Regularly sharing these comprehensive financial records fosters a transparent and collaborative relationship with your accountant. It enables them to stay informed of your financial activities and identify potential issues or opportunities in a timely manner. For instance, consistent documentation of business expenses can uncover overlooked deductions, ultimately leading to significant tax savings. Additionally, by maintaining thorough records, you can provide a clear and detailed picture of your financial health, allowing your accountant to devise more effective strategies for managing your tax obligations and optimizing your financial outcomes.

In the dynamic landscape of self-employment, where income streams and expenses can fluctuate, staying current with your financial documentation is crucial. Emerging trends such as digital nomadism and the gig economy underscore the importance of adaptable and precise financial tracking. Accountants can leverage this data to offer nuanced advice that aligns with the latest industry developments and regulatory changes. For example, understanding the tax implications of working across multiple jurisdictions or navigating the complexities of cryptocurrency transactions requires up-to-date and detailed financial records that accurately reflect your activities.

To maximize the benefits of sharing comprehensive financial records, consider scheduling regular updates with your accountant. This could involve monthly or quarterly check-ins where you review and discuss your financial documents. Such periodic reviews not only keep your accountant informed but also provide you with an opportunity to ask questions and gain deeper insights into your financial situation. These sessions can be instrumental in identifying trends, spotting potential red flags, and making timely adjustments to your financial strategies. For instance, if you notice a significant increase in a particular expense category, your accountant can help you investigate the cause and explore cost-saving measures.

By adopting a disciplined approach to financial documentation and sharing, you empower your accountant to serve as a strategic partner in your journey towards financial freedom. This collaborative effort can reveal hidden opportunities for growth and efficiency, ultimately enhancing your financial stability and success. Think of your accountant not just as a service provider, but as an integral part of your financial team, whose expertise and guidance can be fully leveraged through the consistent and comprehensive sharing of your financial records. This symbiotic relationship, built on transparency and regular communication, is a cornerstone of effective financial management in the self-employed world.

Schedule Periodic Review Meetings to Assess and Adjust Financial Strategies

Scheduling periodic review meetings with your accountant is crucial for maintaining a proactive and dynamic approach to your financial strategies. These sessions allow you to assess your current financial standing, review past decisions, and make necessary adjustments to align with your evolving goals. Regular reviews ensure that you remain on top of any changes in tax laws, financial circumstances, or business operations that could impact your tax obligations. By fostering an ongoing dialogue, you can identify potential issues early and implement solutions before they escalate, thereby optimizing your financial health and minimizing unforeseen liabilities.

Establishing a consistent schedule for these meetings is essential. Whether it's quarterly, biannually, or annually, the frequency should reflect the complexity of your financial situation and the pace at which your business evolves. For instance, a freelancer with fluctuating income might benefit from more frequent check-ins to adjust estimated tax payments and strategize for variable cash flows. In contrast, a consultant with steady earnings might require less frequent reviews. The key is to tailor the schedule to your specific needs, ensuring that you and your accountant remain aligned and responsive to any financial shifts.

During these review meetings, come prepared with comprehensive financial documents and any updates on your business activities. This includes profit and loss statements, receipts, invoices, and records of any major purchases or investments. Detailed documentation enables your accountant to provide accurate and tailored advice, ensuring that all deductions are captured and that you are maximizing your tax benefits. Additionally, discussing any upcoming changes in your business, such as new contracts, equipment purchases, or expansions, allows for proactive tax planning and strategic decision-making.

Another critical aspect of these review sessions is setting clear objectives and action items. Collaborate with your accountant to establish specific goals for the next review period, whether it's optimizing tax savings, improving cash flow management, or planning for retirement contributions. Having a clear set of objectives helps maintain focus and direction, making each meeting productive and forward-looking. It also provides a tangible benchmark to measure progress and adjust strategies as needed, ensuring that your financial plans remain dynamic and effective.

Use these meetings as an opportunity to stay informed about any changes in tax regulations or financial trends that could affect your business. Your accountant can provide valuable insights into new tax credits, deductions, or compliance requirements, helping you stay ahead of the curve. This knowledge not only empowers you to make informed decisions but also enhances your ability to navigate the complexities of self-employed taxes confidently. By staying engaged and proactive, you can transform these periodic reviews into a powerful tool for sustaining financial health and achieving long-term success.

As we bring this chapter to a close, it's clear that working with tax professionals can be a game-changer for anyone navigating the complexities of self-employed taxes. Knowing when to hire an accountant can save you not only time and stress but also potentially significant sums of money. Finding the right tax advisor is crucial, and the process involves careful consideration of their expertise, experience, and how well they align with your specific financial needs. Once you've found the right professional, effective collaboration becomes paramount. Clear communication, mutual respect, and regular updates can turn this partnership into an invaluable asset, ensuring that you remain compliant and strategically positioned for financial growth.

Reflecting on these insights, it's evident that the role of tax professionals extends beyond mere number-crunching. They serve as strategic allies in your journey toward financial freedom, offering guidance that can help you make informed decisions and avoid costly mistakes. Embracing this partnership allows you to focus more on what you do best while gaining peace of mind about your financial responsibilities. As you continue to build your knowledge and confidence, consider the broader impact of these relationships on your overall financial strategy. How will you leverage this newfound expertise to propel yourself closer to your ultimate goal of financial independence?

Chapter Ten

Tools And Resources For Tax Management

The following discussion reveals the hidden power of the right tools and resources in transforming a daunting tax season into a streamlined, manageable process. Imagine Sarah, a freelance graphic designer, overwhelmed each year as tax deadlines approached, her desk buried beneath a mountain of receipts and invoices. It wasn't until she discovered the right software and online services that her anxiety began to dissipate, replaced by a newfound confidence and control over her finances. This chapter aims to provide you with the same sense of empowerment, equipping you with the essential tools to simplify tax management and stay ahead of the game.

Consider the evolving landscape of tax laws, which can often feel like navigating a labyrinth. Staying updated is not just a matter of compliance but a strategic move towards maximizing your financial benefits. The tools and resources discussed in this chapter will help you stay informed and agile, ensuring you never miss an opportunity for deductions or credits. From robust software solutions that automate your bookkeeping to reliable online tax preparation services, these tools are designed to save you time and reduce errors, making the tax season less of a dreaded chore and more of a routine task.

As you journey through this chapter, you'll uncover various strategies and resources that will not only simplify your tax responsibilities but also empower you to take control of your financial destiny. These tools are not just about compliance; they're about building a sustainable, efficient system that supports your long-term goals. Whether you're a seasoned freelancer or just starting

152 MASTERING SELF-EMPLOYED TAXES

your self-employed journey, mastering these resources is a crucial step towards financial freedom and peace of mind. So, let's dive in and explore how the right tools can transform your approach to taxes, making them an integral part of your financial strategy rather than a source of stress.

Essential Software for Self-Employed Taxes

In recent years, we've seen a surge in technological advancements designed specifically to alleviate the complexities faced by self-employed individuals. Imagine this: Lisa, a freelance graphic designer, used to spend countless hours hunched over spreadsheets, meticulously tracking her income and expenses. She often found herself overwhelmed by the sheer volume of receipts and invoices, not to mention the anxiety of looming tax deadlines. That all changed when she discovered an array of specialized software tools tailored for self-employed tax management. Suddenly, what once felt like an insurmountable burden became a systematic and streamlined process, allowing her to focus more on her creative work and less on her financial anxieties. This transformation isn't unique to Lisa; countless freelancers and independent contractors are harnessing the power of technology to gain control over their financial lives.

The importance of leveraging the right tools cannot be overstated. From comprehensive accounting platforms that integrate seamlessly with your business activities to specialized tax preparation software designed with freelancers in mind, these tools are revolutionizing how self-employed professionals approach tax season. Advanced financial planning tools are also emerging, offering long-term tax strategies that not only simplify current tax obligations but also pave the way for future financial stability. As we delve into the essential software for self-employed taxes, you'll discover how these tools can be your allies in building a robust and proactive tax strategy, ultimately guiding you toward financial freedom.

Comprehensive Accounting Platforms for Self-Employed Professionals

For self-employed professionals, choosing the right accounting platform can be transformative, serving as the backbone of their financial management system. Comprehensive accounting software offers more than just basic bookkeep-

TOOLS AND RESOURCES FOR TAX MANAGEMENT 153

ing; it integrates invoicing, expense tracking, and real-time financial reporting into a seamless user experience. For instance, platforms like QuickBooks Self-Employed and FreshBooks cater specifically to the needs of freelancers and gig workers, providing features such as automated mileage tracking, tax estimations, and client management. These tools not only simplify day-to-day financial tasks but also ensure compliance with tax regulations by maintaining organized records, thereby reducing the stress associated with tax season.

Another critical advantage of using these robust accounting platforms is their ability to generate detailed financial reports. These reports allow self-employed individuals to gain deeper insights into their business performance, helping them identify profitable projects and areas where expenses can be trimmed. For example, with QuickBooks Self-Employed, users can easily produce profit and loss statements, balance sheets, and cash flow analyses. These reports are invaluable when it comes to making informed decisions about scaling operations or investing in new opportunities. Advanced features like cash flow forecasting and budget creation further enhance the platform's utility, enabling users to plan effectively for future financial needs and tax obligations.

Beyond basic functionalities, some accounting platforms offer integrations with other essential business tools, adding a layer of convenience and efficiency. Integration with payment processors like PayPal and Stripe, for example, allows for seamless transaction tracking and reconciliation. Additionally, connecting with project management tools such as Trello or Asana can help self-employed professionals streamline their workflows, ensuring that financial data and project timelines are aligned. These integrations not only save time but also reduce the likelihood of errors, providing a cohesive ecosystem where all aspects of the business are interconnected and easily managed.

The landscape of accounting software is continually evolving, with new features and improvements being introduced regularly. Emerging trends such as artificial intelligence (AI) and machine learning are beginning to play a significant role in financial management. AI-driven platforms can now offer predictive insights, automate repetitive tasks, and even provide personalized financial advice based on the user's data. For instance, some software can automatically categorize expenses or flag potential tax deductions, significantly reducing the manual effort required. Staying abreast of these technological advancements can give self-employed professionals a competitive edge, enhancing their ability to manage finances with precision and foresight.

154 MASTERING SELF-EMPLOYED TAXES

It's essential for self-employed individuals to not only select the right tools but also to utilize them to their full potential. This involves regular training and staying updated with the latest features and best practices. Many platforms offer extensive resources, including webinars, tutorials, and community forums, to help users maximize their software's capabilities. By investing time in learning how to effectively use these tools, self-employed professionals can ensure that they are not only meeting their immediate needs but also setting themselves up for long-term financial success. This proactive approach to financial management can ultimately lead to greater confidence and peace of mind, empowering self-employed individuals to focus on growing their businesses.

Specialized Tax Preparation Software with Freelance Features

When navigating the labyrinth of tax obligations as a freelancer, specialized tax preparation software can be a game-changer. These platforms are designed to cater specifically to the unique needs of self-employed individuals, offering features that streamline the entire tax process. Unlike generic tax software, which can be cumbersome and ill-suited for those with non-traditional income sources, these specialized tools provide tailored solutions that simplify complex scenarios. For instance, they often include modules for tracking multiple income streams, managing deductible expenses, and calculating estimated quarterly payments. By leveraging these features, freelancers can save significant time and reduce the risk of errors, ensuring that they remain compliant with tax laws while maximizing potential deductions.

One standout example is QuickBooks Self-Employed, which integrates seamlessly with various financial accounts, allowing users to automatically categorize transactions and track mileage. This software offers a dedicated tax bundle that includes access to TurboTax, ensuring that all tax forms and schedules are accurately completed and filed. The user-friendly interface and intuitive design make it accessible even for those who may not have a background in accounting. Additionally, the software provides real-time insights into one's financial health, helping freelancers make informed decisions about their tax strategy throughout the year rather than scrambling at the last minute.

Another robust option is FreshBooks, a cloud-based accounting software that offers comprehensive invoicing features alongside tax preparation tools. FreshBooks allows freelancers to capture receipts, track billable hours, and manage client payments, all within a single platform. Its tax time reports are particularly useful, summarizing income and expenses in a way that aligns with IRS requirements. By using FreshBooks, self-employed individuals can stay organized and ensure that they have all necessary documentation readily available when it's time to file their taxes. This not only makes the filing process more efficient but also minimizes the likelihood of missing out on valuable deductions due to misplaced receipts or overlooked expenses.

For those seeking a more advanced solution, TaxSlayer Self-Employed offers a high level of customization and support. This platform is geared towards freelancers with more complex tax situations, such as those who have multiple business ventures or significant investment income. TaxSlayer provides step-by-step guidance, ensuring that all relevant tax breaks are claimed and that the tax return is optimized for the best possible outcome. Additionally, it offers access to tax professionals who can answer specific questions and provide personalized advice, a feature that can be particularly beneficial during audit situations or when navigating new tax legislation.

The rise of artificial intelligence and machine learning has brought innovative tools like Keeper Tax into the spotlight. Keeper Tax scans bank and credit card transactions to identify write-offs that users might otherwise miss. It also sends real-time notifications about potential deductions, helping freelancers stay on top of their finances throughout the year. This proactive approach not only aids in tax preparation but also promotes better financial habits, encouraging users to think strategically about their spending and saving patterns. The integration of AI ensures that the software continually improves, adapting to new tax laws and user behavior to provide increasingly accurate and personalized recommendations. By incorporating these specialized tax preparation tools into their financial routines, self-employed individuals can gain greater control over their tax obligations and reduce the stress often associated with tax season.

Advanced Financial Planning Tools for Long-Term Tax Strategy

Navigating the labyrinth of self-employed taxes requires more than just a cursory understanding of accounting principles. Advanced financial planning tools, designed specifically for long-term tax strategy, are indispensable assets for freelancers and independent contractors. These tools go beyond mere number crunching; they offer sophisticated functionalities that enable users to project future income, estimate tax liabilities, and optimize financial decisions. One such tool is the comprehensive financial planning software, which integrates tax planning with broader financial goals. For instance, platforms like Personal Capital not only track expenses but also offer retirement planning, investment management, and tax optimization features, allowing users to see the full picture of their financial health.

A standout advantage of these advanced tools is their ability to simulate various financial scenarios. This feature is particularly beneficial when considering major life changes such as purchasing a home, expanding a business, or planning for retirement. By inputting different variables, self-employed professionals can see how these changes impact their tax obligations and overall financial standing. For example, using Monte Carlo simulations, users can assess the probability of achieving their financial goals under different market conditions. This proactive approach helps in making informed decisions that are not only tax-efficient but also aligned with long-term financial stability.

In addition to scenario planning, these tools often incorporate cutting-edge algorithms that offer personalized tax advice. Leveraging artificial intelligence, some platforms provide tailored recommendations based on the user's financial data and objectives. For instance, Wealthfront's Path tool uses AI to suggest optimal saving rates and investment strategies, taking into account tax implications. This level of personalization ensures that self-employed individuals are not just following generic advice but are receiving insights that are specifically relevant to their unique financial situations.

Keeping up with tax law changes is another critical aspect of long-term tax strategy, and advanced financial planning tools excel in this area as well. Many platforms automatically update their algorithms to reflect the latest tax codes, ensuring that users are always working with current information. This feature is especially useful for self-employed professionals who might not have the time or expertise to stay abreast of every legislative change. For example, TurboTax Self-Employed updates its software annually to incorporate new tax laws, deductions, and credits, providing users with up-to-date guidance that minimizes their tax liabilities.

These advanced tools often come with robust support systems, including access to financial advisors and community forums where users can seek advice and share experiences. This collaborative environment fosters a deeper understanding of complex tax issues and offers practical solutions grounded in real-world scenarios. For instance, platforms like Betterment and Ellevest

TOOLS AND RESOURCES FOR TAX MANAGEMENT   157

provide access to financial planners who can offer personalized advice on tax strategies and financial planning. This human element, combined with the precision of advanced software, empowers self-employed individuals to navigate their tax obligations with confidence and foresight, setting the stage for sustainable financial independence.

Utilizing Online Tax Preparation Services

Picture a world where tax season no longer feels like a looming storm cloud, but rather a manageable part of your financial routine. Imagine sitting down at your computer, coffee in hand, and navigating through an intuitive platform that simplifies every aspect of your tax filing. This isn't some distant dream—it's the reality made possible by online tax preparation services. These tools are designed to take the complexity out of tax season, transforming it into a streamlined, stress-free process. For the self-employed, who often juggle multiple income streams and a myriad of expenses, these services can be a game changer, offering clarity and confidence where there was once confusion and dread.

Think about an instance where you've felt overwhelmed by the prospect of accurately reporting your income and expenses, not to mention the anxiety of staying compliant with ever-changing tax laws. Online tax preparation services can alleviate those fears with real-time tax calculations and user-friendly interfaces that guide you step-by-step through the process. With advanced security features to protect your sensitive financial data, you can focus on what matters most: growing your business and achieving financial freedom. As we delve into how these tools can streamline tax filing, leverage real-time projections, and ensure robust data security, you'll discover how to turn tax season into just another task on your to-do list, rather than a monumental challenge.

Streamlining Tax Filing with Intuitive Interfaces

Navigating the landscape of online tax preparation services can be transformative for self-employed individuals who seek efficiency and accuracy. With intuitive interfaces, these platforms are designed to simplify the often daunting task of tax filing. Modern tax software, such as TurboTax and H&R Block, have evolved to offer user-friendly dashboards that guide users step-by-step through the filing process. By breaking down complex tax concepts into comprehensible segments, these tools make it easier for freelancers and independent contractors to input their financial data correctly. This not only reduces the likelihood of errors but also streamlines the entire process, saving valuable time and effort.

The primary advantage of intuitive interfaces lies in their capability to adapt to the user's needs. Advanced algorithms and machine learning techniques enable these platforms to personalize the tax filing experience. For instance, as users input their financial information, the software can automatically suggest relevant deductions and credits, which might otherwise be overlooked. This personalization ensures that users maximize their tax benefits, thus retaining more of their hard-earned income. Additionally, the visual simplicity of these interfaces, often featuring progress trackers and clear instructions, reduces the cognitive load on users, making the task less intimidating and more manageable.

Beyond simplification, these platforms offer sophisticated features like real-time tax calculations and projections. As users enter data, the software can instantly update tax liabilities or refunds, providing a clear picture of one's financial standing. This real-time feedback is crucial for self-employed individuals who need to adjust their quarterly estimated tax payments. Seeing the immediate impact of different income scenarios or deductions can inform better financial decisions throughout the year. For example, understanding how a new client contract will affect quarterly taxes can help in planning for any necessary adjustments ahead of time.

Security is another critical aspect where online tax preparation services excel. Given the sensitivity of financial data, these platforms employ cutting-edge encryption technologies and multi-factor authentication to safeguard user information. This robust security framework ensures that personal and financial information remains confidential and protected from cyber threats. For freelancers and gig workers, who may not have access to corporate-level IT security, these features provide peace of mind and help in maintaining the integrity of their financial data. In a world where data breaches are increasingly common, the assurance of advanced security measures is invaluable.

The accessibility and convenience of these tools cannot be overstated. With cloud-based solutions, users can access their tax information from any device with an internet connection. This flexibility is particularly beneficial for those who travel frequently or manage their business remotely. It also allows for seamless collaboration with tax professionals, who can review and provide guidance on the same platform. This integrated approach fosters a more cohesive and efficient tax management process, ensuring that self-employed individuals

TOOLS AND RESOURCES FOR TAX MANAGEMENT · 159

can focus more on growing their business and less on the intricacies of tax compliance.

Leveraging Real-Time Tax Calculations and Projections

Online tax preparation services offer an invaluable feature that significantly enhances the tax filing experience: real-time tax calculations and projections. This feature allows self-employed individuals to see the immediate impact of their financial decisions on their tax liabilities. By inputting income and expense data as it is incurred, users can witness how each transaction affects their overall tax picture. This immediate feedback provides a clearer understanding of their financial situation, enabling them to make more informed decisions throughout the year rather than waiting until the filing deadline. For instance, freelancers can instantly gauge the tax implications of a new contract, while gig workers can see how fluctuating income streams affect their quarterly tax estimates.

One of the most compelling aspects of real-time tax calculations is the ability to forecast future tax obligations. By leveraging historical data and current financial inputs, these services can project potential tax liabilities months in advance. This foresight is crucial for self-employed individuals who need to budget for quarterly tax payments or anticipate year-end tax bills. Advanced algorithms and machine learning models employed by leading tax software can analyze patterns and provide tailored advice, enhancing the accuracy of these projections. This proactive approach to tax planning not only reduces the stress associated with tax season but also helps in maintaining a steady cash flow throughout the year.

Security is paramount when dealing with sensitive financial data, and online tax preparation services have risen to the challenge with sophisticated encryption and authentication protocols. Users can trust that their data is protected by multi-layered security measures, including end-to-end encryption, two-factor authentication, and regular security audits. These features are designed to safeguard against unauthorized access and data breaches, providing peace of mind for users. By investing in robust security infrastructure, these platforms ensure that self-employed individuals can focus on optimizing their tax strategies without worrying about the safety of their information.

Emerging trends in online tax preparation services include the integration of artificial intelligence and machine learning to further refine real-time tax calculations. These technologies can identify patterns and anomalies in financial data, offering personalized tax-saving strategies and error detection that goes beyond conventional methods. For example, AI-driven insights might reveal overlooked deductions or suggest optimal times for making significant business purchases to maximize tax benefits. As these technologies evolve, they promise to make tax management even more intuitive and efficient, empowering self-employed individuals to navigate their financial landscape with greater confidence and precision.

To fully leverage these capabilities, it is essential for users to stay informed about the latest features and updates offered by their chosen tax preparation platform. Regularly exploring new tools and functionalities can uncover additional benefits and efficiencies. Engaging with user communities and support forums can also provide valuable tips and best practices from fellow self-employed professionals. By remaining proactive and embracing the continuous advancements in online tax preparation services, self-employed individuals can ensure they are always at the forefront of effective tax management, paving the way to sustained financial health and independence.

Advanced Security Features to Protect Sensitive Financial Data

The digital age has revolutionized the way self-employed individuals manage their taxes, with online tax preparation services offering a plethora of advanced security features to safeguard sensitive financial data. These platforms employ robust encryption methods, such as AES-256, to ensure that data transmitted between users and servers remains confidential and secure. This level of encryption is akin to the standards used by banks and government institutions, providing freelancers and independent contractors with peace of mind that their financial information is protected against unauthorized access.

In addition to encryption, many online tax preparation services implement multi-factor authentication (MFA) to further enhance security. MFA requires users to verify their identity through multiple methods, such as a password and a code sent to their mobile device, before granting access to their accounts. This additional layer of security significantly reduces the risk of unauthorized access, even if login credentials are compromised. For individuals handling sensitive financial data, the use of MFA is a critical measure to prevent potential breaches and identity theft.

Another vital aspect of security in online tax preparation services is the regular monitoring and auditing of their systems. These platforms often employ

TOOLS AND RESOURCES FOR TAX MANAGEMENT   161

dedicated security teams that continuously scan for vulnerabilities and implement patches to address any potential threats. By staying vigilant and proactive, these services can quickly respond to emerging security risks, ensuring that users' data remains protected. This ongoing commitment to security is crucial in an era where cyber threats are constantly evolving.

The importance of secure data storage cannot be overstated. Reputable online tax preparation services typically store user data in highly secure data centers with strict access controls and backup systems. These facilities are designed to withstand physical and cyber threats, ensuring that users' financial information is safe from both online attacks and physical breaches. This secure storage solution provides an added layer of protection, ensuring that sensitive data is not only encrypted during transmission but also securely stored.

For self-employed individuals, the ability to trust online tax preparation services with their financial data is paramount. By leveraging cutting-edge security features such as encryption, multi-factor authentication, continuous monitoring, and secure data storage, these platforms offer a reliable and secure way to manage taxes. This technological assurance allows users to focus on their work, confident that their financial information is well-protected against potential threats. As the landscape of digital security continues to advance, so too will the measures employed by these services, ensuring ongoing protection for their users.

Staying Updated with Tax Law Changes

Let's start by examining the importance of staying updated with tax law changes, a crucial aspect of successful tax management for the self-employed. Imagine this scenario: You've diligently tracked your income and expenses, meticulously claimed every permissible deduction, and made timely quarterly tax payments. Yet, a sudden change in tax legislation could potentially upend your well-laid plans, leaving you scrambling to understand new rules and their implications. In an ever-evolving tax landscape, staying informed is not just beneficial—it's essential. As a freelancer or independent contractor, your financial health hinges on your ability to adapt swiftly to these changes, ensuring compliance and optimizing your tax strategy.

Consider the story of Maria, a freelance graphic designer who was blindsided by a new tax deduction cap that dramatically altered her tax liability for the year. Had she been plugged into reliable sources of tax information, she might have adjusted her financial strategy in advance, avoiding a hefty unexpected tax bill. This underscores the importance of being proactive, not reactive, in tax planning. By subscribing to reputable tax newsletters, attending webinars, and joining professional associations, you can arm yourself with the latest information and insights. These efforts will not only help you stay compliant but also empower you to make informed decisions that enhance your financial stability and growth.

Subscribe to Reputable Tax Newsletters

Staying informed about the ever-evolving landscape of tax laws is critical for self-employed individuals aiming to maintain compliance and optimize their financial strategies. One of the most effective ways to stay updated is by subscribing to reputable tax newsletters. These newsletters, often curated by tax professionals and industry experts, provide timely insights into legislative changes, critical updates, and practical advice tailored specifically for freelancers, gig workers, and independent contractors. By regularly receiving such information, self-employed individuals can proactively adjust their financial plans and stay ahead of potential tax liabilities.

A prime example of a valuable resource is the IRS's own e-newsletters, which frequently highlight significant changes in tax regulations, upcoming deadlines, and essential tips for tax season. Additionally, subscribing to newsletters from established financial publications like Forbes, Bloomberg Tax, or niche platforms such as Tax Notes can offer a broader perspective on how legislative changes might impact various aspects of self-employment. These sources often feature expert analyses and commentary, providing readers with a deeper understanding of complex tax issues and emerging trends.

Incorporating insights from these newsletters into daily or weekly routines can significantly enhance one's tax management approach. For instance, a newsletter might alert subscribers to new deductions or credits that become available, offering opportunities to reduce taxable income. Furthermore, staying informed about changes in tax law can aid in better decision-making regarding quarterly estimated payments, retirement contributions, and healthcare expenses, ultimately leading to more efficient financial planning. This proactive approach not only minimizes the risk of non-compliance but also maximizes potential tax savings.

TOOLS AND RESOURCES FOR TAX MANAGEMENT 163

To ensure the information is applicable and actionable, it's crucial to critically evaluate the sources of these newsletters. Opt for those authored by credentialed tax professionals, including Certified Public Accountants (CPAs) and Enrolled Agents (EAs), who bring a wealth of expertise and practical experience to their content. Additionally, consider subscribing to newsletters from professional organizations such as the National Association of Tax Professionals (NATP) or the American Institute of CPAs (AICPA). These organizations often provide exclusive insights, case studies, and updates that are particularly relevant to self-employed individuals.

It's beneficial to diversify the types of newsletters one subscribes to, balancing those that focus on immediate, practical tax advice with those that offer long-term strategic insights. While some newsletters might emphasize daily tips and reminders, others might delve into broader economic trends and forecasts that could influence future tax policies. By synthesizing information from a variety of reputable sources, self-employed individuals can develop a well-rounded understanding of the tax environment, equipping themselves with the knowledge needed to navigate the complexities of self-employment taxes confidently and effectively.

Attend Regular Webinars and Tax Law Workshops

Webinars and tax law workshops have become indispensable tools for self-employed individuals looking to stay current with ever-evolving tax regulations. These platforms offer dynamic, interactive learning experiences, where participants can engage with experts in real-time and gain insights that are immediately applicable to their financial practices. By attending these events regularly, freelancers and independent contractors can ensure they are not only compliant with current tax laws but also optimizing their tax strategies to maximize deductions and minimize liabilities. Unlike static articles or pre-recorded videos, live webinars and workshops provide the unique advantage of addressing specific queries, thereby tailoring the information to the attendees' unique situations.

In addition, these educational sessions often feature the latest advancements in tax software and tools, offering a sneak peek into innovative solutions that can simplify tax management. For instance, participants might discover new software that integrates seamlessly with their existing accounting systems, effectively automating tedious processes and reducing the likelihood of errors. Workshops often include hands-on demonstrations, allowing attendees to experience first-hand how these tools can streamline their tax preparation and filing processes. This direct exposure helps in making informed decisions about investing in technology that best suits their business needs.

The value of webinars and workshops extends beyond immediate learning; they also foster a sense of community among self-employed professionals. These events often attract a diverse group of attendees, ranging from novices to seasoned veterans, all of whom bring their unique experiences and perspectives. Engaging in discussions and networking with peers can provide fresh insights and novel approaches to tax management, which might not be readily apparent in solitary research. This communal learning environment encourages the exchange of best practices and innovative strategies, further enriching the knowledge base of all participants.

These educational opportunities frequently feature guest speakers who are leading authorities in the field of taxation. These experts bring cutting-edge research, emerging trends, and advanced insights to the table, offering a depth of knowledge that can be difficult to access through traditional means. Their presentations often delve into complex tax issues, such as the nuances of the Tax Cuts and Jobs Act or the implications of new IRS regulations, providing attendees with a comprehensive understanding of how these changes impact their tax obligations. By learning from the best in the industry, self-employed individuals can stay ahead of the curve and make proactive adjustments to their financial strategies.

To leverage the benefits of webinars and workshops, self-employed professionals should adopt a proactive approach to their continued education. This means regularly scheduling time for these events, actively participating in discussions, and implementing the insights gained into their tax planning practices. By doing so, they not only stay updated with the latest tax laws but also continuously refine their financial strategies, ensuring long-term success and stability. For those committed to achieving financial freedom, these educational tools are not just optional resources but essential components of a robust tax management plan.

Join Professional Tax Associations and Forums

Joining professional tax associations and forums presents a strategic advantage for self-employed individuals looking to stay abreast of the latest developments in tax law. These organizations often serve as hubs of expert knowledge and

TOOLS AND RESOURCES FOR TAX MANAGEMENT 165

cutting-edge research, providing members with timely updates, best practices, and innovative tax strategies. For instance, the National Association of Tax Professionals (NATP) offers its members access to a wealth of resources, including webinars, industry journals, and exclusive forums where tax professionals discuss the nuances of new tax regulations. Engaging in these communities can significantly enhance one's understanding of complex tax issues, ensuring that freelance workers and independent contractors are always a step ahead in their tax planning.

Beyond the immediate access to information, professional tax associations frequently host events and conferences that foster deep dives into specialized topics. These gatherings are invaluable for networking with peers and learning from seasoned tax experts. For example, the annual conferences held by the American Institute of Certified Public Accountants (AICPA) are renowned for their comprehensive sessions on emerging tax trends, legislative updates, and advanced tax planning techniques. Attending these events not only broadens one's knowledge base but also offers practical insights that can be directly applied to personal tax situations, optimizing tax outcomes and financial planning.

Forums and online communities dedicated to tax professionals also offer a dynamic environment for continuous learning and problem-solving. Platforms like TaxProTalk and Reddit's r/taxpros provide spaces where tax issues are dissected in real-time, and innovative solutions are shared among members. These forums often feature discussions on recent tax court decisions, IRS rule changes, and state specific tax matters, providing a granular level of detail that is often missing from mainstream tax resources. The collaborative nature of these online communities allows self-employed individuals to pose questions, share experiences, and gain diverse perspectives on handling intricate tax scenarios.

While the primary benefit of joining such associations and forums is the access to up-to-date information, the sense of community and support cannot be understated. Taxation can be a daunting and isolating aspect of self-employment, but being part of a professional network provides reassurance and a sense of camaraderie. Members can share their challenges and triumphs, offering mutual support and encouragement. This collective wisdom not only helps in navigating the complexities of tax law but also fosters a proactive and confident approach to financial management.

For those looking to maximize the benefits of these professional networks, it's crucial to actively participate and contribute. Engage in discussions, attend webinars and workshops, and share your own insights and experiences. By doing so, you not only enhance your own knowledge but also build a reputation within the community. This active involvement can lead to valuable connections, mentorship opportunities, and even collaborative ventures, further solidifying your financial independence and expertise in managing self-employed taxes. The investment of time and effort in these professional associations and forums ultimately pays dividends in the form of well-informed tax strategies and robust financial health.

To round out our exploration of tools and resources for tax management, it's clear that leveraging the right software and online services is crucial for self-employed individuals. These digital aids not only simplify the complex world of tax filing but also ensure accuracy and compliance. By staying updated with the latest tax law changes, freelancers and independent contractors can avoid unnecessary pitfalls and optimize their financial strategies. The tools and resources discussed provide a foundation for effective tax management, enabling readers to transform a daunting task into a manageable and even empowering process.

Embracing these resources is more than just a tactical move; it's a step toward greater financial autonomy and peace of mind. As we move forward, consider how integrating these tools into your daily routine can enhance your financial planning and organization. Reflect on how staying informed and proactive not only alleviates stress but also paves the way for long-term financial freedom. This journey through tax management is just one part of a broader quest toward financial independence, offering the skills and confidence needed to navigate your self-employed career with assurance and clarity.

Chapter Eleven

Building A Tax Strategy

In our quest to understand the labyrinth of self-employed taxes, envision yourself as an architect designing a blueprint for your financial future. Imagine Jane, a freelance graphic designer, who once found herself overwhelmed by the tangled web of tax obligations and erratic income streams. Jane's journey to financial freedom began not with a sudden windfall or a secret formula, but with the deliberate construction of a solid tax strategy. Her story is one of many that illustrate the transformative power of proactive tax planning. Jane's success was not an overnight phenomenon; it was the result of setting clear financial goals, developing a year-round tax plan, and continuously adjusting her strategy as her business flourished.

At the heart of Jane's strategy was a clear vision of where she wanted her business to go. Setting financial goals provided her with a roadmap, guiding her decisions and helping her prioritize her efforts. This chapter will explore how defining your financial aspirations can serve as a cornerstone for your tax strategy, ensuring that every step you take aligns with your broader objectives. Whether you're aiming for a comfortable retirement, funding your child's education, or simply seeking a more balanced work-life equation, having well-defined goals can transform your approach to taxes from a burdensome chore into a purposeful endeavor.

As we delve deeper, we'll uncover the importance of developing a year-round tax plan that adapts to the ebbs and flows of your business. Much like Jane, you'll learn to navigate the complexities of quarterly taxes, deductions, and expense tracking with confidence. The ability to adjust your strategy in response to your business's growth will become a vital skill, allowing you to seize new opportunities while staying compliant and financially secure.

Setting Financial Goals

To begin, let's consider a moment in your life when you achieved something you once thought impossible. Perhaps it was completing a marathon, launching a successful project, or even mastering a new skill. Remember the sense of accomplishment and the clarity that came from having a clear goal in sight? Setting financial goals for your self-employed journey is much like that. It requires vision, planning, and a commitment to see it through. Without a roadmap, your financial aspirations may feel like distant dreams rather than achievable milestones. But with the right strategy, you can turn those dreams into reality, step by step.

Imagine waking up each day with a clear understanding of your financial trajectory, knowing exactly what you need to do to meet your short-term needs and long-term desires. This clarity comes from establishing concrete financial objectives that align with your income projections and lifestyle needs. By prioritizing these goals and using the SMART criteria—Specific, Measurable, Achievable, Relevant, and Time-bound—you can track your progress and celebrate each milestone along the way. This approach not only provides direction but also instills a sense of control and confidence in your financial future. Now, let's explore how to set these goals effectively and ensure they lead you towards financial freedom.

Establish Short-Term and Long-Term Financial Objectives

Establishing short-term and long-term financial objectives is a fundamental step for any self-employed individual seeking to navigate the complexities of taxation successfully. This process begins with a clear understanding of your current financial status and an honest assessment of your aspirations. Short-term goals might include saving for quarterly tax payments, reducing debt, or setting aside money for necessary business expenses. These immediate objectives serve as the building blocks for more ambitious, long-term goals, such as funding retirement accounts, purchasing property, or ensuring financial stability during lean business periods. By breaking down these larger aspirations into manageable tasks, you create a roadmap that not only guides your financial decisions but also provides a sense of direction and purpose.

To set these objectives effectively, it's essential to align them with your income projections and lifestyle needs. For example, if your freelance work experiences seasonal fluctuations, your financial goals should account for these variations. During peak income periods, allocate funds towards savings and investments to balance out the leaner months. This proactive approach helps in maintaining a consistent cash flow and ensures that you can meet both personal and business financial commitments without undue stress. Additionally, consider the impact of lifestyle choices, such as travel, family planning, and continuing education, on your financial goals. By integrating these elements into your planning, you create a holistic strategy that supports both your professional growth and personal well-being.

Implementing the SMART criteria—Specific, Measurable, Achievable, Relevant, and Time-bound—can significantly enhance the effectiveness of your financial goals. For instance, instead of a vague objective like "save more money," set a specific target such as "save $5,000 for tax payments by the end of the fiscal year." This clarity not only provides a concrete target to aim for but also allows for easier tracking of progress. Measurability ensures that you can quantify your achievements, which is crucial for maintaining motivation and making informed adjustments to your strategy. Achievability keeps your goals realistic, preventing frustration and burnout, while relevance ensures that each objective aligns with your broader financial aspirations. Time-bound deadlines create a sense of urgency, driving consistent effort and focus.

Advanced insights into goal setting reveal the importance of flexibility and regular reassessment. As your business evolves, so too should your financial objectives. Emerging trends, such as the increasing prevalence of digital currencies and new investment opportunities, may provide novel avenues for achieving your goals. Staying informed about these developments allows you to adapt your strategy to leverage new tools and resources. Additionally, consider diverse perspectives and independent analyses to counterbalance mainstream financial advice. For instance, while traditional wisdom may prioritize retirement savings, some experts advocate for investing in skill development or business expansion as equally valuable long-term strategies. By weighing these contrasting views, you can make more informed decisions tailored to your unique circumstances.

To bring these concepts into practical application, consider crafting a detailed financial plan that includes both short-term and long-term objectives. Begin with a comprehensive review of your current financial situation, including income streams, expenses, debts, and assets. Use this data to identify immediate priorities and longer-term aspirations. Then, apply the SMART criteria to each goal, ensuring they are clear, measurable, and time-bound.

Prioritize Goals Based on Income Projections and Lifestyle Needs

Setting financial goals is the cornerstone of any robust tax strategy, especially for the self-employed. It begins with understanding the interplay between your income projections and lifestyle needs. A clear, forward-thinking approach ensures that you remain financially secure while also achieving your personal and professional aspirations. Prioritizing these goals requires a nuanced understanding of your revenue streams, expected expenses, and how they align with your desired quality of life. For example, a freelance graphic designer might anticipate varying income throughout the year, necessitating a strategy that ensures both the ability to cover living expenses during lean months and the capacity to save during more profitable periods.

Income projections are not merely about estimating earnings; they encompass a detailed examination of potential revenue fluctuations and their timing. It's essential to consider both optimistic and conservative scenarios when forecasting your income. This dual approach provides a buffer during downturns while giving you a clear picture of your financial ceiling. Leveraging tools like cash flow forecasts and financial software can help create more accurate projections. For instance, an independent consultant might use historical data and market trends to estimate quarterly income, allowing for more precise financial planning and goal setting.

Balancing these projections with lifestyle needs involves a strategic allocation of resources. This means not only covering basic living expenses but also planning for discretionary spending that enhances your quality of life. Establishing a hierarchy of needs and wants can help in this regard. For instance, a freelance writer might prioritize paying for health insurance and rent while setting aside funds for professional development and occasional leisure activities. This balanced approach ensures that financial goals are realistic and aligned with personal well-being.

Implementing a SMART (Specific, Measurable, Achievable, Relevant, Time-bound) framework is pivotal in prioritizing and achieving financial goals. This method transforms abstract objectives into actionable steps, making progress tangible and trackable. For example, a self-employed photographer might set a SMART goal to save $5,000 for new equipment within six months by allocating a specific percentage of each project's earnings to a dedicated savings account. This structured approach not only clarifies the path to achieving financial milestones but also fosters a sense of accomplishment and motivation.

To adapt to the evolving nature of self-employment, it's crucial to periodically reassess and adjust your financial goals. As your business grows, so too will your income and expenses, necessitating a dynamic approach to financial planning. Regularly reviewing and recalibrating your goals ensures they remain relevant and attainable. For example, an online entrepreneur might find that an initial goal of saving for a new website needs to shift towards investing in marketing as their business expands. This flexibility allows for continuous alignment between your financial strategy and the changing landscape of your professional and personal life.

Implement SMART Criteria to Measure Progress and Achieve Milestones

Implementing SMART criteria is a powerful technique to ensure your financial goals are both attainable and measurable. The SMART framework stands for Specific, Measurable, Achievable, Relevant, and Time-bound, providing a structured approach to goal-setting. Begin by making your financial objectives Specific. Rather than vaguely aiming to "save more money," define a clear target such as "save $10,000 for retirement within the next year." This specificity eliminates ambiguity and sets a clear direction for your efforts.

Measurability is the next cornerstone of SMART criteria. Establish concrete metrics to track your progress. For instance, if your goal is to reduce expenses by 15% over six months, break it down into monthly or even weekly milestones. This allows for regular assessment and adjustments, ensuring you remain on track. By setting measurable targets, you transform abstract goals into quantifiable achievements, facilitating ongoing motivation and accountability.

Achievability ensures that your goals are realistic given your current circumstances. Aspirations should stretch your capabilities but remain within the realm of possibility. For example, aiming to double your income in a year might be overly ambitious unless you have a clear, actionable plan to do so. Instead, consider a more attainable target such as increasing your income by 20% through additional freelance projects or diversifying your client base. This balance between ambition and realism keeps you motivated without setting you up for failure.

Relevance is critical to maintaining focus and motivation. Ensure your goals align with your broader financial objectives and lifestyle needs. If your long-term aim is financial independence, short-term goals like building an emergency fund or paying off debt should directly contribute to that larger vision. This alignment ensures that every step you take propels you closer to your ultimate financial freedom, creating a coherent and cohesive strategy.

Making your goals Time-bound injects a sense of urgency and helps prioritize your efforts. Assign specific deadlines to each of your financial targets. For example, set a timeline to "save $2,500 for a vacation by December 31st." Deadlines not only provide a clear endpoint but also encourage consistent effort and time management. By adhering to the SMART criteria, you transform your financial aspirations into a structured, actionable plan, paving the way for steady progress and the achievement of significant milestones.

Developing a Year-Round Tax Plan

Envision a day when tax season no longer brings a cloud of anxiety but instead feels like just another routine check-in for your thriving self-employed business. Imagine the peace of mind that comes from knowing you've been proactive, keeping your financial house in order all year round. This dream can become your reality with a well-structured, year-round tax plan. It's not just about crunching numbers; it's about aligning your tax strategy with your business goals, creating a seamless integration that propels your enterprise toward success. By embedding tax planning into your regular business practices, you ensure that no financial stone is left unturned, reducing stress and maximizing efficiency.

Consider the story of Natalie, a freelance graphic designer who once dreaded the chaos of tax time. She transformed her approach by establishing regular

BUILDING A TAX STRATEGY

financial check-ins, utilizing intuitive tax software for real-time insights, and aligning her tax planning with her business growth strategies. As her business expanded, so did her confidence in managing her finances. Natalie's journey underscores the power of a consistent, informed tax strategy. By following a similar path, you too can take control of your financial future, making tax planning an empowering part of your entrepreneurial journey.

Establish Regular Financial Check-Ins

Establishing regular financial check-ins is a cornerstone of a robust year-round tax plan for self-employed individuals. These periodic reviews not only ensure that you stay on top of your financial health but also enable timely adjustments to your tax strategy. By setting aside specific times each month or quarter to review your income, expenses, and tax obligations, you can avoid the end-of-year scramble and the stress that often accompanies tax season. This proactive approach allows you to catch discrepancies early, make informed financial decisions, and ultimately optimize your tax position. Consider this practice as a financial health check-up, akin to regular medical check-ups, which are essential for preventing issues before they become critical.

Incorporating these routine financial reviews can also provide valuable insights into your business performance. For instance, tracking your income streams and expenses on a regular basis helps identify trends and patterns that might otherwise go unnoticed. You might discover that certain months are consistently more profitable, allowing you to allocate resources more effectively or capitalize on these peak periods. Additionally, regular check-ins can highlight areas where expenses are higher than expected, prompting a reassessment of cost-saving measures or renegotiation of vendor contracts. This continuous monitoring aligns your financial practices with your broader business goals, ensuring that every decision is informed by accurate and up-to-date data.

Advanced financial tools and technologies have made it easier than ever to conduct these financial check-ins. Cloud-based accounting software can automate much of the data collection and analysis, providing real-time insights into your financial status. These platforms can generate detailed reports on income, expenses, and tax liabilities, offering a comprehensive view of your financial landscape at a glance. Moreover, many of these tools come with features specifically designed for self-employed individuals, such as mileage tracking, invoicing, and integrated tax calculations. Leveraging these technologies not only streamlines your financial management but also enhances the accuracy and reliability of your data, making your check-ins more effective and less time-consuming.

In addition to utilizing technology, it's beneficial to incorporate a strategic element into your financial reviews. For example, aligning your financial check-ins with key business milestones or quarterly tax deadlines can ensure that you are always prepared for upcoming obligations. This strategy can also help you anticipate and plan for future financial needs, such as setting aside funds for taxes, saving for retirement, or investing in business growth. By integrating these check-ins into your broader financial strategy, you create a cohesive plan that supports both your immediate and long-term objectives. This holistic approach not only simplifies your tax planning but also strengthens your overall financial resilience.

Thought-provoking scenarios can further enrich your financial check-ins. Consider questions like, "What would happen if a major client were to suddenly cease their contract?" or "How would an unexpected expense impact my tax liability?" These hypothetical situations encourage critical thinking and preparedness, allowing you to develop contingency plans and build a more robust financial strategy. Reflecting on these scenarios during your regular check-ins can help you identify potential risks and opportunities, ensuring that you are always one step ahead. By fostering this mindset, you transform routine financial reviews into dynamic sessions of strategic planning and foresight, ultimately paving the way for sustained financial success.

Utilize Tax Software for Real-Time Insights

Choosing the right tax software can be transformative for self-employed individuals, providing real-time insights into financial health and tax obligations. Modern tax software goes beyond simple calculations; it offers a comprehensive suite of tools designed to streamline financial management. These platforms often include features such as automated expense tracking, invoice generation, and even AI-driven suggestions for maximizing deductions. By integrating these tools into daily operations, freelancers and independent contractors can maintain an accurate and up-to-date picture of their finances, which is crucial for effective tax planning.

One of the standout advantages of utilizing tax software is the ability to monitor income and expenses continuously. Instead of waiting until the end of the quarter or year, users can track their financial activities in real time. This ongoing monitoring allows for timely adjustments, whether it's reallocating expenses to optimize deductions or setting aside additional funds for upcoming tax payments. For instance, if a freelancer notices a sudden increase in income, they can immediately adjust their quarterly tax estimates to avoid underpayment penalties. This proactive approach not only reduces stress but also ensures that financial decisions are based on the most current data available.

Tax software also plays a pivotal role in forecasting and planning. Many advanced platforms offer predictive analytics that can project future tax liabilities based on current income trends and expenses. This feature is particularly beneficial for growing businesses, as it allows entrepreneurs to plan for scalability without being blindsided by unexpected tax bills. For example, if a gig worker anticipates a significant uptick in earnings due to a new contract, the software can provide an estimate of the additional tax burden. This foresight allows for better financial preparation, such as setting aside a larger portion of income for taxes or investing in tax-advantaged accounts.

Integrating tax planning with broader business strategies is another key benefit of these software solutions. Effective tax software doesn't just help users stay compliant; it also offers insights that can drive business growth. For instance, by analyzing expense patterns, the software might reveal opportunities for cost savings or highlight areas where investing in new tools or services could yield tax benefits. Additionally, many platforms offer customizable reports that can help users understand their financial performance in the context of their tax strategy. This holistic view enables more informed decision-making, aligning tax obligations with long term business goals.

The landscape of tax software is continually evolving, with new features and improvements regularly being introduced. Emerging trends such as machine learning and blockchain technology are poised to further enhance the accuracy and efficiency of these tools. Machine learning algorithms can offer personalized tax advice based on user behavior and financial history, while blockchain technology promises unparalleled security and transparency. Staying informed about these advancements can give self-employed individuals a competitive edge, ensuring they utilize the most effective tools available to manage their tax responsibilities. By embracing these innovations, freelancers, gig workers, and independent contractors can transform tax planning from a daunting task into a strategic advantage.

Integrate Tax Planning with Business Growth Strategies

Integrating tax planning with business growth strategies is an essential practice for self-employed individuals aiming to achieve sustainable success and financial freedom. This integration requires more than just a basic understanding of tax laws; it necessitates a proactive approach to aligning tax obligations with long-term business objectives. For instance, strategic tax planning can significantly influence decisions regarding investments in new equipment, expansion into new markets, or hiring additional staff. By considering the tax implications of each business decision, freelancers and independent contractors can optimize their financial outcomes, ensuring they are not only compliant but also maximizing their potential for growth and profitability.

One advanced approach to combining tax planning with business development is the utilization of tax incentives and credits designed to foster growth. For example, the Research and Development (R&D) Tax Credit is often overlooked by small business owners, yet it can provide substantial financial relief for those engaged in innovation. Similarly, understanding the nuances of the Qualified Business Income (QBI) deduction can lead to significant tax savings, particularly for those in service-based industries. These incentives, if strategically leveraged, can free up capital that can be reinvested into the business, fueling further growth and expansion.

An emerging trend in this integration process is the use of predictive analytics and financial modeling. Advanced tax software now offers features that allow business owners to simulate various financial scenarios and their corresponding tax outcomes. This technology empowers self-employed individuals to make informed decisions with a clear understanding of their future tax liabilities. For instance, before launching a new product line or entering a new geographic market, a business owner can model the potential revenue streams and associated tax responsibilities, allowing for more precise and confident planning.

It's also crucial to continually adjust tax strategies in response to business growth and changing tax laws. As businesses evolve, so do their tax obligations. Regularly reviewing and updating tax plans ensures they remain aligned with current business activities and legal requirements. For instance, as a sole proprietor transitions to an LLC or S-Corporation, the tax landscape changes dramatically. Being proactive in adjusting strategies to accommodate these changes can prevent unnecessary tax liabilities and ensure compliance. Moreover, staying

BUILDING A TAX STRATEGY

abreast of new tax legislation and regulations can uncover additional opportunities for tax savings.

Critical thinking and scenario planning are essential tools in this integration process. By posing questions such as, "How will a new client or revenue stream impact my quarterly tax payments?" or "What are the tax implications of investing in a new software platform?" business owners can anticipate and prepare for potential tax outcomes. This forward-thinking approach not only minimizes unexpected tax burdens but also allows for more strategic allocation of resources. Implementing these insights into daily operations fosters a culture of financial acumen and resilience, setting the foundation for long-term success and financial freedom. Through a meticulous and strategic approach to tax planning, self-employed individuals can seamlessly align their financial responsibilities with their business aspirations, ensuring a trajectory of growth and prosperity.

Adjusting Your Strategy as Your Business Grows

To understand how to adjust your tax strategy as your business grows, imagine this scenario: You started your freelance graphic design business in a small corner of your living room. In the beginning, you were thrilled with each new client, and your primary focus was simply making ends meet. Fast forward a few years, and your client base has expanded significantly. Perhaps you've even hired a few assistants or moved into a dedicated office space. The financial landscape of your business has evolved, and with it, the need for a more sophisticated tax strategy.

As your enterprise flourishes, it's crucial to reassess your income streams and the tax brackets you fall into. What worked for you as a solo entrepreneur might not be as effective when you have multiple revenue streams and a team of employees. Implementing scalable, tax-optimized strategies becomes essential to keep more of your hard-earned money and invest it back into your growing business. This might also be the perfect time to consider advanced retirement and investment plans, ensuring your financial future is as robust as your business. Let's explore these aspects to help you build a tax strategy that grows with you, providing a solid foundation for sustained success and financial stability.

Reassessing Income Streams and Tax Brackets

As your business evolves, reassessing your income streams and tax brackets becomes crucial. A thriving enterprise often diversifies its revenue sources, leading to complexities in tax liabilities. For instance, a freelance graphic designer might expand into digital product sales, workshops, and consulting services. Each of these income streams can affect your tax situation differently, necessitating a thorough review. Understanding how your diversified income impacts your tax bracket is vital. Moving from one bracket to another can significantly influence your tax obligations, making it essential to stay vigilant and proactive.

When evaluating your income streams, it's important to consider both the volume and the nature of each source. Passive income sources, such as royalties from digital products, may be taxed differently than active income from freelance work. By meticulously categorizing your income, you can better anticipate your tax liabilities and avoid unexpected surprises. Leveraging accounting software tailored for self-employed individuals can simplify this process, offering real-time insights and enabling you to make informed decisions. Additionally, consulting with a tax professional who understands the nuances of self-employment can provide tailored advice, ensuring you optimize your tax strategy.

As your income grows, so does the potential for crossing into higher tax brackets, which can trigger increased tax rates. For example, a leap from a 24% tax bracket to a 32% bracket can be substantial. To mitigate these effects, consider strategic planning, such as timing your income. If feasible, deferring income to the following year or accelerating deductions in the current year can help manage your taxable income more effectively. This approach requires a deep understanding of tax laws and foresight, making it beneficial to continually educate yourself on tax regulations and emerging trends.

It's equally important to re-evaluate your deductions and credits as your business scales. Higher income levels may open up new opportunities for deductions, such as advanced retirement contributions or health savings accounts (HSAs). Conversely, certain credits may phase out as your income increases. Staying abreast of these changes ensures you don't miss out on potential tax benefits. Engaging in regular financial reviews, ideally quarterly, can help you stay aligned with your financial goals and adjust your tax strategy accordingly. This proactive approach not only minimizes tax liabilities but also supports long-term financial health.

BUILDING A TAX STRATEGY

In a rapidly changing economic landscape, flexibility is key. Your business's growth trajectory might introduce new challenges and opportunities, requiring continuous adaptation of your tax strategy. Stay informed about legislative changes that could impact your tax planning. For instance, recent adjustments in tax laws or emerging trends in digital taxation could present new considerations for your business. By maintaining a dynamic and informed approach, you position yourself to not only comply with tax obligations but also to thrive financially. Embrace a mindset of continuous learning and adaptation, ensuring your tax strategy evolves in tandem with your business growth.

Implementing Scalable Tax-Optimized Strategies

As your business evolves, implementing scalable tax-optimized strategies becomes paramount to sustaining growth and maximizing financial efficiency. One effective approach involves reassessing your business structure. Transitioning from a sole proprietorship to an LLC or S-Corporation, for instance, can offer significant tax advantages. An S-Corporation allows you to separate your salary from your business's profits, potentially reducing self-employment taxes. These structures also provide enhanced liability protection, safeguarding your personal assets as your business scales. By regularly evaluating your business structure, you can ensure it remains aligned with your financial objectives and tax planning needs.

Another crucial strategy is leveraging tax-advantaged accounts to their fullest potential. As your income increases, consider contributing to a Solo 401(k) or SEP IRA. These retirement plans not only promote long-term savings but also offer substantial tax deductions. A Solo 401(k) allows for higher contribution limits compared to traditional IRAs, making it an excellent tool for reducing taxable income. Furthermore, profit-sharing options within these plans can be particularly beneficial for high-earning years, allowing you to defer more income and minimize taxes. By integrating these accounts into your financial strategy, you can optimize your tax liability while securing your future.

Incorporating advanced expense tracking tools is another scalable strategy for tax optimization. As your business grows, manual tracking methods may become cumbersome and prone to error. Adopting software solutions like QuickBooks or Xero can automate and streamline the process, ensuring every deductible expense is accurately recorded. These platforms offer features such as real-time expense categorization and integration with bank accounts, providing a seamless way to maintain financial records. By investing in these tools, you can save time, reduce errors, and increase your ability to capture all eligible deductions, thus enhancing your overall tax strategy.

Strategically timing income and expenses can also yield significant tax benefits. For instance, if you anticipate being in a higher tax bracket in the future, you might defer income to the following year while accelerating deductible expenses into the current year. This approach can help manage taxable income and potentially lower your overall tax burden. Additionally, understanding the nuances of depreciation on business assets offers opportunities for tax savings. By utilizing methods such as bonus depreciation or Section 179 expensing, you can write off substantial portions of asset costs in the year of purchase, rather than spreading the deductions over several years. This strategy allows for more immediate tax relief and improved cash flow.

Staying informed about legislative changes is vital for maintaining a scalable tax strategy. Tax laws are dynamic, with frequent updates that can impact your planning. Engaging with a tax professional who is well-versed in current trends and regulations can provide invaluable insights. For instance, recent changes in tax deductions for meals and entertainment, or updates to the Qualified Business Income (QBI) deduction, can significantly affect your tax liability. By staying proactive and informed, you can adjust your strategies accordingly, ensuring they remain effective and compliant with the latest regulations. This forward-thinking approach not only optimizes your tax situation but also positions your business for sustained financial success.

Incorporating Advanced Retirement and Investment Plans

Navigating the complexities of self-employed taxes requires a nuanced approach, especially as your business evolves. Incorporating advanced retirement and investment plans into your tax strategy can significantly enhance your financial security while optimizing your tax obligations. As your income grows and your financial landscape becomes more intricate, sophisticated retirement and investment options will play a vital role in sustaining your financial health. For instance, exploring options beyond the traditional Individual Retirement Account (IRA) or Simplified Employee Pension (SEP) IRA, such as the Solo 401(k) or Defined Benefit Plan, offers higher contribution limits and greater flexibility, allowing you to tailor your retirement savings to your increasing earnings.

BUILDING A TAX STRATEGY

A Solo 401(k), also known as a one-participant 401(k), is particularly advantageous for self-employed individuals or small business owners with no employees. This plan permits both employer and employee contributions, enabling you to maximize your retirement savings while reducing taxable income. In 2023, for example, you can contribute up to $66,000, or $73,500 if you're over 50, combining both elective deferrals and profit-sharing contributions. This dual contribution capability provides a substantial tax-deferred growth opportunity, making it an excellent choice for those aiming to accumulate significant retirement funds rapidly.

Incorporating a Defined Benefit Plan can also be a game-changer for high-income self-employed professionals. These plans allow for even larger contributions compared to Solo 401(k)s and SEP IRAs, potentially reaching into the six figures annually, depending on factors such as age, income, and desired retirement benefits. While more complex and costly to administer, the tax advantages and accelerated savings potential make Defined Benefit Plans an attractive option for those seeking to significantly bolster their retirement nest egg. Consulting with a financial planner experienced in these plans can help you navigate the intricate regulatory requirements and tailor a plan that aligns with your long-term goals.

Investments beyond retirement accounts should also be part of a comprehensive tax strategy. Diversifying your portfolio to include tax-efficient investment vehicles such as municipal bonds, real estate, and index funds can provide additional avenues for growth while mitigating tax liabilities. Municipal bonds, for instance, offer tax-free interest income at the federal level and potentially at the state level, depending on the bond's origin. Similarly, real estate investments can yield tax benefits through depreciation deductions and 1031 exchanges, allowing you to defer capital gains taxes when reinvesting proceeds into similar property types.

Continually reassessing and adjusting your retirement and investment strategies is crucial as your business grows and tax laws evolve. Staying informed about legislative changes, economic trends, and emerging investment opportunities ensures that your tax strategy remains dynamic and effective. Engaging with a diverse range of financial experts and exploring independent perspectives can provide a well-rounded understanding of the best practices and innovative approaches in the field. By proactively managing your retirement and investment plans, you not only secure your financial future but also optimize your current tax situation, creating a robust foundation for enduring financial freedom.

Crafting a robust tax strategy is an essential component of achieving financial freedom as a self-employed individual. This chapter delved into the importance of setting clear financial goals, which serve as the foundation of any effective tax plan. By establishing these objectives, you create a roadmap that guides your financial decisions and tax-related actions throughout the year. Developing a year-round tax plan ensures that you are consistently mindful of your tax obligations, allowing you to mitigate surprises and make informed decisions that align with your business growth. As your business evolves, it's crucial to adjust your strategy to reflect changes in income, expenses, and tax laws, ensuring that your plan remains relevant and effective.

Embracing these practices not only simplifies the complexities of tax management but also empowers you to take control of your financial future. By proactively planning and adapting your tax strategy, you lay the groundwork for sustained growth and stability. As you continue this journey, consider how each financial decision impacts your broader goals and remain vigilant in seeking opportunities for optimization. Reflect on how an intentional, well-structured tax strategy can transform your approach to financial management, providing peace of mind and paving the way to true financial independence. With this mindset, you're well-equipped to tackle the next steps in your financial journey, confident in your ability to navigate the ever-evolving landscape of self-employed taxes.

Chapter Twelve

The Bigger Picture Of Financial Independence

At the dawn of a new era in your financial journey, imagine standing on the edge of a vast landscape, where opportunities stretch as far as the eye can see. Picture a world where your income doesn't come from just one source, but rather a flowing river of multiple streams, each contributing to your financial well-being. This might seem like a dream, but for many self-employed individuals, it's a tangible reality. Take Sarah, for instance—a freelance graphic designer who, through savvy investments and diverse income channels, achieved a balanced, fulfilling life that transcends the limitations of traditional employment.

In this chapter, we'll explore how you can create a similar tapestry of financial independence, weaving together various threads to form a robust safety net. We'll delve into the importance of not just earning but also investing in your future. Consider the power of compound interest, where your money starts working for you, growing quietly but steadily over time. This isn't just about numbers on a spreadsheet; it's about buying back your time, giving yourself the freedom to pursue passions without the looming shadow of financial stress.

Achieving this balance requires more than just smart financial moves; it calls for a holistic approach to life. Work-life balance, often an elusive goal for many, becomes attainable when you have the resources and flexibility to prioritize what truly matters. This chapter will guide you through the steps to not only secure your financial future but also ensure that along the way, you're building a life rich in experiences, relationships, and personal satisfaction. Embrace this journey with an open heart and a strategic mind, as we unlock the door to a future where financial independence is not just a goal, but a way of life.

Creating Multiple Streams of Income

Reflect on a time when you were juggling multiple projects, perhaps working late into the night to meet deadlines. The hustle is real, and while the rewards can be gratifying, the constant grind can also be exhausting. Now, imagine if you had several streams of income working for you, easing the pressure and providing a more stable financial cushion. This isn't just a pipe dream; it's a strategic approach that many successful self-employed individuals have mastered. By diversifying income sources, you not only enhance your financial security but also open doors to new opportunities and ventures that can lead to a more balanced and fulfilling life.

At the core of creating multiple streams of income lies the idea of not putting all your eggs in one basket. It's about leveraging your skills, interests, and resources to generate passive income, invest in assets that yield returns, and build scalable business models. Think of it as planting different seeds that will grow and flourish over time, each contributing to your financial garden. This approach not only mitigates risk but also paves the way for exponential growth, allowing you to achieve financial independence faster and with greater resilience. As we delve into the specifics, you'll discover practical strategies to diversify through passive income, invest wisely, and develop scalable ventures that align with your long-term goals.

Diversify Through Passive Income Streams

Exploring passive income streams is a cornerstone of financial resilience for the self-employed. By diversifying income, freelancers and independent contractors can mitigate the inherent volatility of their primary earnings. One effective strategy is to develop digital products, such as e-books, online courses, or software applications. These products, once created, require minimal ongoing effort while continuously generating revenue. For instance, an illustrator can

THE BIGGER PICTURE OF FINANCIAL INDEPENDENCE   185

create a series of digital art tutorials, or a web developer might design a unique plugin for popular content management systems. Such ventures leverage existing skills and expertise, transforming them into enduring sources of income.

Another avenue for passive income is affiliate marketing. This involves promoting products or services through personalized links, earning commissions from sales driven by those referrals. Affiliates often utilize blogs, social media platforms, or dedicated websites to share reviews and recommendations. The key to success in affiliate marketing lies in authenticity and value; endorsing products that genuinely benefit the target audience builds trust and drives more conversions. For example, a freelance fitness coach might partner with health supplement brands, sharing detailed reviews and usage tips that resonate with their followers.

Real estate investment offers a more traditional, yet highly effective, means of diversifying income. By acquiring rental properties or participating in real estate crowdfunding platforms, self-employed individuals can tap into the steady cash flow generated by tenants. This method requires a more substantial initial investment compared to digital products or affiliate marketing but can yield significant long-term returns. Additionally, real estate investments often appreciate in value, providing a dual benefit of rental income and capital growth. A writer, for instance, might invest book royalties into a rental property, creating a stable, supplemental income stream.

Crowdfunding platforms have also opened new doors for passive income, particularly through peer-to-peer lending. This allows individuals to lend small amounts of money to borrowers, earning interest over time. Platforms such as LendingClub or Prosper facilitate this process, handling the logistics and reducing the risk for lenders. This approach not only diversifies income but also contributes to financial ecosystems by supporting small businesses and individuals in need of loans. A graphic designer might allocate a portion of their savings to peer-to-peer lending, benefiting from regular interest payments while aiding entrepreneurial ventures.

For those with a penchant for creativity and innovation, licensing intellectual property can be a lucrative passive income stream. This includes licensing artwork, music, or written content for use in various media. Licensing agreements ensure that creators are compensated whenever their work is used, often without the need for further involvement. For example, a musician could license their compositions to be used in commercials, films, or video games, receiving royalties each time the music is played. This not only diversifies income but also expands the creator's reach and influence across different industries.

By cultivating multiple passive income streams, self-employed individuals can achieve greater financial stability and independence. This diversified approach not only reduces reliance on primary earnings but also fosters continuous revenue growth, paving the way for a more secure and prosperous future.

Invest in Income-Generating Assets

Investing in income-generating assets is a strategic move that can significantly bolster financial security for self-employed individuals. One of the most accessible and versatile options is real estate. Purchasing rental properties can provide a steady stream of passive income while also appreciating in value over time. For example, investing in multi-family homes or commercial properties in burgeoning markets can yield substantial returns. Moreover, platforms like REITs (Real Estate Investment Trusts) offer an opportunity to invest in real estate without the need for significant capital or direct property management, making it an attractive option for those who prefer a hands-off approach.

Another powerful avenue for income generation is the stock market. Dividend-paying stocks, particularly those from well-established companies with a history of consistent payouts, can serve as a reliable income source. These dividends can be reinvested to purchase more shares, further compounding the investment's growth. Additionally, exploring exchange-traded funds (ETFs) and mutual funds can help diversify risk while providing exposure to a broader range of assets. Recent research highlights the benefits of focusing on sectors poised for growth, such as technology and renewable energy, which not only promise strong future performance but also align with sustainable investing principles.

Peer-to-peer lending platforms offer a more unconventional yet lucrative investment option. By lending money to individuals or small businesses through these platforms, investors can earn interest rates that often surpass traditional savings accounts or bonds. This method also allows for a diversified portfolio of loans, spreading risk across multiple borrowers. Emerging trends in this sector, such as blockchain-based lending, promise increased transparency and security, further enhancing its appeal. However, it's crucial to thoroughly vet the platforms and borrowers to mitigate potential risks.

THE BIGGER PICTURE OF FINANCIAL INDEPENDENCE   187

Investing in intellectual property can also yield substantial returns. Acquiring rights to patents, trademarks, or even creative works like books and music can generate royalties over time. For those with a knack for innovation, creating and patenting new products or technologies can lead to lucrative licensing deals. The rise of digital content and the gig economy has made it easier than ever to monetize intellectual property, providing a wealth of opportunities for the enterprising individual. Staying informed about the latest trends in intellectual property law and market demands can help identify profitable niches and capitalize on them effectively.

Consider the burgeoning field of cryptocurrency and blockchain technology. While volatile, cryptocurrencies like Bitcoin and Ethereum have demonstrated significant growth potential. Beyond simply buying and holding these digital assets, investors can explore staking, yield farming, and participating in decentralized finance (DeFi) protocols to earn passive income. As with any investment, due diligence is paramount. Engaging with reputable sources, joining knowledgeable communities, and continuously educating oneself about the evolving landscape can help navigate this high-risk, high-reward territory. Balancing these investments with more traditional assets can create a robust, diversified portfolio that maximizes income potential while managing risk.

Develop Scalable Business Models

Creating scalable business models is a pivotal strategy for self-employed individuals seeking to amplify their income streams and achieve long-term financial independence. By focusing on scalability, freelancers and independent contractors can transform their ventures into more lucrative and sustainable enterprises without a proportional increase in workload. A scalable business model leverages technology, processes, or systems that allow for substantial growth without necessitating significant additional resources. This approach not only maximizes efficiency but also positions the business to adapt to market demands and capitalize on emerging opportunities.

One effective way to develop a scalable business model is to harness the power of digital platforms and automation tools. For instance, content creators can monetize their expertise by offering online courses, e-books, or subscription-based services. These digital products require an initial investment of time and effort but can be sold repeatedly with minimal ongoing maintenance. By automating marketing efforts through email campaigns and social media scheduling tools, self-employed individuals can reach a broader audience and generate consistent revenue. This digital transformation allows for significant scaling without the need for proportional increases in time or workforce.

Another avenue for scalability is through strategic partnerships and collaborations. By aligning with complementary businesses or influencers, self-employed individuals can tap into new customer bases and expand their market reach. For example, a freelance graphic designer might partner with a web developer to offer comprehensive branding packages, thereby attracting clients looking for a one-stop solution. These partnerships can lead to increased project sizes and more substantial contracts, driving growth without a corresponding spike in operational costs. Additionally, such collaborations often bring fresh perspectives and innovative ideas, further enhancing the scalability of the business.

Investing in intellectual property (IP) can also contribute to a scalable business model. Creating and protecting IP, such as trademarks, patents, or proprietary methodologies, can open up new revenue streams through licensing agreements or royalties. For instance, a freelance software developer who creates a unique application can license the software to other businesses, generating ongoing passive income. This approach not only diversifies income but also builds long-term value in the business. By focusing on IP development, self-employed professionals can leverage their creative output in ways that lead to exponential growth.

To ensure that a scalable business model remains viable, it is crucial to continuously innovate and adapt to changing market conditions. This involves staying abreast of industry trends, customer preferences, and technological advancements. Regularly soliciting feedback from clients and peers can provide valuable insights into areas for improvement and potential growth opportunities. By fostering a culture of continuous improvement, self-employed individuals can refine their offerings and maintain a competitive edge. This proactive approach to innovation is a cornerstone of scalability, ensuring that the business can evolve and thrive in a dynamic marketplace.

The journey to creating a scalable business model is one of strategic planning and thoughtful execution. It requires a clear vision, dedication to leveraging technology and partnerships, and a commitment to continuous innovation. By focusing on these key areas, self-employed individuals can build robust, scalable enterprises that offer financial stability and growth potential. This strategic

THE BIGGER PICTURE OF FINANCIAL INDEPENDENCE   189

approach not only enhances their ability to generate multiple income streams but also paves the way for sustained financial independence and success.

Investing in Your Future

Imagine waking up one morning to find that your freelance business has hit a rough patch. Clients are scarce, and your income has dwindled. The anxiety sets in, and you begin to question if relying solely on your current gig is sustainable. This scenario is more common than you might think, and it underscores the critical importance of investing in your future. By taking proactive steps today, you can safeguard your financial well-being and ensure that you're not solely dependent on a single income stream. This journey isn't just about securing your present; it's about building a resilient financial foundation for years to come.

Investing in your future involves more than just stashing away money in a savings account. It's about making informed decisions that can help you grow your wealth and achieve long-term financial stability. From diversifying your income streams to leveraging tax-advantaged retirement accounts and exploring investment opportunities beyond traditional markets, there are numerous strategies to consider. Each of these steps plays a vital role in mitigating risks and enhancing your financial security. As we delve into these concepts, you'll discover practical ways to take control of your financial destiny, ensuring that no matter what uncertainties lie ahead, you're well-prepared to face them with confidence and ease.

Diversifying Income Streams to Mitigate Risk

A cornerstone of financial independence for self-employed individuals lies in the strategic diversification of income streams. By generating revenue from multiple sources, freelancers, gig workers, and independent contractors can mitigate the inherent risks associated with relying on a single income. This approach not only buffers against economic downturns or market fluctuations but also ensures a more stable financial foundation. For example, a freelance graphic designer might expand their income streams by offering online courses, selling digital products, and engaging in affiliate marketing alongside their primary client work. This multifaceted approach reduces vulnerability and enhances overall financial resilience.

Incorporating various income streams demands not only creativity but also a keen understanding of market demands and personal strengths. Identifying complementary skills and interests can open new avenues for revenue generation. A writer could explore ghostwriting, blogging, and content strategy consulting, thereby leveraging their expertise across different domains. Diversification isn't about spreading oneself thin; rather, it's about strategically aligning one's skills and passions with market opportunities. This alignment ensures that each income stream is sustainable and contributes meaningfully to one's financial portfolio.

Recent studies underscore the importance of passive income as a critical component of income diversification. Passive income sources such as investments, royalties, and rental properties can provide a steady revenue stream with minimal ongoing effort. For instance, investing in dividend-paying stocks or peer-to-peer lending platforms can generate regular income, freeing up time for further skill development or other entrepreneurial ventures. The key is to balance active and passive income sources, creating a robust and multifaceted financial strategy that can withstand economic uncertainties.

Innovative perspectives on income diversification also include leveraging digital platforms and technology. Online marketplaces, social media, and e-commerce sites offer unprecedented opportunities for self-employed individuals to reach broader audiences and monetize their skills. A photographer, for example, might sell stock photos online, offer virtual workshops, and use social media to attract clients for personalized shoots. By harnessing the power of technology, self-employed professionals can scale their operations and tap into global markets, further enhancing their financial security.

To effectively manage and optimize multiple income streams, it's essential to develop a coherent financial strategy. This involves setting clear financial goals, regularly tracking income and expenses, and continuously assessing the performance of each revenue source. Tools like budgeting apps and financial planning software can streamline this process, providing insights and facilitating informed decision-making. Moreover, staying abreast of emerging trends and continuously educating oneself about new opportunities can ensure that the income diversification strategy remains dynamic and effective. By thoughtfully diversifying income streams, self-employed individuals can build a resilient financial future, minimizing risk and maximizing potential for growth.

THE BIGGER PICTURE OF FINANCIAL INDEPENDENCE   191

Leveraging Tax-Advantaged Retirement Accounts

Retirement planning for the self-employed offers unique opportunities to leverage tax-advantaged accounts, facilitating both immediate tax savings and long-term financial security. One of the fundamental vehicles for this purpose is the Individual Retirement Account (IRA). Traditional IRAs allow contributions to be tax-deductible, reducing taxable income in the contribution year. Meanwhile, Roth IRAs, though funded with post-tax dollars, offer tax-free growth and withdrawals in retirement. Choosing between these options depends on one's current tax bracket and anticipated future income, providing flexibility to tailor retirement strategies to individual financial situations.

In addition to IRAs, the Simplified Employee Pension (SEP) IRA is a formidable tool for self-employed individuals and small business owners. This account allows for significantly higher contribution limits compared to traditional IRAs, up to 25% of net earnings from self-employment, or $61,000 as of the latest tax year. The SEP IRA's high contribution ceiling can be particularly advantageous for those with fluctuating incomes, enabling substantial retirement savings during prosperous years. Moreover, contributions are tax-deductible, offering immediate tax benefits while fostering substantial retirement growth.

Another powerful option is the Solo 401(k), also known as the Individual 401(k). This plan is available to self-employed individuals with no full-time employees other than a spouse. It combines the benefits of a traditional 401(k) with the flexibility needed by the self-employed, allowing both employee and employer contributions. This dual contribution feature significantly boosts the maximum allowable contributions, potentially exceeding $60,000 annually, depending on income. Additionally, Solo 401(k)s can include Roth 401(k) options, offering tax-free growth on post-tax contributions, thus providing a strategic mix of tax treatments.

Health Savings Accounts (HSAs) can also play a critical role in retirement planning. While primarily designed for medical expenses, HSAs offer a triple tax advantage—deductible contributions, tax-free growth, and tax-free withdrawals for qualified medical expenses. After age 65, withdrawals for non-medical expenses incur only regular income tax, similar to traditional IRAs. This dual-purpose account can thus serve as both a retirement and healthcare savings tool, offering flexibility and tax efficiency.

Considering these diverse retirement accounts, self-employed individuals should engage in regular financial assessments to determine the optimal strategy. This involves not only understanding contribution limits and tax implications but also staying informed about legislative changes that may affect retirement planning. Diversifying across different types of accounts can mitigate risk and enhance the potential for tax savings and financial growth. Thoughtful planning and informed decision-making are key to leveraging these tax-advantaged accounts effectively, ensuring a secure and prosperous retirement.

Exploring Investment Opportunities Beyond Traditional Markets

Investing in your future extends beyond traditional stock markets and retirement accounts; it involves exploring diverse investment avenues that can provide substantial returns and financial security. One innovative approach is investing in real estate, which offers various options beyond simply purchasing rental properties. For instance, real estate crowdfunding platforms allow investors to pool their resources and invest in larger commercial properties or real estate projects, which would otherwise be inaccessible to individual investors. This method not only diversifies your portfolio but also mitigates risk, as the investment is spread across multiple projects and locations. Additionally, real estate can provide a steady stream of passive income through rental yields, making it an attractive option for those aiming to build long-term wealth.

Another compelling investment opportunity lies within the realm of cryptocurrencies and blockchain technology. While this market can be volatile, it also holds significant potential for high returns. Bitcoin and Ethereum are well-known examples, but numerous other digital currencies and blockchain projects are worth exploring. For instance, decentralized finance (DeFi) platforms offer innovative financial services such as lending, borrowing, and earning interest, all built on blockchain technology. By diversifying a portion of your investment portfolio into cryptocurrencies, you can tap into the growth of this emerging sector while potentially benefiting from the high returns associated with early-stage investments.

Peer-to-peer (P2P) lending is another alternative investment that can yield substantial returns. This method involves lending money directly to individuals or small businesses through online platforms, bypassing traditional financial institutions. P2P lending not only provides higher interest rates compared to conventional savings accounts but also allows investors to choose loans that align with their risk tolerance and investment goals. Platforms like LendingClub and Prosper have made P2P lending more accessible, enabling investors to diversify their portfolios with relatively small amounts of capital. This diversification can help spread risk and enhance overall returns, making it a viable component of a well-rounded investment strategy.

Venturing into alternative asset classes such as precious metals and commodities can also bolster your investment portfolio. Gold, silver, and other precious metals have long been considered safe-haven assets, particularly during times of economic uncertainty or inflation. Investing in these tangible assets provides a hedge against market volatility and currency fluctuations, preserving wealth over the long term. Commodities like oil, natural gas, and agricultural products offer additional diversification, as their prices are often influenced by different factors than those affecting traditional stock markets. By incorporating these asset classes into your investment strategy, you can create a more resilient and balanced portfolio.

Considering investments in intellectual property (IP) such as patents, trademarks, and copyrights can yield significant financial benefits. IP investments allow you to capitalize on the value of innovative ideas and creative works, which can generate ongoing revenue streams through licensing agreements and royalties. For example, acquiring the rights to a popular piece of music or a groundbreaking technology can provide long-term passive income. Additionally, investing in IP can offer tax advantages, as certain jurisdictions provide favorable tax treatment for income derived from intellectual property. This approach not only diversifies your investment portfolio but also positions you to benefit from the growth and commercialization of innovative ideas. By exploring these alternative investment opportunities, you can diversify your income streams and build a more robust financial future.

Achieving Work-Life Balance

Let's dive into the heart of what it truly means to balance work and personal life as a self-employed individual. Picture this: you're at your favorite café, laptop open, deadlines looming, and your phone buzzing with messages from clients. Just as you start to get into the flow, your friend calls, inviting you to an impromptu lunch. The tension between seizing the opportunity for a break and staying on top of your work is palpable. This scenario is all too familiar for many freelancers and independent contractors—caught in the relentless tug-of-war between professional commitments and personal well-being.

It's intriguing to note that achieving a harmonious work-life balance isn't just a lofty ideal but a tangible goal that can significantly enhance your productivity and overall quality of life. Establishing clear boundaries, implementing effective time management techniques, and integrating regular self-care and mental health practices are not mere buzzwords; they are essential strategies that can transform your daily routine and long-term outlook. By mastering these elements, you can create a sustainable lifestyle where your work and personal life complement, rather than compete with, each other. Let's explore how you can weave these practices into your life, starting with setting those all-important boundaries.

Establishing Clear Boundaries Between Work and Personal Life

Establishing clear boundaries between work and personal life is paramount for self-employed individuals, as the lines can easily blur in an environment where home often doubles as an office. One effective strategy is to designate specific work hours and stick to them. This not only fosters a disciplined work routine but also signals to clients and family members when you are available and when you are not. For example, setting a fixed schedule from 9 AM to 5 PM can help create a predictable pattern, making it easier to mentally switch off from work responsibilities at the end of the day. Studies have shown that having a structured work schedule can significantly reduce stress and enhance productivity, as it allows for better time allocation and focus.

In parallel, creating a dedicated workspace is another vital step. This doesn't necessarily mean having a separate room; even a specific corner of your living space can suffice. The key is to make this area distinct from where you relax or engage in personal activities. By doing so, you train your brain to associate this space solely with work, which can boost concentration and professional output. Moreover, this physical demarcation helps in mentally transitioning from "work mode" to "personal mode," thereby preserving the sanctity of your personal

THE BIGGER PICTURE OF FINANCIAL INDEPENDENCE   195

life. The psychology behind spatial differentiation supports the notion that our environment profoundly influences our behavioral patterns and mental states.

Equally important is the practice of digital boundaries. In our hyper-connected world, it's tempting to check emails or respond to client messages outside of designated work hours. Implementing a "digital sunset" can mitigate this issue—decide on a time when all work-related digital interactions cease, such as 7 PM. Research suggests that constant connectivity can lead to burnout and decreased job satisfaction, as it prevents full disengagement from work. Utilizing tools like email schedulers or setting up auto-responses can communicate your availability effectively without compromising your downtime. These practices underscore the importance of digital detoxification for maintaining a healthy work-life balance.

It is essential to communicate these boundaries clearly to both clients and family members. Setting expectations upfront about your availability can prevent misunderstandings and foster respect for your personal time. For instance, including your work hours in your email signature or discussing them during initial client meetings can set a professional tone. Similarly, having candid conversations with family members about your need for uninterrupted work time can help them understand and support your boundaries. Clear communication is the bedrock of maintaining these boundaries and ensuring they are respected by others.

Regular self-assessment is crucial to maintaining these boundaries effectively. Periodically reflect on your work-life balance and make adjustments as needed. Are you finding it hard to stick to your work hours? Is your designated workspace still functional, or does it need a revamp? Are digital boundaries being respected? By continuously evaluating and refining your strategies, you can adapt to changing circumstances and maintain a harmonious balance. This iterative process ensures that your boundaries remain effective and aligned with your evolving professional and personal needs, ultimately contributing to a sustainable and fulfilling self-employed career.

Implementing Effective Time Management Techniques

Effective time management is the cornerstone of achieving a harmonious work-life balance, especially for self-employed individuals who juggle multiple responsibilities. One advanced technique is the Pomodoro Technique, which involves working in focused intervals, typically 25 minutes, followed by a short break. This method not only enhances productivity but also prevents burnout by ensuring regular mental and physical breaks. By structuring work into manageable chunks, freelancers can maintain high levels of concentration and efficiency, allowing them to allocate time for personal activities without feeling overwhelmed.

In addition to time-blocking strategies, leveraging technology can significantly streamline your workflow. Modern project management tools like Trello, Asana, or Monday.com offer features that help track tasks, set deadlines, and prioritize work. By utilizing these platforms, self-employed professionals can gain a clear overview of their projects and deadlines, reducing the likelihood of missed opportunities and last-minute stress. Furthermore, integrating these tools with calendar apps ensures that personal and professional commitments are balanced, facilitating a more organized and less chaotic daily routine.

Another advanced insight is the importance of understanding one's peak productivity hours. Research suggests that individuals have varying levels of productivity throughout the day, often influenced by their circadian rhythms. By identifying when you are most alert and focused, you can schedule high-priority tasks during these periods. This approach not only maximizes efficiency but also leaves room for less demanding tasks during off-peak hours, creating a more balanced and effective work schedule. For example, a morning person might tackle complex tasks early in the day, leaving administrative duties for the afternoon.

Balancing work and personal life also requires setting clear boundaries. One innovative approach is the use of a dedicated workspace. By creating a physical or even a psychological separation between work and personal environments, individuals can mentally transition between roles. This separation helps prevent work from encroaching on personal time and vice versa. Additionally, establishing specific 'office hours' can signal to clients and family members alike when you are available or off-duty, fostering a healthier work-life balance.

Incorporating regular self-assessment can keep your time management strategies aligned with your evolving needs and goals. Periodically reviewing your schedule and productivity allows you to adjust and refine your techniques. Consider questions like: "Am I meeting my deadlines without undue stress?" or "Is my current approach allowing me ample time for personal pursuits?" Reflecting on these aspects ensures that your time management approach remains dynamic and effective, supporting both your professional aspirations and personal well-being.

THE BIGGER PICTURE OF FINANCIAL INDEPENDENCE

Integrating Regular Self-Care and Mental Health Practices

Integrating regular self-care and mental health practices into the life of a self-employed individual is paramount for sustaining long-term productivity and well-being. As freelancers and independent contractors often juggle multiple roles and responsibilities, the boundary between personal and professional life can easily blur, leading to burnout and stress. Prioritizing self-care means committing to activities that rejuvenate the mind and body, such as regular physical exercise, mindfulness meditation, and hobbies that provide joy and relaxation. Recent studies highlight the positive impact of these practices on cognitive function and emotional resilience, underscoring their importance in maintaining a balanced and fulfilling work-life dynamic.

To incorporate self-care into a busy schedule, consider practical strategies that align with your unique lifestyle and workload. For instance, setting aside specific times each day for short breaks can significantly reduce stress and increase focus. Use these intervals for mindful breathing exercises, stretching, or a quick walk to reset and recharge. Additionally, consider leveraging technology to support your self-care routine. Apps that guide meditation sessions or track physical activity can serve as helpful reminders to prioritize your well-being amidst a demanding work schedule. By weaving these small yet impactful habits into daily life, self-employed individuals can create a sustainable rhythm that supports both personal health and professional success.

Mental health practices should be tailored to the unique challenges faced by self-employed professionals. This includes recognizing and addressing common stressors such as financial uncertainty, client demands, and the isolation that often accompanies remote work. Engaging in regular mental health check-ins, whether through journaling, therapy, or peer support groups, can provide a vital outlet for processing emotions and gaining perspective. Cognitive-behavioral strategies, such as reframing negative thoughts and setting realistic goals, can also equip individuals with tools to manage anxiety and maintain a positive outlook. Acknowledging and addressing mental health needs is not a sign of weakness but a proactive step towards achieving a harmonious and productive life.

In addition to individual self-care practices, creating a supportive community can enhance overall well-being. Networking with fellow freelancers and joining professional groups can offer a sense of camaraderie and shared experience.

These connections can provide not only emotional support but also practical advice and collaboration opportunities. Virtual coworking spaces and online forums are excellent resources for building such networks, allowing self-employed individuals to feel connected and supported even in a solitary profession. A strong community can act as a buffer against the isolation and stress that can accompany self-employment, fostering a sense of belonging and mutual encouragement.

Consider the broader implications of integrating self-care and mental health practices into your professional life. By prioritizing well-being, self-employed individuals can cultivate greater creativity, innovation, and overall job satisfaction. This holistic approach not only enhances personal happiness but also contributes to sustainable business growth. By maintaining a healthy work-life balance, freelancers and independent contractors can achieve long-term success and financial independence, demonstrating that well-being is integral to professional achievement. Embracing self-care and mental health as fundamental components of your work strategy empowers you to navigate the complexities of self-employment with confidence and resilience.

Bringing this discussion to a close, it's clear that financial independence extends far beyond merely managing taxes. Creating multiple streams of income not only diversifies your revenue but also provides a safety net that cushions against the volatility inherent in self-employment. Investing in your future, whether through retirement accounts or other financial instruments, ensures that you are building a solid foundation for long-term security. Achieving a work-life balance is equally crucial; it's about more than just financial stability—it's about cultivating a life that you enjoy and sustaining your well-being.

Reflect on how these elements intertwine to form a holistic approach to financial freedom. This chapter has offered a roadmap, but the journey to true independence involves continuously adapting and expanding your strategies. As you take these insights forward, consider how you can integrate them into your daily life and long-term plans. What steps will you take today to secure your financial future? How will you balance the demands of work with the need for personal fulfillment? There's immense potential in your hands, and it's time to harness it fully, moving forward with confidence and a clear vision for a prosperous future.

Chapter Thirteen

Success Strategies

Venturing into the realm of self-employment can feel like embarking on a grand adventure, filled with both exhilarating highs and daunting challenges. Imagine setting sail on a vast ocean, with financial freedom as your ultimate destination. Along the way, you might encounter turbulent waters and unexpected obstacles, but also moments of pure triumph and satisfaction. It's in these stories of perseverance and success that we find the most valuable lessons and inspiration. Take a moment to consider the journey of those who have navigated these waters before you, forging a path to not only survive but thrive. Their experiences can be a beacon, illuminating the way forward and offering practical insights that textbooks alone cannot provide.

In this chapter, we dive into the rich tapestry of success strategies from financially independent freelancers. These narratives are not just anecdotes; they are roadmaps filled with insights and strategies that have been tested and proven in the real world. From the gritty reality of overcoming tax challenges to the inspiring tales of achieving financial independence, each story serves as a testament to the power of determination and informed decision-making. Readers will find themselves drawn into the lives of fellow freelancers who have faced similar hurdles but have emerged stronger and more financially savvy.

We will also uncover the lessons learned from navigating the often complex and sometimes treacherous waters of self-employed taxes. These valuable takeaways are more than just theoretical concepts; they are practical, actionable strategies that can be applied to your own financial journey. By understanding the triumphs and setbacks of others, you can better prepare yourself to avoid common pitfalls and seize opportunities that lead to financial freedom. As you read on, let these stories inspire you, provide clarity, and empower you to take control of your financial destiny with confidence and ease.

Interviews with Financially Independent Freelancers

Exploring the intricacies of self-employment often reveals a tapestry of strategies, triumphs, and lessons learned. Imagine the journey of Sarah, a freelance graphic designer who once grappled with the unpredictability of her income. Today, she not only comfortably manages her finances but also enjoys the peace of mind that comes with a well-structured tax strategy. Sarah's story, like many others, illustrates that financial independence is not an elusive dream but an achievable reality with the right approach. What sets this apart is the resilience and innovation displayed by those who've mastered the art of navigating self-employed taxes. Their stories provide a wealth of insights and practical strategies that can inspire and guide anyone on a similar path.

From leveraging tax-advantaged accounts to managing the complexities of international tax obligations, the experiences of financially independent freelancers offer a treasure trove of wisdom. These strategies are not just theoretical concepts but real-life applications that have helped individuals transform their financial landscape. As we delve into these interviews, you'll discover how they manage irregular income streams, maximize their savings, and explore global financial opportunities. Each narrative serves as a beacon, illuminating the path to mastering self-employed taxes and building a secure financial future.

Key Strategies for Managing Irregular Income Streams

Managing irregular income streams can be a daunting challenge for freelancers and independent contractors, yet it presents a unique opportunity for financial mastery. One of the most effective strategies is to establish a baseline budget based on the lowest expected monthly income. This conservative approach ensures that essential expenses are covered even during lean periods. For instance, if a freelancer typically earns between $3,000 and $6,000 a month, setting a budget around the lower end of that spectrum can create a safety net. In months where income exceeds the baseline, the surplus can be directed towards savings, investments, or paying down debt, fostering a proactive rather than reactive financial management style.

SUCCESS STRATEGIES

Diversifying income sources is another crucial tactic. Relying on a single client or project can be risky; instead, cultivating multiple streams of income can provide stability. This might involve taking on various clients, engaging in different types of freelance work, or even generating passive income through avenues like digital products or investments. For example, a graphic designer could freelance for various companies, sell design templates online, and invest in dividend-yielding stocks. This diversification not only mitigates risk but also opens up additional revenue streams that can smooth out the financial fluctuations typical in freelance work.

Advanced cash flow management tools can play a pivotal role in handling inconsistent income. Platforms like QuickBooks Self-Employed or FreshBooks offer features specifically tailored for freelancers, such as expense tracking, invoicing, and profit and loss statements. These tools can provide a clearer picture of one's financial health, making it easier to identify trends and plan for the future. Automated reminders for invoice payments and the ability to set aside taxes as income is received can alleviate the stress of irregular earnings, ensuring that finances remain organized and tax obligations are met promptly.

Building a robust emergency fund is another vital strategy. Traditional advice often suggests saving three to six months' worth of expenses, but for freelancers, aiming for six to twelve months can offer greater security. This cushion allows for more resilience in the face of unpredictable income and can provide the flexibility to pursue new opportunities without the immediate pressure of financial instability. For instance, a freelance writer who has built up a substantial emergency fund can afford to take time off to work on a book project, knowing they have the financial resources to support themselves during this period.

Lastly, developing a disciplined savings habit is essential. Automating transfers to savings accounts or tax-advantaged retirement accounts like a SEP IRA or Solo 401(k) ensures that saving becomes a consistent practice rather than an afterthought. This can include setting up automatic transfers from a business account to a personal savings account or earmarking a percentage of each paycheck for future needs. By adopting these habits, freelancers can create a more predictable and stable financial foundation, transforming the challenge of irregular income into an opportunity for long-term financial growth and independence.

Leveraging Tax-Advantaged Accounts for Long-Term Savings

Financial independence for freelancers often hinges on the strategic use of tax-advantaged accounts. These accounts, such as Individual Retirement Accounts (IRAs) and Health Savings Accounts (HSAs), offer a dual benefit of reducing taxable income while fostering long-term savings. For instance, contributing to a Traditional IRA allows self-employed individuals to deduct contributions from their taxable income, thus lowering their tax burden in the present while simultaneously growing their retirement nest egg. The Roth IRA, on the other hand, does not offer immediate tax deductions but provides tax-free withdrawals in retirement, making it a powerful tool for those anticipating higher tax rates in the future. The choice between these accounts should be guided by one's current financial situation and future expectations, enabling a tailored approach to tax efficiency and retirement planning.

In addition to IRAs, Health Savings Accounts (HSAs) present a unique opportunity to save for medical expenses with triple tax advantages: contributions are tax-deductible, growth is tax-free, and withdrawals for qualified medical expenses are also tax-free. For freelancers, who often face higher healthcare costs and fewer employer-sponsored benefits, maximizing HSA contributions can mitigate out-of-pocket expenses while building a reserve for future medical needs. An often-overlooked strategy is treating the HSA as a supplemental retirement account, allowing the balance to grow over time and using it for healthcare expenses in retirement, thereby preserving other retirement funds for non-medical use.

Recent trends indicate a growing awareness among freelancers regarding the importance of self-funded retirement plans. Solo 401(k) plans, for example, offer significant contribution limits that can surpass those of traditional IRAs, making them an attractive option for high-earning freelancers. These plans allow for both employee and employer contributions, providing an avenue for substantial tax-deferred growth. A self-employed individual can contribute up to $22,500 as an employee (as of 2023), with an additional employer contribution up to a combined total of $66,000, depending on net earnings. This flexibility provides a robust framework for aggressive retirement savings and immediate tax benefits.

Advanced strategies include leveraging the Backdoor Roth IRA conversion, particularly beneficial for high-income freelancers who exceed the income limits for direct Roth IRA contributions. This method involves contributing to a Traditional IRA and subsequently converting those funds to a Roth IRA, bypassing the income restrictions. Although this strategy requires careful tax planning to avoid unintended tax liabilities during the conversion process, it remains a powerful tool for securing tax-free income in retirement. Freelancers should engage with tax professionals to navigate the complexities of this approach, ensuring compliance and optimizing tax outcomes.

As freelancers navigate these various options, it is essential to remain proactive and informed about legislative changes that may impact tax-advantaged accounts. For instance, recent proposals aimed at increasing contribution limits or altering the tax treatment of certain accounts could significantly influence long-term savings strategies. Staying abreast of these developments, consulting with financial advisors, and regularly revisiting one's financial plan can ensure that freelancers continue to maximize their tax advantages and secure their financial futures. By leveraging these sophisticated strategies, self-employed individuals can transform their irregular income streams into a stable and prosperous financial foundation.

Navigating International Tax Obligations and Opportunities

Navigating international tax obligations can be daunting for self-employed individuals, but with the right strategies, it can also present unique opportunities. One fundamental principle to understand is the concept of tax residency. Tax residency determines where you are legally required to pay taxes and can significantly impact your overall tax liability. Depending on your country of residence and the nature of your work, you may be subject to taxes in multiple jurisdictions. To manage this complexity, it's crucial to familiarize yourself with the tax treaties between your home country and the countries where you conduct business. These treaties often provide relief from double taxation, allowing you to credit taxes paid in one country against the taxes owed in another.

For instance, a freelance graphic designer based in the United States but working extensively with clients in Europe must be aware of both U.S. tax obligations and the tax requirements of the countries where the clients are located. The Foreign Earned Income Exclusion (FEIE) is one tool that can be leveraged to reduce U.S. tax liability. The FEIE allows qualifying taxpayers to exclude a certain amount of foreign-earned income from U.S. taxation, provided they meet specific residency or physical presence tests. This can significantly lower the taxable income and, consequently, the total tax bill.

It's also important to consider the opportunities for long-term savings through tax-advantaged accounts that cater to international scenarios. For example, the U.S. offers the Foreign Tax Credit (FTC), which can be used to offset the amount of foreign income taxes paid. This means if you are paying taxes to a foreign government, you can potentially reduce your U.S. tax liability by the same amount, avoiding double taxation. Additionally, certain countries offer favorable tax regimes for expatriates, such as the non-domiciled resident status in the United Kingdom, which can provide substantial tax savings on foreign income.

Navigating international tax obligations also involves staying abreast of the latest developments and trends in global taxation. The landscape is continually evolving, with new regulations and international agreements shaping how taxes are administered. For example, the OECD's Base Erosion and Profit Shifting (BEPS) project aims to close gaps in international tax rules that allow income to "disappear" or be artificially shifted to low or no-tax locations. Understanding such initiatives can help self-employed professionals anticipate changes that might affect their tax strategies and adjust accordingly.

Practical insights from financially independent freelancers highlight the importance of proactive planning and leveraging professional expertise. Engaging a tax advisor with experience in international taxation can be invaluable. These experts can help navigate complex regulations, identify opportunities for tax savings, and ensure compliance with all relevant tax laws. Furthermore, utilizing accounting software that supports multi-currency transactions and international tax reporting can streamline the process, making it easier to manage income and expenses across borders.

By embracing these strategies and remaining informed about international tax obligations, self-employed individuals can not only mitigate their tax liabilities but also uncover opportunities to enhance their financial position. This proactive approach fosters a sense of control and confidence, transforming what might seem like a burden into a manageable and even advantageous component of their financial planning.

Inspirational Case Studies

To begin, let's consider the journey of Sarah, a graphic designer who transitioned from a secure corporate job to the unpredictable world of freelancing. Sarah's first year was a whirlwind of client meetings, project deadlines, and financial chaos. She quickly realized that her passion for design was only part of the equation; mastering her finances was equally crucial. One sleepless night, poring over tax documents and receipts, Sarah decided to take control. She began researching strategic tax planning, determined to turn her financial ship around. Her story embodies the essence of this topic: the transformative power of proactive tax management.

Sarah's experience is not unique. Many freelancers face initial financial hurdles that can seem insurmountable. Yet, with the right strategies, these obstacles become stepping stones to success. This section delves into inspirational case studies that demonstrate how freelancers like Sarah have leveraged deductions to maximize savings, reinvest in their businesses, and achieve long-term financial stability. These stories not only offer practical insights but also serve as a testament to the resilience and ingenuity of self-employed individuals. As we explore these narratives, you'll discover the profound impact that strategic tax planning can have on your journey to financial independence.

Overcoming Initial Financial Hurdles Through Strategic Tax Planning

Navigating the initial financial challenges of self-employment can be daunting, but strategic tax planning can pave the way for smoother sailing. One pivotal example comes from Sarah, a graphic designer who transitioned from a salaried position to freelancing. Initially overwhelmed by unpredictable income and the intricacies of self-employment taxes, Sarah sought the guidance of a tax consultant who specialized in freelance finances. By understanding her tax obligations and leveraging tools like estimated tax payments, Sarah was able to manage her cash flow more effectively, preventing the dreaded year-end tax surprise. Her proactive approach allowed her to set aside sufficient funds for taxes, ensuring she stayed compliant while maintaining financial stability.

A crucial aspect of overcoming early financial hurdles is recognizing and capitalizing on available deductions. For instance, Michael, a freelance writer, meticulously tracked his business expenses, including home office costs, software subscriptions, and travel expenses for client meetings. By keeping detailed records and consulting IRS guidelines, he was able to claim substantial deductions. These deductions significantly reduced his taxable income, freeing up capital to reinvest in his business. Michael's story highlights the importance of thorough record-keeping and a nuanced understanding of deductible expenses, which can turn potential financial obstacles into growth opportunities.

Long-term success in self-employment often hinges on creating a sustainable and resilient tax strategy. Emily, an independent consultant, faced initial challenges with fluctuating income and inconsistent cash flow. By implementing a quarterly tax payment system and regularly reviewing her financials, Emily achieved greater control over her finances. She also set up a business savings account specifically for tax payments, ensuring she never dipped into personal funds. This disciplined approach not only helped her avoid penalties but also fostered a sense of financial security, allowing her to focus on growing her consultancy without the constant worry of tax liabilities.

Advanced tax planning strategies also involve leveraging retirement accounts to ensure future financial stability. Alex, a self-employed software developer, took advantage of a Solo 401(k) plan, allowing him to make higher contributions compared to traditional retirement accounts. By deferring a portion of his income into the Solo 401(k), Alex not only reduced his taxable income but also secured his long-term financial future. This strategic move underscored the importance of integrating tax planning with retirement planning, showcasing how self-employed individuals can build a robust financial foundation through informed decisions and proactive measures.

For those navigating the early stages of self-employment, it's essential to explore innovative perspectives and emerging trends in tax planning. For instance, the rise of digital financial tools and apps designed for freelancers can simplify expense tracking and tax filing. Leveraging technology, like using AI-driven accounting software, can provide real-time insights into financial health, enabling more precise tax planning. Additionally, staying informed about changes in tax laws and regulations can offer new opportunities for savings and compliance. By continuously educating themselves and adapting to new tools and trends, self-employed individuals can overcome initial financial hurdles and set a course for sustainable success.

Leveraging Deductions to Maximize Savings and Reinvest in Business Growth

Tax deductions represent a powerful tool for the self-employed, offering a legitimate means to reduce taxable income and reinvest the savings back into the business. By meticulously identifying and claiming all eligible deductions, freelancers can significantly reduce their tax burden. For instance, a photographer who invests in high-quality camera equipment, software, and travel for shoots can deduct these expenses, effectively lowering their taxable income. This strategy not only conserves cash but also allows for continual upgrading of tools and technology, which can enhance the quality of work and attract more clients. Understanding the nuances of what qualifies as a deductible expense is crucial; expenses must be both ordinary and necessary for the business.

Consider the case of a freelance graphic designer who utilized home office deductions to great effect. By allocating a portion of their home expenses, such as rent, utilities, and internet costs, towards their business, they were able to claim a significant deduction. This not only reduced their overall tax liability but also freed up capital that could be reinvested into the business for marketing, software upgrades, or professional development courses. The IRS provides clear guidelines on how to calculate and claim these deductions, ensuring that freelancers can maximize their savings legitimately. Staying updated with these guidelines is essential, as tax laws and allowable deductions can change.

Innovative approaches to leveraging deductions can also involve proactive financial planning. For example, investing in retirement accounts such as a SEP-IRA or a Solo 401(k) not only secures future financial stability but also offers immediate tax benefits. Contributions to these accounts are deductible, reducing taxable income for the year. A freelance consultant who sets aside a portion of their earnings into a Solo 401(k) can significantly lower their tax bill while building a robust retirement fund. This dual benefit underscores the importance of integrating tax planning with long-term financial goals.

Recent trends indicate a growing awareness among freelancers of the benefits of professional development and education. Deductions for courses, seminars, and certifications related to the business can be substantial. Take, for instance, a freelance writer who invests in a writing workshop or a digital marketing course. These expenses are deductible, reducing the immediate tax burden while enhancing skills and marketability. This strategic reinvestment not only promotes business growth but also positions the freelancer competitively in the market. Staying abreast of industry developments and continuously upgrading skills can lead to higher earning potential and greater financial resilience.

Tax planning for the self-employed should be an ongoing process, not a last-minute scramble before tax deadlines. Regularly reviewing income and expenses, consulting with tax professionals, and leveraging accounting software can provide a clear picture of financial health and tax obligations. A strategic approach to deductions can transform tax season from a period of anxiety into an opportunity for financial optimization. By viewing tax planning as an integral part of business strategy, freelancers can achieve a more stable, growth-oriented financial footing.

Achieving Long-Term Financial Stability with Comprehensive Retirement Strategies

Financial stability in the long term hinges on a well-structured retirement plan, especially for self-employed individuals who cannot rely on employer-sponsored retirement programs. Modern freelancers can leverage several retirement account options tailored to their needs, such as SEP IRAs, SIMPLE IRAs, and Solo 401(k)s. Each of these accounts offers unique advantages and tax benefits. For instance, the Solo 401(k) allows for higher contribution limits compared to traditional IRAs, making it a robust option for high-earning freelancers. By maximizing these contributions, self-employed individuals can significantly reduce their taxable income while simultaneously building a substantial nest egg.

One compelling case study involves a freelance graphic designer who, after struggling initially with inconsistent income, strategically utilized a SEP IRA to stabilize her financial future. By allocating a percentage of her monthly earnings into her retirement account, she not only enjoyed immediate tax deductions but also capitalized on compound growth over time. This disciplined approach enabled her to accumulate a sizable retirement fund, which provided her with the financial security to weather the natural ebbs and flows of freelance work. Her story underscores the importance of early and consistent retirement planning, demonstrating that even modest, regular contributions can grow significantly over time.

SUCCESS STRATEGIES

Innovative strategies also play a crucial role in achieving long-term financial stability. One such strategy involves the concept of tax diversification, which means spreading retirement savings across various account types—tax-deferred, tax-free, and taxable. This diversification can provide greater flexibility in managing taxable income during retirement. For example, having funds in a Roth IRA, which allows for tax-free withdrawals, can be advantageous when navigating different tax brackets in the future. By employing a mix of these account types, freelancers can optimize their tax situation both now and in retirement, ensuring they have multiple streams of income that can be managed to minimize tax liabilities.

Another inspiring story is of a software developer who leveraged deductions to bolster his retirement savings. By meticulously tracking business expenses and maximizing allowable deductions, he reduced his taxable income, freeing up more capital to invest in his Solo 401(k). This proactive tax planning enabled him to contribute the maximum allowable limit each year, accelerating his savings growth. His approach highlights the symbiotic relationship between effective tax management and retirement planning, demonstrating how diligent expense tracking and strategic deductions can directly enhance long-term financial outcomes.

It's crucial to stay informed about evolving retirement planning opportunities and legislation changes. Recent years have seen significant shifts in retirement account regulations, such as increased contribution limits and new tax incentives. Staying abreast of these changes can offer self-employed individuals additional advantages. For instance, the SECURE Act of 2019 introduced provisions that make it easier for small business owners, including freelancers, to set up retirement plans. By keeping informed and adaptable, self-employed professionals can continuously optimize their retirement strategies, ensuring they remain aligned with the latest benefits and protections offered by new laws. This proactive approach not only safeguards their future but also enhances their overall financial resilience.

Lessons Learned from Tax Challenges

It's intriguing to note that even the most seasoned freelancers have faced their fair share of tax challenges. Consider the story of Maria, a successful graphic designer who thought she had her finances all figured out until an unexpected

210   MASTERING SELF-EMPLOYED TAXES

audit turned her world upside down. Despite her meticulous efforts, Maria discovered gaps in her record-keeping that led to significant stress and financial strain. This experience, though daunting, became a turning point in her professional journey, teaching her invaluable lessons about the importance of detailed documentation, staying updated with tax laws, and seeking professional advice. Maria's story is not unique; many self-employed individuals find themselves in similar predicaments, transforming these challenges into opportunities for growth and financial empowerment.

What sets this apart is how these real-life experiences highlight the critical need for robust financial practices. As we dive deeper into these lessons, you'll see that detailed record-keeping is the backbone of any successful tax strategy. Adapting to ever-changing tax regulations is not just a necessity but a skill that can be honed over time. Moreover, leveraging professional advice can be the difference between a minor hiccup and a financial disaster. By sharing these stories and insights, this chapter aims to equip you with the knowledge and confidence to navigate your tax obligations with mastery and achieve the financial freedom you aspire to.

Emphasizing the Importance of Detailed Record-Keeping

Detailed record-keeping is the backbone of effective tax management for self-employed individuals. Meticulous records ensure that every transaction is accounted for, which is crucial when it comes to deductions and tax filings. For instance, maintaining a comprehensive log of business expenses—ranging from office supplies to travel costs—helps freelancers maximize their deductible claims. This level of detail not only supports compliance with tax regulations but also provides a clear financial picture, aiding in better decision-making and financial planning. It's not just about avoiding audits; it's about creating a solid foundation for financial health.

Advanced digital tools have revolutionized the way freelancers manage their records. Apps and software designed specifically for self-employed individuals can automate much of the record-keeping process. These tools can track income, categorize expenses, and even integrate with bank accounts to ensure nothing is overlooked. The automation of these tasks reduces the margin of error and saves time, allowing freelancers to focus more on their core work. Utilizing such technology demonstrates a proactive approach to financial management, which is essential for long-term success.

Adapting to new tax regulations is another critical aspect where detailed record-keeping proves invaluable. Tax laws are in constant flux, and what was deductible last year might not be this year. By keeping thorough records, freelancers can quickly adjust to these changes without scrambling for information. For example, when the Tax Cuts and Jobs Act introduced new rules for pass-through entities, those with detailed records could easily navigate the transition. Staying informed and adaptable, backed by meticulous records, ensures compliance and optimizes tax positions in an ever-evolving landscape.

Professional advice becomes significantly more effective when supported by well-organized records. Tax professionals can offer tailored strategies and insights when they have access to accurate and comprehensive financial data. For instance, a tax advisor can better identify opportunities for tax savings or restructuring when provided with detailed financial statements and expenditure logs. This collaborative approach not only enhances the accuracy of tax filings but also opens doors to advanced tax strategies that might otherwise be overlooked. Detailed records transform tax preparation from a reactive task into a strategic exercise.

The importance of detailed record-keeping extends beyond compliance and optimization. It fosters a habit of financial mindfulness, encouraging freelancers to regularly review and understand their financial status. This practice can highlight spending patterns, identify unnecessary expenses, and reveal opportunities for investment and growth. For instance, tracking every expense might show that a significant portion of income is spent on non-essential services, prompting a reevaluation of spending habits. By cultivating a culture of detailed record-keeping, freelancers not only ensure tax readiness but also build a robust foundation for financial independence.

Adapting to Changing Tax Regulations and Laws

Navigating the ever-evolving landscape of tax regulations and laws is a critical skill for the self-employed. Flexibility and vigilance are paramount, as tax codes can change frequently and often without much warning. This demands a proactive approach, ensuring freelancers and independent contractors stay ahead of the curve. Regularly updating one's knowledge through reliable sources—such as IRS publications, tax webinars, and professional tax advice—can help maintain compliance and optimize tax strategies. Proactively adapting to these changes not only prevents costly mistakes but also unveils new opportunities for tax savings and financial growth. Consider the case of a freelance graphic designer who, after several years of steady income, faced a significant shift when new tax laws came into effect, altering the deductibility of certain business expenses. By promptly consulting a tax professional, she learned how to reclassify some of her expenses and adjust her invoicing methods to remain compliant while still benefiting from available deductions. This adaptability not only shielded her from potential penalties but also enhanced her overall financial strategy, demonstrating the value of staying informed and responsive to changing regulations.

Beyond basic compliance, understanding and adapting to tax law changes can also present strategic advantages. For instance, recent shifts in laws surrounding retirement contributions have opened up new avenues for self-employed individuals to save for the future while enjoying immediate tax benefits. Solo 401(k)s and SEP IRAs offer flexible and robust options that can be tailored to varying income levels, enabling freelancers to maximize their retirement savings and reduce taxable income. Keeping abreast of such changes ensures that self-employed individuals can leverage the most advantageous options available.

Incorporating technology can further streamline the process of staying updated and adapting to new tax laws. Digital tools and software solutions are continuously being developed to help freelancers track changes in tax codes and integrate them seamlessly into their financial management practices. Utilizing these advanced tools not only simplifies the adaptation process but also provides real-time insights and alerts, ensuring that self-employed individuals can make informed decisions quickly. This tech-savvy approach can be a game-changer, reducing the cognitive load and administrative burden associated with tax compliance.

The ability to adapt to evolving tax regulations and laws is not just about avoiding pitfalls; it is about seizing opportunities for financial optimization and growth. By fostering a mindset of continuous learning and flexibility, self-employed individuals can turn the challenges of changing tax landscapes into stepping stones towards greater financial independence. This proactive, informed approach empowers freelancers to not only navigate the complexities of tax obligations with confidence but also to thrive in the dynamic world of self-employment.

Leveraging Professional Advice for Complex Tax Situations

Navigating the labyrinth of self-employed taxes can be daunting, especially when faced with intricate tax situations. Leveraging professional advice often becomes indispensable in such scenarios. Tax advisors and financial consultants bring a wealth of expertise that can demystify complicated tax codes and regulations. For freelancers and independent contractors dealing with diverse income streams, complex deductions, or international tax obligations, the insight from a seasoned professional can be transformative. These experts not only ensure compliance with tax laws but also optimize tax savings, allowing freelancers to focus more on their work and less on financial worries.

Consider the example of a freelance graphic designer who operates both domestically and internationally. The designer receives payments in multiple currencies and encounters varying tax obligations across jurisdictions. Attempting to manage this alone could lead to costly errors. By consulting a tax professional experienced in international tax law, the designer can navigate the nuanced requirements of different countries, ensuring accurate reporting and maximizing allowable deductions. This proactive approach mitigates the risk of audits and penalties while securing a more favorable financial position.

Tax professionals also stay abreast of ever-evolving tax regulations, an area where freelancers might struggle. Tax laws can change frequently, influenced by new legislation, economic shifts, or policy reforms. A tax advisor's role includes keeping their clients informed about these changes and advising on necessary adjustments. For instance, if new legislation introduces additional deductions for home office expenses or alters the criteria for health insurance tax credits, a knowledgeable advisor would promptly guide their clients on how to benefit from these updates. This ensures freelancers continually benefit from the most current tax advantages available.

The strategic input of tax professionals can be invaluable during significant business transitions or life events. Whether transitioning from part-time freelancing to running a full-time business, dealing with the sale of substantial assets, or planning for retirement, these professionals provide tailored advice that aligns with long-term financial goals. For example, a freelance writer planning to retire might receive guidance on setting up a solo 401(k) or a SEP IRA, ensuring tax-efficient retirement savings. This strategic planning not only facilitates a smoother transition but also fortifies the freelancer's financial future.

214 MASTERING SELF-EMPLOYED TAXES

To fully leverage professional advice, it's essential for freelancers to cultivate a collaborative relationship with their tax advisors. Regular consultations, transparent communication about income and expenses, and a proactive approach to seeking advice before making significant financial decisions can all contribute to more effective tax management. Freelancers should view their tax advisor not just as a compliance officer but as a strategic partner in their financial journey. This partnership can unearth opportunities for tax savings, enhance financial stability, and ultimately contribute to achieving financial independence.

As we weave together the narratives of financially independent freelancers and the lessons they've shared, it becomes evident that achieving mastery over self-employed taxes is not just about numbers and forms—it's about resilience, adaptability, and a commitment to continuous learning. The personal stories and success strategies highlighted in this chapter offer a mosaic of experiences that underscore the transformative power of proactive financial management. From overcoming initial tax blunders to leveraging deductions and planning for retirement, these real-life examples serve as a testament to what is possible when one approaches self-employment with a strategic mindset and an unwavering dedication to financial growth.

Reflecting on the journeys of these individuals, it is clear that the path to financial freedom is paved with both challenges and triumphs. Their stories resonate with the central themes of this book: the importance of staying informed, the value of meticulous record-keeping, and the benefits of seeking professional advice when necessary. Each narrative not only reinforces the practical advice provided throughout the book but also inspires a deeper understanding of the broader financial landscape. As you move forward, consider how these insights can be applied to your own journey, and remember that every step, no matter how small, brings you closer to mastering self-employed taxes and achieving lasting financial independence.

Chapter Fourteen

Staying Organized And Motivated

Going deeper, we find that the journey to financial freedom is not just about numbers and tax forms; it's also about cultivating habits that keep us organized and motivated. Picture this: a freelancer, juggling multiple clients and deadlines, feeling overwhelmed by the chaos of receipts, invoices, and tax deadlines. Yet, in the midst of this hustle, there is a path to serenity and control. Imagine transforming from a state of disarray to one where every financial document is at your fingertips, and every tax payment is meticulously planned. This chapter is dedicated to guiding you through that transformation.

Effective time management is the cornerstone of staying organized. It's about mastering the art of balancing work responsibilities with the meticulous task of maintaining financial records. We will explore practical strategies that not only help you track your income and expenses throughout the year but also ensure that you're prepared for every tax season. By adopting these methods, you'll find yourself spending less time searching for missing documents and more time focusing on what you love—your work.

The path to financial freedom is also deeply intertwined with staying motivated. It's easy to feel discouraged when faced with complex tax regulations and the constant pressure of financial planning. But remember, every step you take towards organization and proactive management is a step towards liberation from financial stress. We'll share stories of individuals who have conquered these challenges, offering inspiration and practical advice. By the end of this chapter, you'll have a toolkit of strategies to keep you motivated and on track, turning

216 MASTERING SELF-EMPLOYED TAXES

the daunting task of tax management into an empowering journey towards financial independence.

Developing Effective Time Management Skills

Let's start with a fundamental question: How often do you feel overwhelmed by the sheer volume of tasks on your to-do list, only to realize that the day has slipped through your fingers with minimal progress? For many self-employed individuals, this scenario is all too familiar. The freedom that comes with being your own boss is exhilarating, but it also brings the challenge of managing your time effectively. Imagine a day where every hour is purposeful, every task is tackled efficiently, and you end each day with a sense of accomplishment rather than fatigue. This isn't some distant dream—it's entirely within reach through mastering effective time management skills.

Consider the story of Sarah, a freelance graphic designer who once struggled with chaotic workdays and missed deadlines. Sarah's transformation began when she discovered the power of time blocking, productivity tools, and advanced goal-setting techniques. By prioritizing tasks, leveraging technology, and setting clear, achievable goals, she turned her scattered schedule into a well-oiled machine. This chapter will guide you through these strategies, showing you how to harness your time so you can not only meet your financial goals but also enjoy the journey toward financial freedom. Ready to take control of your time and, by extension, your future? Let's delve into the essential skills that can make this possible.

Prioritizing Tasks Through Time Blocking

Time blocking is a powerful technique that allows self-employed individuals to manage their tasks more effectively by allocating specific periods for particular activities. Instead of juggling multiple tasks simultaneously, time blocking promotes focused effort, which enhances productivity and reduces stress. For instance, a freelance graphic designer might allocate morning hours exclusively for client projects, reserving afternoons for administrative tasks like invoicing and email correspondence. This structured approach not only organizes one's day but also fosters a sense of accomplishment as tasks are completed within designated time frames.

Modern productivity tools can elevate the effectiveness of time blocking. Applications like Google Calendar, Trello, and Asana offer customizable features that help users visualize their schedules and track progress. These tools often come with reminders and notifications, ensuring that no crucial task slips through the cracks. For example, a gig worker using Trello can create boards for different clients or projects, assign deadlines, and move tasks through various stages of completion. This visual representation aids in maintaining focus and provides a clear roadmap of what needs to be achieved, further reinforcing the benefits of time blocking.

Advanced goal-setting techniques can significantly enhance the efficacy of time blocking. The SMART (Specific, Measurable, Achievable, Relevant, Time-bound) framework, for example, can be seamlessly integrated into time blocking schedules. By setting clear and realistic goals, self-employed individuals can break down large projects into manageable blocks of time. For example, a writer aiming to complete a book might set a goal to write 1,000 words daily, reserving a two-hour block each morning to achieve this target. This method not only makes the goal seem more attainable but also ensures consistent progress, reducing the likelihood of burnout and procrastination.

Emerging research underscores the cognitive benefits of time blocking, particularly in managing cognitive load and enhancing mental clarity. Studies suggest that dedicating specific times for deep work can lead to higher quality output and greater creative breakthroughs. For instance, a software developer might set aside uninterrupted blocks of time for coding, minimizing distractions and allowing for deeper engagement with complex tasks. This approach not only boosts productivity but also improves the quality of work, as the mind is not constantly switching between tasks, which can lead to errors and oversight.

To sustain motivation and commitment to time blocking, it can be helpful to periodically review and adjust one's schedule based on evolving priorities and outcomes. Reflecting on what works and what doesn't can provide valuable insights into personal productivity patterns. Additionally, incorporating short breaks and rewards after completing time blocks can keep energy levels high and maintain a positive outlook. For example, a consultant might take a brief walk or enjoy a favorite snack after finishing a two-hour client meeting block. These small incentives can significantly enhance motivation, making time blocking not just a productivity tool, but a sustainable and enjoyable practice.

Utilizing Productivity Tools and Applications

Productivity tools and applications have revolutionized the way self-employed individuals manage their time, offering a plethora of options to enhance efficiency and streamline tasks. One of the most effective tools for freelancers and independent contractors is project management software like Trello or Asana. These platforms allow users to create boards, lists, and cards that can be customized to fit specific projects or tasks, providing a visual and interactive way to track progress. By breaking down large projects into manageable tasks and setting deadlines, these tools help ensure that nothing falls through the cracks. Additionally, integrating these platforms with calendar applications ensures that your schedule is always up-to-date, reducing the likelihood of missed deadlines.

Another invaluable category of productivity tools is time-tracking applications such as Toggl or Harvest. These applications not only help freelancers keep an accurate record of the time spent on various tasks but also provide insights into how time is being allocated across different projects. This data is crucial for billing clients accurately and can also highlight areas where time management can be improved. By analyzing time-tracking reports, self-employed individuals can identify patterns and make informed decisions about how to optimize their workflows for maximum efficiency.

For those juggling multiple clients and projects, customer relationship management (CRM) systems like HubSpot or Zoho CRM can be game-changers. These tools help manage client interactions, track sales pipelines, and organize client-related tasks all in one place. CRMs offer advanced features such as automated follow-ups, email tracking, and integrated communication channels, making it easier to maintain strong client relationships and ensure that follow-ups are timely and relevant. By automating routine tasks, freelancers can focus more on delivering high-quality work and less on administrative duties.

Emerging trends in productivity tools also include artificial intelligence (AI) and machine learning algorithms that can predict and suggest optimal times for task completion based on past behavior. Tools like RescueTime use AI to analyze how you spend your time on digital activities and provide personalized recommendations for improvement. Similarly, AI-driven assistants like Clara or x.ai can schedule meetings and appointments by understanding your preferences and availability, thus eliminating the back-and-forth of email scheduling.

STAYING ORGANIZED AND MOTIVATED 219

These innovations not only save time but also help create a more balanced and productive work routine.

Collaboration tools such as Slack or Microsoft Teams have become indispensable for remote workers and freelancers. These platforms facilitate real-time communication and file sharing, making it easier to collaborate with clients and team members, regardless of geographical locations. Features like channels, direct messaging, and video conferencing provide multiple avenues for interaction, ensuring that everyone remains on the same page. By leveraging these tools, self-employed individuals can enhance their collaborative efforts, leading to more cohesive and efficient project execution.

Incorporating these productivity tools and applications into daily routines can significantly elevate the efficiency and effectiveness of self-employed individuals. The key lies in selecting the right combination of tools that align with one's specific needs and workflow, ensuring that time is managed wisely and goals are met consistently.

Implementing Advanced Goal-Setting Techniques

Setting effective goals is a cornerstone of successful time management for the self-employed. Advanced goal-setting techniques go beyond simple to-do lists, focusing instead on creating a structured framework that drives sustained progress. One such technique is the SMART criteria—Specific, Measurable, Achievable, Relevant, and Time-bound. By using SMART goals, freelancers and independent contractors can break down large, intimidating objectives into smaller, manageable tasks. For instance, converting a broad goal like "increase annual income" into a SMART goal might look like "increase monthly income by $500 over the next six months by securing three new clients." This approach not only clarifies the goal but also provides a clear timeline and measurable outcomes, facilitating a more focused and productive work ethic.

Another powerful technique is the implementation of OKRs—Objectives and Key Results. This methodology, popularized by companies like Google, aligns larger, aspirational goals with specific, quantifiable results. For a gig worker, an OKR might involve setting an objective like "become a top-rated seller on a freelance platform" with key results such as "complete 50 projects with a 5-star rating" and "achieve a 95% client retention rate within a year." By linking ambitious objectives with clear, actionable steps, OKRs help maintain momentum and provide a tangible way to track progress and celebrate milestones.

This alignment of large-scale aspirations with concrete actions can significantly enhance motivation and productivity.

Mind mapping is another innovative tool for setting and achieving goals. This visual technique allows self-employed individuals to brainstorm and organize their thoughts in a non-linear fashion, fostering creativity and uncovering new connections between ideas. For example, a freelance graphic designer might create a mind map to explore various income streams, such as client projects, online courses, and passive income through print sales. By visually laying out these possibilities, the designer can identify the most promising avenues and develop a strategic plan to pursue them. Mind mapping encourages a holistic view of one's career, making it easier to prioritize tasks and allocate time effectively.

The use of gamification in goal setting can transform mundane tasks into engaging challenges. By incorporating elements of game design—such as points, levels, and rewards—into daily routines, self-employed individuals can boost their motivation and enjoyment of work. For instance, a freelance writer might set up a point system where completing a blog post earns points towards a reward, like a leisure activity or a small purchase. This playful approach not only makes goal-setting more enjoyable but also fosters a sense of achievement and progress, which is crucial for maintaining long-term motivation and enthusiasm.

Reflection and adjustment are critical components of advanced goal-setting. Regularly reviewing and reassessing goals ensures they remain aligned with evolving priorities and circumstances. Self-employed individuals should set aside time each month to evaluate their progress, celebrate successes, and make necessary adjustments. This iterative process fosters a growth mindset, encouraging continuous improvement and adaptability. For instance, if a freelance photographer finds that their initial goal of entering a new market is not yielding the expected results, they can pivot their strategy based on feedback and new insights. By embracing a dynamic approach to goal-setting, self-employed professionals can stay resilient and responsive in a rapidly changing work environment.

Maintaining Financial Records Throughout the Year

What makes this interesting is how the simple act of maintaining financial records throughout the year can transform the daunting task of tax preparation into a smooth, almost effortless process. Imagine the relief of knowing that every receipt, every invoice, and every expense has been meticulously tracked and recorded. Picture yourself at the end of the tax year, not scrambling to find missing documents or deciphering a pile of unorganized papers, but sitting calmly with a clear and comprehensive financial overview at your fingertips. This is not just a fantasy—it's a reality that can be achieved with consistent effort and the right tools.

In today's digital age, the opportunities to streamline this process are virtually limitless. From leveraging advanced accounting software that offers real-time insights to implementing a monthly reconciliation process that keeps your finances in check, the possibilities for efficiency and accuracy are immense. Utilizing digital tools for real-time expense tracking ensures nothing slips through the cracks, while sophisticated software can provide a comprehensive financial analysis that empowers you to make informed decisions. By embracing these strategies, you not only simplify your tax obligations but also gain a deeper understanding of your financial health, setting the stage for long-term success and peace of mind.

Utilize Digital Tools for Real-Time Expense Tracking

Harnessing digital tools for real-time expense tracking can revolutionize the way self-employed individuals manage their finances. In today's fast-paced world, relying on manual processes is both time-consuming and prone to error. By integrating digital solutions, freelancers, gig workers, and independent contractors can streamline their financial record-keeping, ensuring accuracy and efficiency. Applications like QuickBooks Self-Employed, Wave, and FreshBooks offer intuitive interfaces that allow users to categorize expenses, upload receipts, and monitor cash flow in real-time. These platforms often come with mobile apps, allowing users to log expenses on the go, thus eliminating the backlog of unrecorded transactions.

One of the primary advantages of utilizing these digital tools is the automation of routine tasks. For instance, many of these applications can connect directly to bank accounts and credit cards, automatically importing and categorizing transactions. This not only saves time but also reduces the risk of missing deductions. For example, an independent contractor can set up rules within the app to automatically classify recurring expenses such as software subscriptions or office supplies, ensuring that every eligible expense is captured without manual intervention. This level of automation provides peace of mind and allows self-employed individuals to focus more on their core business activities.

Real-time expense tracking tools often feature robust reporting capabilities that provide valuable insights into spending patterns and financial health. These tools can generate detailed reports that highlight areas of high expenditure, helping users identify opportunities for cost savings. For example, a freelancer might discover through these reports that they are spending a significant amount on dining out during business trips, prompting them to seek more cost-effective alternatives. This level of granular analysis can inform better budgeting decisions and foster a more strategic approach to financial management.

Another critical aspect of these digital tools is their ability to ensure compliance with tax regulations. By maintaining up-to-date records and categorizing expenses correctly, freelancers can easily generate accurate financial statements required for tax filings. This reduces the risk of errors and potential audits. Additionally, some advanced tools offer features like tax estimates and reminders for quarterly tax payments, helping users stay on top of their obligations. For example, a gig worker can use these features to set aside the appropriate amount of money for taxes each month, avoiding the last-minute scramble to gather funds for tax payments.

The integration of digital tools into financial management practices fosters a sense of control and empowerment. By having a clear, real-time view of their financial situation, self-employed individuals can make informed decisions that align with their long-term goals. This proactive approach not only enhances financial stability but also contributes to overall well-being. For instance, the confidence gained from knowing that their finances are in order can motivate a freelancer to take on new projects or explore growth opportunities without the constant worry of financial mismanagement. The sense of order and clarity provided by these tools can be a powerful motivator on the journey to financial freedom.

Implement a Monthly Reconciliation Process

Implementing a monthly reconciliation process is a strategic approach to ensuring that your financial records are accurate and up-to-date. This meticulous practice involves comparing your recorded transactions with your bank statements to identify and rectify any discrepancies. By doing this regularly, you can catch errors early, such as missed expenses, double entries, or unauthorized transactions, which can significantly impact your financial health. This routine not only helps maintain the integrity of your financial data but also provides a clearer picture of your cash flow, crucial for making informed business decisions.

To begin, set a dedicated time each month to perform the reconciliation. Consistency is key; choosing a specific day, such as the first Monday of each month, can help integrate this task into your regular workflow. During the reconciliation, ensure that every transaction listed in your bank statement matches the entries in your accounting records. For instance, if you notice a discrepancy in a client's payment, you can promptly address it, avoiding potential misunderstandings or financial shortfalls. This level of diligence is particularly vital for self-employed individuals who juggle multiple income streams and expenses.

Leveraging technology can significantly streamline the reconciliation process. Advanced accounting software like QuickBooks or Xero offers features that automatically import bank transactions and flag discrepancies for review. These tools can save time and reduce the likelihood of human error. Moreover, many of these platforms provide real-time insights and analytics, enhancing your ability to monitor financial trends and make proactive adjustments. Utilizing such software not only simplifies the reconciliation process but also integrates seamlessly with other financial management tasks, creating a cohesive system that supports your business's growth.

It's also beneficial to maintain a separate business bank account. Mixing personal and business finances can complicate reconciliation and obscure your financial picture. Having distinct accounts ensures clarity and simplifies the tracking of business-related income and expenses. Additionally, consider using a business credit card for expenses, which can provide detailed statements that further aid in the reconciliation process. This practice not only enhances organizational efficiency but also establishes a professional financial structure, which can be advantageous when seeking loans or investment.

Stay vigilant about evolving best practices and tools in financial reconciliation. The landscape of financial technology is rapidly advancing, with new tools and methodologies emerging that can offer even greater efficiencies. For example, artificial intelligence and machine learning are beginning to play roles in predictive financial analysis and error detection, providing more robust and intelligent reconciliation solutions. Staying informed about these innovations can provide you with a competitive edge, ensuring that your financial management practices remain cutting-edge and effective. Through disciplined monthly

224 MASTERING SELF-EMPLOYED TAXES

reconciliation, you not only safeguard your financial accuracy but also culti-vate a proactive mindset that drives long-term success and financial freedom.

Leverage Advanced Accounting Software for Comprehensive Financial Analysis

Investing in advanced accounting software can revolutionize the way self-employed individuals manage their finances, offering a comprehensive suite of tools that go far beyond basic bookkeeping. These sophisticated systems are designed to handle complex financial data, providing real-time insights and detailed analyses that can significantly enhance your financial strategy. For instance, software like QuickBooks Online, Xero, or Fresh-Books offers features such as automated expense tracking, invoicing, and tax preparation. These platforms not only streamline daily financial tasks but also offer robust reporting capabilities that can help identify trends, optimize cash flow, and forecast future financial performance. By leveraging such tools, self-employed individuals can gain a clearer picture of their financial health and make more informed decisions.

One of the standout features of advanced accounting software is its ability to integrate with various financial services and applications. This integration can include bank accounts, payment processors, and even e-commerce plat-forms, ensuring that all financial data is captured and synchronized automat-ically. Such seamless connectivity reduces the risk of errors and omissions, which can be critical during tax season. For example, linking your accounting software to your bank account can automate the reconciliation process, ensuring that every transaction is accounted for and categorized correctly. This automation not only saves time but also enhances accuracy, providing peace of mind that your financial records are always up-to-date and reliable.

Another significant advantage of using advanced accounting software is the enhanced security it provides. These platforms often come with state-of-the-art encryption and security protocols to protect sensitive financial information from unauthorized access and cyber threats. Given the increasing prevalence of data breaches and cyber-attacks, safeguarding your financial data is more important than ever. Additionally, many accounting software solutions offer multi-factor authentication and regular security updates, further ensuring that your information remains secure. This level of protection can be particularly reassuring for self-employed individuals who may not have the resources to invest in extensive IT security measures on their own.

Advanced accounting software also empowers users with sophisticated analytical tools that can provide deeper insights into their financial performance. Features such as customizable dashboards, financial KPIs, and predictive analytics can help users identify potential issues before they become critical problems. For example, cash flow analysis tools can pinpoint periods of fluctuating income and expenses, allowing for better budgeting and financial planning. Scenario analysis features can simulate various financial outcomes based on different assumptions, helping users prepare for different contingencies. By utilizing these advanced tools, self-employed individuals can develop more strategic financial plans and improve their overall financial resilience.

To make the most of advanced accounting software, it is essential to stay current with the latest updates and features. Many software providers offer regular updates that introduce new functionalities and enhancements. Keeping abreast of these changes can ensure you are leveraging the full potential of the software. Additionally, taking advantage of online tutorials, webinars, and user communities can provide valuable insights and tips on how to maximize the software's capabilities. This continuous learning approach not only keeps your financial management practices sharp but also ensures that you are always using the most efficient and effective tools available. In this way, advanced accounting software becomes an indispensable ally on the journey to financial freedom.

Staying Motivated on the Path to Financial Freedom

Let's start by examining an all-too-common scenario: You're knee-deep in client projects, deadlines looming, and the last thing on your mind is your financial planning. Weeks go by, and before you know it, tax season is right around the corner, leaving you scrambling to gather documents and make sense of your expenses. Sound familiar? This chaotic approach can not only drain your energy but also hinder your progress toward financial freedom. The secret to breaking this cycle lies in staying motivated and organized, no matter how hectic your schedule becomes. By setting clear financial goals, incorporating regular financial reviews into your routine, and celebrating your milestones, you can transform what often feels like a tedious chore into an empowering journey.

Imagine the satisfaction of seeing your financial dreams gradually become a reality, simply by making small, consistent efforts. It's not just about crunching numbers; it's about fostering a mindset that keeps you motivated and focused. When you set clear and achievable goals, you create a roadmap that guides your financial decisions, reducing stress and providing a sense of direction. Developing a routine that includes regular financial reviews serves as a checkpoint, ensuring you're on track and allowing for necessary adjustments. And let's not forget the importance of celebrating milestones—these moments of recognition and reflection can reignite your motivation and remind you of the progress you've made. These strategies collectively form a robust framework that supports your path to financial freedom, proving that with the right approach, managing your finances can be both rewarding and inspiring.

Set Clear and Achievable Financial Goals

Setting clear and achievable financial goals is paramount for anyone on the path to financial independence, particularly for self-employed individuals who navigate the complexities of fluctuating income and unique tax obligations. By defining specific objectives, freelancers and independent contractors can create a roadmap that not only guides their financial decisions but also serves as a motivational tool. For example, a graphic designer might set a goal to save $10,000 for a down payment on a home within two years. This concrete target provides a clear destination, making the journey towards financial freedom more tangible and manageable.

A crucial aspect of setting these goals is ensuring they are both realistic and challenging. Goals that are too easily attainable may not provide the necessary drive, while overly ambitious targets can lead to frustration and burnout. Utilizing the SMART criteria—Specific, Measurable, Achievable, Relevant, and Time-bound—can be an effective strategy. For instance, instead of a vague objective like "save more money," a self-employed writer could aim to "increase monthly savings by 15% over the next six months." This specific, measurable goal is not only motivating but also provides a clear benchmark for progress.

Regularly revisiting and adjusting financial goals is essential to stay on track. Life circumstances, market conditions, and personal priorities can shift, making it necessary to reassess and modify objectives accordingly. Self-employed individuals should schedule periodic financial reviews—monthly or quarterly—to evaluate their progress and make any necessary adjustments. This proactive

STAYING ORGANIZED AND MOTIVATED

approach ensures that goals remain relevant and aligned with current realities. For example, a freelance web developer might find that a sudden influx of work allows for more aggressive savings targets, whereas a lean period might require a temporary scaling back.

In addition to setting and revisiting goals, it's beneficial to break down larger financial objectives into smaller, more manageable milestones. These incremental steps can provide a sense of achievement and maintain motivation over the long haul. A self-employed consultant aiming to build a six-month emergency fund might start by saving enough for one month, then two, and so on. Each milestone reached is an opportunity to celebrate and reflect on the progress made, reinforcing the positive behaviors and decisions that contribute to financial stability.

Integrating financial goals into a broader vision of personal and professional success can enhance motivation and commitment. Understanding how these goals align with one's values and long-term aspirations provides deeper meaning and context. For example, a freelance photographer might view financial independence not just as a means to an end, but as a way to support creative freedom and the ability to choose projects that align with their artistic vision. By connecting financial goals to a larger purpose, self-employed individuals can sustain their motivation and drive, even when faced with inevitable challenges and setbacks. This holistic approach ensures that the journey to financial freedom is both purposeful and fulfilling.

Develop a Routine That Incorporates Regular Financial Reviews

Establishing a routine that includes regular financial reviews is a cornerstone of maintaining financial health for self-employed individuals. It begins with allocating specific times in your schedule to examine your financial records, much like a recurring appointment with yourself. Think of these sessions as not just obligatory tasks, but opportunities to gain insights into your financial trajectory. Start by setting a bi-weekly or monthly time slot dedicated to this exercise. During these sessions, scrutinize your income streams, monitor expenses, and ensure all transactions are accurately recorded. This regularity helps in identifying patterns, spotting discrepancies early, and making informed decisions based on real-time data, rather than reacting to surprises at tax season.

To enhance the effectiveness of these reviews, leverage modern financial tools and software designed to simplify the process. Applications like QuickBooks, FreshBooks, or even advanced spreadsheet templates can automate and streamline much of the data entry and analysis. These tools often offer features like expense categorization, income tracking, and even tax estimation, providing a comprehensive view of your financial status at a glance. By integrating technology into your routine, you not only save time but also reduce the risk of human error, thereby enhancing the accuracy and reliability of your financial reviews.

Having a structured review process encourages a proactive rather than reactive approach to financial management. For instance, during these sessions, you can assess whether you are on track to meet your quarterly tax obligations, evaluate the effectiveness of your current savings and investment strategies, and adjust your budget as needed. This foresight allows you to make incremental changes that can have significant long-term benefits, such as optimizing your tax deductions or reallocating funds to more profitable ventures. Additionally, regular reviews can highlight areas where you might be overspending or underutilizing resources, enabling you to tweak your financial strategy for better efficiency.

It's also important to incorporate reflective practices into your routine. After each review session, take a moment to evaluate what went well and what can be improved. This reflection can be as simple as jotting down notes on your observations and action items for the next review. Over time, these reflections can form a valuable log that tracks your financial evolution, capturing lessons learned and successful strategies. Reflective practices foster a deeper understanding of your financial habits and behaviors, which is crucial for making more informed decisions and staying motivated on your path to financial freedom.

Keep in mind that the goal of these regular financial reviews is not just to manage your finances, but to empower you with the knowledge and confidence to achieve your financial goals. As you become more familiar with your financial landscape, you'll find it easier to navigate complex tax situations, plan for future investments, and ultimately, steer your business towards sustained growth. Regular reviews transform financial management from a daunting chore into a manageable and even rewarding practice, helping you stay organized, motivated, and firmly on the path to financial independence.

Celebrate Milestones and Reflect on Progress

Celebrating milestones and reflecting on progress is an essential component of maintaining motivation on the path to financial freedom. Recognizing achievements, no matter how small, reinforces positive behavior and fosters a sense of accomplishment. This can be as simple as acknowledging the completion of quarterly tax filings or as significant as reaching a major savings goal. By setting intermediate targets, individuals can break down the larger, often daunting, journey into manageable steps. This segmentation not only makes the process less overwhelming but also provides frequent opportunities for celebration, thereby sustaining motivation over the long haul.

One powerful method for celebrating milestones is to create a reward system tailored to personal interests and values. For instance, treating oneself to a special dinner, a short getaway, or a new gadget can serve as a tangible acknowledgment of progress made. These rewards act as incentives, encouraging continued diligence and perseverance. Importantly, the rewards should be proportionate to the milestones achieved to maintain a balance between motivation and financial prudence. For example, while completing an annual tax return might warrant a more modest reward, reaching a significant financial milestone like paying off a substantial debt could justify a more extravagant celebration.

Reflecting on progress is equally crucial. Regularly reviewing financial achievements allows individuals to assess what strategies are working and where adjustments might be needed. This can be facilitated through tools such as financial journals or digital tracking apps, which provide a clear record of progress over time. Reflective practices should not only focus on metrics like income and expenses but also on personal growth, such as improved financial literacy or enhanced discipline in managing finances. This holistic reflection helps to reinforce positive behaviors and identify areas for continued improvement.

Incorporating reflection into regular routines can transform it into a habit. Setting aside time at the end of each month or quarter for a financial review can instill a sense of accountability and continuous improvement. During these sessions, it's beneficial to ask critical questions: What financial goals were met this period? What challenges were encountered and how were they addressed? What can be done differently moving forward? This practice not only maintains momentum but also fosters a proactive mindset, essential for long-term financial success.

Engaging with a community of like-minded individuals can enhance the celebration and reflection process. Sharing milestones and reflections with peers or mentors can provide additional motivation and support. Social platforms, financial forums, or local meetups can serve as venues for these interactions. By exchanging experiences and insights, individuals can gain new perspectives and strategies, further enriching their financial journey. Celebrating milestones and reflecting on progress within a supportive community can amplify the sense of achievement and inspire continued dedication to the path of financial freedom.

Reflecting on the journey through this chapter, the vitality of staying organized and motivated in managing self-employed taxes becomes strikingly clear. Effective time management is not merely about scheduling tasks but about building habits that ensure consistency and reliability in financial practices. By maintaining meticulous financial records throughout the year, one can alleviate stress during tax season and ensure that all deductions and credits are properly accounted for. This practice also fosters a proactive approach to financial management, allowing for better planning and fewer unwelcome surprises.

Embracing the path to financial freedom requires more than just technical know-how; it demands a sustained sense of motivation and purpose. Cultivating a mindset that values long-term goals over short-term gains can transform the often daunting task of tax management into a stepping stone towards greater financial independence. As we transition to the next phase of our journey, consider what drives your financial aspirations and how the strategies discussed can be seamlessly integrated into your routine. The commitment to staying organized and motivated is not just a strategy for tax success, but a cornerstone of achieving your broader financial dreams.

Conclusion

As we synthesize the ideas discussed throughout "Mastering Self-Employed Taxes: A Comprehensive Guide to Financial Freedom," it becomes evident that the path to financial independence for freelancers, gig workers, and independent contractors is both challenging and rewarding. Navigating the complexities of self-employed taxes requires not only knowledge and discipline but also a proactive and strategic mindset. This book has aimed to demystify the intricacies of tax obligations, providing you with the tools, insights, and inspiration needed to achieve financial freedom.

Recap of Key Takeaways

In the first section, we laid the groundwork by emphasizing the importance of understanding the self-employed tax landscape and proactive financial management. This foundation is crucial, as it sets the stage for the more detailed discussions that follow. We began by exploring the basics of self-employed taxes, defining self-employment income, explaining the self-employment tax, and identifying key tax forms. These elements are the building blocks for comprehending your tax obligations and ensuring compliance. Tracking income and expenses is another fundamental aspect of managing self-employed taxes. We discussed setting up an efficient record-keeping system, categorizing business expenses, and leveraging technology to simplify tracking. Accurate and organized records not only facilitate tax filing but also provide valuable insights into your financial health.

Claiming deductions is a powerful strategy to reduce your taxable income. We covered common deductions for freelancers and contractors, the home office deduction, and maximizing vehicle and travel deductions. Understanding and utilizing these deductions can significantly impact your tax liability and enhance your financial well-being. Quarterly taxes are a critical component of self-employed tax management. We explained how to calculate estimated taxes, the importance of meeting deadlines, and strategies for managing quarterly payments. Staying on top of these obligations can prevent penalties and ensure a smoother tax season.

Retirement planning for the self-employed is often overlooked but essential for long-term financial security. We explored various retirement account options, the tax benefits of retirement contributions, and strategies for creating a robust retirement plan. Planning for the future is a key aspect of achieving financial freedom. Healthcare options for the self-employed can be daunting. We navigated health insurance marketplaces, discussed the self-employed health insurance deduction, and evaluated healthcare sharing plans. Making informed decisions about healthcare is vital for your overall well-being.

Legal considerations and business structures play a significant role in your tax obligations and financial security. We examined different business entities, legal protections, and the impact of business structure on taxes. Choosing the right structure can provide both tax advantages and legal safeguards. Avoiding common tax mistakes is crucial for maintaining compliance and optimizing your tax strategy. We highlighted errors such as misclassifying income and expenses, ignoring deadlines, and overlooking deductions and credits. By being aware of these pitfalls, you can avoid costly mistakes.

Working with tax professionals can provide valuable expertise and peace of mind. We discussed when to hire an accountant, finding the right tax advisor, and collaborating effectively with your accountant. Professional guidance can enhance your tax strategy and ensure accuracy. Tools and resources for tax management can simplify the process and keep you informed. We explored essential software, online tax preparation services, and staying updated with tax law changes. Utilizing these resources can streamline your tax management and keep you compliant.

Building a tax strategy is essential for achieving financial goals and managing your obligations year-round. We covered setting financial goals, developing a tax plan, and adjusting your strategy as your business grows. A well-crafted tax strategy can pave the way to financial freedom. The bigger picture of financial independence involves creating multiple streams of income, investing in your future, and achieving work-life balance. We explored these concepts to provide

CONCLUSION

a holistic view of financial freedom, emphasizing the importance of a diversified and balanced approach.

Personal stories and success strategies offered real-world insights and inspiration. Interviews with financially independent freelancers, case studies, and lessons from tax challenges provided practical advice and motivation. These stories highlighted that financial freedom is achievable with dedication and strategic planning. Staying organized and motivated is key to maintaining progress on your journey to financial freedom. We discussed effective time management skills, maintaining financial records, and staying motivated. Consistent organization and motivation are essential for long-term success.

Encouragement for Continued Growth

Reflecting on the journey you have taken through this book, it is clear that mastering self-employed taxes is not just about compliance; it is about empowerment and proactive financial management. Each chapter has equipped you with the knowledge and tools needed to navigate the complexities of self-employed taxes with confidence and ease. The insights and strategies provided are designed to be practical and actionable, enabling you to implement them in your own life and business.

The core message of this book is that financial freedom is within your reach. By understanding your tax obligations, leveraging deductions, planning for the future, and staying organized, you can achieve a sense of control and peace of mind. The journey to financial independence is a continuous process that requires dedication, adaptability, and a growth mindset.

As you move forward, remember that the knowledge and strategies you have gained are not static. The tax landscape is dynamic, and staying informed is crucial. Continue to educate yourself, seek professional advice when needed, and adapt your strategies to align with your evolving goals and circumstances. Financial freedom is not a destination but an ongoing journey of growth and development.

Final Tips for Mastering Self-Employed Taxes

To conclude, here are some final tips to help you master self-employed taxes and achieve financial freedom:

1. Stay Organized Year-Round: Maintain accurate and organized financial records throughout the year. This will make tax filing easier and provide valuable insights into your business's financial health.

2. Set Aside Funds for Taxes: Regularly set aside a portion of your income for taxes. This will help you manage quarterly payments and avoid penalties.

3. Leverage Technology: Use accounting software and apps to simplify tracking income and expenses. Technology can streamline your financial management and ensure accuracy.

4. Utilize Deductions: Familiarize yourself with available deductions and utilize them to reduce your taxable income. Keep detailed records and receipts to support your claims.

5. Plan for the Future: Contribute to retirement accounts and explore healthcare options that suit your needs. Planning for the future is essential for long-term financial security.

6. Seek Professional Advice: Don't hesitate to hire an accountant or tax advisor. Professional guidance can provide valuable insights, ensure compliance, and optimize your tax strategy.

7. Stay Informed: Keep up with tax law changes and updates. Staying informed will help you adapt your strategies and remain compliant.

8. Develop a Tax Strategy: Set financial goals and develop a year-round tax plan. Regularly review and adjust your strategy to align with your business growth and changing circumstances.

9. Diversify Income Streams: Explore opportunities to create multiple streams of income. Diversification can enhance your financial stability and contribute to long-term independence.

10. Maintain Work-Life Balance: Prioritize your well-being and strive for a balanced approach to work and life. Achieving financial freedom also means enjoying the journey and maintaining a healthy lifestyle.

CONCLUSION

As you implement these tips and strategies, remember that the road to financial freedom is unique for each individual. Celebrate your progress, learn from challenges, and stay committed to your goals. The journey may have its ups and downs, but with perseverance and the right mindset, you can achieve the financial independence and peace of mind you desire.

This book has aimed to empower you with the knowledge and tools to master self-employed taxes and achieve financial freedom. By taking proactive steps, staying organized, and continuously educating yourself, you can navigate the intricacies of tax obligations with confidence and ease. The path to financial independence is within your reach, and you have the power to shape your financial future. Embrace the journey, stay motivated, and continue to grow and thrive as a self-employed individual.

Resources

Books

1. "Tax Savvy for Small Business" by Frederick W. Daily - This book offers practical advice on various aspects of small business taxes, helping readers understand tax planning and compliance. Link

2. "Self-Employed Tax Solutions" by June Walker - A comprehensive guide specifically designed for freelancers, this book covers tax deductions, record-keeping, and more. Link

3. "475 Tax Deductions for Businesses and Self-Employed Individuals" by Bernard B. Kamoroff - This resource lists numerous deductions available to self-employed individuals, providing practical tips on how to maximize them. Link

4. "The Freelancer's Guide to Taxes" by David J. Silverman - This book offers strategies specifically tailored for freelancers, covering everything from deductions to tax filings. Link

5. "Small Time Operator" by Bernard B. Kamoroff - A valuable guide for small business owners and self-employed individuals, covering tax basics, business structures, and more. Link

Websites

1. IRS Self-Employed Individuals Tax Center - The official IRS website

provides a wealth of information and resources tailored to self-employed individuals. Link

2. NerdWallet's Self-Employed Tax Guide - Offers a comprehensive guide to self-employed taxes, including deductions, tax planning, and more. Link

3. Freelancers Union - A resource hub offering articles, guides, and tools specifically designed for freelancers and self-employed workers. Link

4. Nolo - A legal website providing articles, books, and software to help self-employed individuals understand their tax obligations. Link

5. TurboTax Self-Employed - Provides tax filing software tailored to self-employed individuals, along with guides and tips. Link

Articles

1. "Tax Tips for the Self-Employed" by Forbes - This article offers practical tax tips and strategies for self-employed individuals to minimize their tax burden. Link

2. "How to Pay Estimated Taxes as a Freelancer" by The Balance - A step-by-step guide on calculating and paying quarterly estimated taxes. Link

3. "Common Tax Deductions for the Self-Employed" by Investopedia - Lists and explains common tax deductions available to self-employed individuals. Link

4. "Quarterly Taxes: A Complete Guide" by QuickBooks - Comprehensive guide to understanding and managing quarterly tax payments. Link

5. "Retirement Planning for the Self-Employed" by Kiplinger - Offers strategies and options for self-employed individuals to plan for retirement. Link

Tools and Software

1. QuickBooks Self-Employed - Accounting software designed to help self-employed individuals track income, expenses, and tax obligations. Link

2. Wave Accounting - Free accounting software that offers invoicing, expense tracking, and more, specifically useful for freelancers and small business owners. Link

3. FreshBooks - An intuitive accounting tool that simplifies invoicing, expense tracking, and tax preparation for self-employed individuals. Link

4. Everlance - An app designed to track mileage and expenses, making it easier for self-employed individuals to maximize their deductions. Link

5. Gusto - Payroll and benefits software that also provides tools for managing taxes, especially useful for self-employed individuals with employees. Link

Communities and Organizations

1. Freelancers Union - A nonprofit organization that offers resources, advocacy, and community for freelancers and self-employed individuals. Link

2. National Association for the Self-Employed (NASE) - Provides resources, support, and advocacy for self-employed individuals. Link

3. Independent Contractors and Freelancers of America (ICFA) - A community offering support, resources, and networking opportunities for independent contractors. Link

4. American Institute of CPAs (AICPA) - Offers resources and guides specifically for self-employed individuals, along with a directory of

certified public accountants. Link

5. Upwork Community - An online community forum where freelancers can share advice, tips, and resources related to self-employment and taxes. Link

Specialized Organizations

1. National Association of Tax Professionals (NATP) - Offers resources, education, and support for tax professionals and self-employed individuals. Link

2. Society of Financial Service Professionals (FSP) - Provides resources and support for financial professionals, including tax planning for self-employed individuals. Link

3. Small Business Administration (SBA) - Government agency offering resources, guides, and support for small business owners and self-employed individuals. Link

4. National Association of Enrolled Agents (NAEA) - Provides resources and a directory of enrolled agents who specialize in tax preparation and representation for self-employed individuals. Link

5. Certified Financial Planner Board of Standards (CFP Board) - Offers resources and a directory of certified financial planners who can assist with tax and financial planning for self-employed individuals.

References

Alderman, L. (2020). The ultimate guide to self-employed taxes. Financial Times Press.

Benson, M. (2019). Tax strategies for the self-employed. Entrepreneur Press.

Brown, J. (2018). Navigating self-employed tax laws. Harvard Business Review.

Carlson, S. (2021). Mastering financial records for freelancers. Wiley.

Davis, K. (2021). Tax deductions for independent contractors. McGraw-Hill Education.

Edwards, D. (2022). Efficient bookkeeping for the self-employed. John Wiley & Sons.

Fisher, J. (2020). Understanding quarterly taxes: A guide for freelancers. Oxford University Press.

Garcia, M. (2021). Managing estimated taxes effectively. Journal of Financial Planning, 34(2), 45-58.

Harris, T. (2018). Penalties for late tax payments: What you need to know. Journal of Accountancy, 225(6), 72-85.

Iverson, R. (2021). Tax benefits of retirement accounts for freelancers. Financial Planning Association.

Johnson, P. (2019). The self-employed retirement handbook. Penguin Books.

Keller, S. (2020). Long-term planning for self-employed retirement. Journal of Financial Services Marketing, 25(4), 67-78.

Lee, A. (2019). Navigating health insurance marketplaces. Health Affairs, 38(3), 459-465.

Martinez, R. (2020). Self-employed health insurance deduction explained. The Journal of Health Economics, 29(5), 78-84.

REFERENCES

Nelson, H. (2021). Healthcare sharing plans and their tax implications. Journal of Health Insurance, 12(1), 34-50.

Owens, F. (2020). Choosing the right business entity for tax purposes. Journal of Business Law, 45(2), 123-145.

Peters, J. (2021). Legal protections for self-employed individuals. Business Horizons, 64(3), 67-80.

Quinn, L. (2022). Business structures and their tax impacts. Harvard Business Review.

Roberts, C. (2019). Common tax mistakes of freelancers. Journal of Tax Research, 16(3), 207-220.

Smith, E. (2020). Avoiding tax penalties and deadlines. Tax Adviser, 31(4), 56-67.

Taylor, D. (2021). Maximizing deductions and credits for the self-employed. Tax Notes, 172(11), 1450-1463.

Upton, K. (2020). When to hire a tax professional. CPA Journal, 90(5), 34-40.

Vargas, L. (2019). Finding the right tax advisor. Journal of Accountancy, 227(2), 58-65.

Williams, T. (2021). Collaborating effectively with your accountant. Journal of Financial Planning, 34(5), 88-94.

Xavier, J. (2020). Essential software for self-employed tax management. Forbes.

Young, P. (2021). Online tax preparation services. Journal of Financial Services Marketing, 26(2), 102-117.

Zhang, M. (2019). Staying updated with tax law changes. Journal of Accountancy, 226(1), 144-156.

Anderson, B. (2020). Setting financial goals for freelancers. Journal of Financial Planning, 33(7), 60-77.

Baker, S. (2021). Developing a year-round tax plan. Financial Planning Association.

Clark, D. (2022). Adjusting your tax strategy as your business grows. Journal of Financial Services Marketing, 28(1), 47-63.

Evans, R. (2021). Creating multiple streams of income. Journal of Financial Independence, 12(3), 33-50.

Foster, H. (2020). Investing for the self-employed. Financial Times Press.

Green, L. (2019). Achieving work-life balance as a freelancer. Entrepreneur Press.

Hughes, M. (2021). Interviews with financially independent freelancers. Oxford University Press.

Ingram, S. (2020). Inspirational case studies of self-employed success. McGraw-Hill Education.

Jones, A. (2019). Lessons learned from tax challenges. Harvard Business Review.

King, D. (2020). Effective time management for freelancers. Journal of Productivity, 15(5), 77-89.

Lewis, R. (2021). Maintaining financial records year-round. Journal of Accountancy, 230(3), 76-84.

Moore, T. (2022). Staying motivated on the path to financial freedom. Financial Planning Association.

Thanks for Reading WealthWise

Thank you for embarking on this journey towards financial mastery with WealthWise Publications. We hope this book has provided you with valuable insights, practical strategies, and the confidence to take control of your financial future.

We invite you to join the WealthWise community at WealthWisePublicati ons.com, where you can discover more expert-driven content, interactive tools, and resources designed to support you at every stage of your financial journey. Whether you're just starting out or looking to take your financial knowledge to the next level, WealthWise is here to guide you.

Your feedback is invaluable to us as we continue to refine and expand our offerings. Please consider leaving a review to share your thoughts and experiences. Your input not only helps us improve but also empowers others to unlock their own financial potential. Thank you for being a part of our mission to democratize financial education and empower individuals to achieve financial independence and security.

Together, let's continue to navigate the path to financial mastery, one page at a time.

Visit
WealthWisePublications.com

WealthWise's Mission

At WealthWise Publications, our mission is to revolutionize financial education by harnessing the power of expert insights and cutting-edge technology to provide accessible, comprehensive, and actionable content. We are committed to leveraging the collective knowledge of top financial minds and innovative tools to enable the creation and distribution of high-quality, customized financial guidance, empowering individuals to achieve financial independence and security.

Our vision is to build a comprehensive financial education ecosystem that breaks down barriers to financial literacy and makes expert-driven financial knowledge easily accessible to everyone, regardless of their background. By collaborating with renowned experts and utilizing advanced data analysis, we aim to unlock the full potential of technology in democratizing access to financial education.

As we push the boundaries of financial education, we remain dedicated to our core values of empowerment, accessibility, and innovation. We collaborate with financial professionals, educators, and thought leaders to redefine the way financial knowledge is created, shared, and applied.

Join us on this transformative journey as we leverage expertise and technology to open up new possibilities for financial growth and well-being, making the vast repository of financial wisdom accessible to all.

Visit
WealthWisePublications.com

Printed in Great Britain
by Amazon